CREATIVE EXPERIENCE

CREATIVE EXPERIENCE

BY

M. P. FOLLETT

GYAN

Published by

GYAN

Gyan Publishing House
5, Ansari Road
Daryaganj, New Delhi-110002
Phone: 011-47034999, 9811692060
E-mail: books@gyanbooks.com

Distribution Network
gyanbooks.com
India, USA, Canada, UK, Australia

ISBN: 978-81-212-5949-1 (PB)
First Published, 1924

2nd Impression 2024

Printed at: Gyan Press, Delhi.

CREATIVE EXPERIENCE
Author: M. P. FOLLETT

CREATIVE EXPERIENCE

BY

M. P. FOLLETT

AUTHOR OF

"THE SPEAKER OF THE HOUSE OF REPRESENTATIVES,"

"THE NEW STATE"

LONGMANS, GREEN AND CO.

55 FIFTH AVENUE, NEW YORK

39 PATERNOSTER ROW, LONDON, E.C. 4

TORONTO, BOMBAY, CALCUTTA AND MADRAS

1930

TO

RICHARD CLARKE CABOT

AND

ELLA LYMAN CABOT

With affection, with warm gratitude for the help they have so generously given me, and with appreciation of their faith in that crescent power of the human spirit to which I have tried to give some expression in this book.

First Edition April 1924
Reprinted January 1930

CONTENTS

Part II

AN EXPERIMENTAL ATTITUDE TOWARD EXPERIENCE

INTRODUCTION

THE social sciences are not gathering all the fruits of certain recent developments of thought; they are not all of them even using the most modern *method* of study, which is wholly to abandon the region of abstract speculation and to study the behavior of men. Many political scientists talk about conferring power without analyzing power; many economists talk about representation in industry without analyzing representation; there are sociologists who talk about individual and social interests without sufficiently analyzing the difference, if there is one, between individual and social interests. In a book by a recent writer on politics these four words are used in a sentence of three lines: power, purpose, freedom, service. But the author has not told us what these words mean—and we do not know. We can find out only by watching in thousands of cases the working of power, purpose, freedom, only by watching the behavior of men.

The greatest need of today is a keen, analytical, objective study of human relations. We preach "compromise" as the apex of the ethical life, we laud the "balance of power" as our political and international faith, we give our substance and ourselves to establish an "equilibrium" of nations. But compromise sacrifices the integrity of the individual, and balance of power merely rearranges what already exists; it produces no new values. No fairer life for men will ever be the fruit of such doctrine. By adherence to such a creed we bind ourselves to equivalents, we do not seek the plusvalents of experience. If experience is to be progressive, another principle of human association must be found. I know of but one way to seek it. The conceptions of politics, economics and sociology should be studied while they are still living in the lives of men. We need to study not the "conception" of a general will but concrete joint activity. We should, without disregarding whatever light the past has thrown on these questions, now look at men in their daily occupations at factory or store, at town meeting or congress, and see what we can learn. We should abandon the region of mere statement and counter-statement where so much controversy takes place. We should take our language too from the concrete daily happenings; the words we now use have nearly always ethical connotations which prejudge, which merely in themselves attribute praise or blame to individuals or groups or state.

The biologist, the physiologist and the experimental psychologist are studying "response" in their laboratories. Infant behavior, the behavior of animals both in laboratory and field, the behavior of primitive tribes, have all been carefully observed, but much less study has been given to the relation of adults among civilized peoples. Thousands of students have watched birds building their nests and told us of their "purpose"; the same study has not been given to purpose in human relations and yet it is perhaps the most important conception of social psychology. I suppose we have thought we already understood sufficiently the behavior of men, that we knew how to make the intercourse of men serve the ends of men; yet the Genoa Conference broke up, labor and capital arrive at no peace, the farmers wage bitter war against the middlemen. To be sure, sociology tells us much of the crowd, but the large accomplishments of men are not made in crowd-association. As for philosophy, this is not its richest moment: idealism is in disrepute, pragmatism has still bits of intellectualism sticking to it, and realism has not yet found itself. The time is ripe for empirical studies of human relations, social situations.

But we wish to do far more than observe our experience, we wish to make it yield up for us its riches; observation alone may give only negative results, prompt useful guesses, suggest interesting prophecies. Moreover, we must face the fact, if social research is to be made valuable for us, that it is seldom possible to "observe" a social situation as one watches a chemical experiment; the presence of the observer usually changes the situation. We need then those who are frankly participant-observers, those who will try experiment after experiment and note results, experiments in making human interplay productive—in industry and business, in legislative committees and administrative commissions, in trade unions and shop committees and joint boards of control, in athletic committees and college faculties, in our families, in parliamentary cabinets and international conferences. Brilliant empiricists have poked much pleasant fun at those who tell us of some vague should-be instead of what is. We want something more than either of these; we want to find out what *may* be, the possibilities now open to us. This we can discover only by experiment. Observation is not the only method of science. The methods of physical science are observation and experiment; these should be the methods of the social sciences.

Above all, we should remember that good intentions are not sufficient to solve our problems. Sympathy with labor will not alone solve the labor question; a sympathy with labor that is not founded on understanding often makes matters worse, for any attempt to work out a method of industrial democracy must begin with a frank recognition that the interests involved are different and must be dealt with as such. It is the ethics of the sentimentalist to say that men's interests are the same; if they were, life would stagnate. Our present experience invalidates all facile prescriptions for superficial reform. We want to know how men can interact and coact better: (1) to secure their ends; (2) to understand and so broaden their ends.

What is the central problem of social relations? It is the question of power; this is the problem of industry, of politics, of international affairs. But our task is not to learn where to place power; it is how to develop power. We frequently hear nowadays of "transferring" power as the panacea for all our ills. Transfer power to occupational groups, we are told, and all will be well; but the transference of power has been the whole course of history—power passing to priests or king or barons, to council or soviet. Are we satisfied to continue this puss-in-the-corner game? We shall certainly do so as long as we think that the transference of power is the way of progress. Genuine power can only be grown, it will slip from every arbitrary hand that grasps it; for genuine power is not coercive control, but coactive control. Coercive power is the curse of the universe; coactive power, the enrichment and advancement of every human soul.

We need a technique of human relations based on the preservation of the integrity of the individual. Of late years we have heard too much of the collective life as an aim in itself. But who cares for "the collective life"? It is usually a mere shibboleth of empty words. What we care about is the *productive* life, and the first test of the productive power of the collective life is its nourishment of the individual. The second test is whether the contributions of individuals can be fruitfully united. Moralist after moralist tells us to give ourselves to the general good, but we need to know far more than this, to do far more than this; our ideal of society is not a kaleidoscope of pretty *bits*.

The nineteenth century talked of the "will" of the people, the "rights" of man. The early twentieth based its hopes for social progress on the doctrine of interests, but long before that doctrine has grown cold, another is emerging. Psychology now gives us "desire" as the key word of our individual life. Students of social relations see desire as the basis of all the actions and interactions of men. It is the word used by Dean Pound in his latest books on law. The pregnant question for the social scientist becomes, then, whether we are to be ruled by the desires of the strongest, whether we are to live in a Power-Society, or whether there is any process possible by which desires may interweave. This is the problem of judge and statesman. The way to rid ourselves of economic determinism is not to deny that it exists; the way to weaken the domination of majorities is not by denunciation.

The object of this book is to suggest that we seek a way by which desires may interweave, that we seek a method by which the full integrity of the individual shall be one with social progress, that we try to make our daily experience yield for us larger and ever larger spiritual values. The confronting of diverse desires, the thereby revealing of "values," the consequent revaluation of values, a uniting of desires which we welcome above all because it means that the next diversity will emerge on a higher social level—this is progress. With many writers "adjustment" has been the controlling principle of the social sciences, but the idea of adjustment has been broadened and developed by the term we have now gained, that of integration. This expression has large implications, some of which are given in this volume. To stick to the word adjustment keeps us enmeshed in the thought which this word once connoted, whereas our thinking has now gone beyond that stage. We do not want capitalism to "adjust" itself to trade unionism; we want something better than either of these. We want the plus values of the conflict. This is still adjustment, if you will, but with a more comprehensive meaning than of old. Or rather, if we used the word adjustment in the social sciences with scientific accuracy, it might still be a good word, but in the social sciences adjustment as the outcome of conflict has too often been used quite loosely, meaning not the method of evolution, but rather reciprocal abandonments based on the idea that by some system of magic subtraction may become a process of addition.

The acceptance of the doctrine of circular or integrative behavior which I have tried to give in this book, lends a new significance to adjustment. This doctrine gives us hints of that "mystery moment" which leads from the existing to the new, shows us a *progressive* experience, the way of individual and social development. Yet it is not from the psychological field alone that our thought is receiving this impetus. The rapprochement of results from widely different fields of research is as striking as it is significant. The psychobiologist and the political scientist, physiologist and philosopher, jurist and psychologist, are reaching certain conclusions which bear a most suggestive resemblance to one another. And these conclusions lead to a conception of creative experience which is perhaps seminal for our future thinking, a conception which is surely destined to influence largely the social sciences.

The pairings made above were not fortuitous ones: Lippmann, a student of politics, quotes Kempf, the psychobiologist; Bok, the Dutch physiologist, hints at a connection between his conclusions and a certain tendency in philosophy; the most progressive juristical thinking has marked kinship with recent psychological thought;[1] Köhler brings to us from his field of work some striking resemblances to the observations of the psychiatrists; the results of one social worker[2] are in some respects most interestingly like the conclusions of some of our contemporary psychologists; the same might be said of the ideas worked out in regard to methods by a successful labor manager[3] who, from his study of how to deal with the complaints of his work-

[1] See pp. 268–9. [2] See pp. 105–7. [3] See pp. 79–80.

men, has discerned principles which are similar to some of the present-day psychological conceptions in regard to relation. In Chapters III, IV and V, I have written of these conceptions, but as psychology is a domain in which the more general student may easily lose his bearings, I have tried to give some of the implications of recent psychological thought without venturing on difficult technicalities. If, however, an encounter with these has sometimes been unavoidable, and I have not been able to escape all the dangers involved, I hope it will be recognized that I am not writing on psychology, but merely indicating certain correspondences in different fields of thinking which seem to me suggestive. I do not wish to overwork these correspondences or to treat as more than analogy that which is only analogy. We have always to guard against substituting for observation of social relations facile and interesting analogies from psychological studies of the individual. We cannot equip ourselves with the results of research on one level and "apply" them to another. But, interested chiefly in the seeking of a new method, as are most students of the social sciences today, I have taken illustrations of a method which I think vital wherever I could find them; that is, I have used as illustrative material certain parallels (although not wishing to force their standing as parallels) which seem to me to indicate a new attitude towards method. The social sciences are in some respects in the state of the physical sciences before Newton. The great contribution of Newton to the physical sciences was his showing of the relation of quantitative analysis to qualitative analysis. This must be worked out for the social sciences where we have not always understood the relation between quantitative and qualitative analysis.

I should like to add, since my position in regard to some of the matters touched on in this volume might otherwise be misunderstood, that I have often referred to the results of psychological research in discussing social phenomena when my inclination would sometimes have been to refer to philosophical discussion of the points involved. I have done this partly because the experimental verification which psychology is bringing to certain philosophical conceptions seems to me very valuable, and also because since what is called social psychology is coming to have more and more standing as a subject of study, it has seemed to me useful to bring together present psychological and social data as far as I could in regard to the one idea in this book. In addition to this I have thought that the correlation of the results of entirely independent observation in different fields might be interesting, that we might get an appreciation of the full import of certain conceptions in one field of study by a cognizance of their value in other fields, that the cross-fertilizations, so to speak, which are now going on in our thinking are worthy of recognition.

I have, therefore, because I have entered other fields of study than my own in writing this book, more acknowledgments to make than is usual. So many people have given me most generously of their time, either to discuss particular problems or to read and criticize manuscript, that their names would make too long a list to print here, yet my sense of indebtedness for the many suggestions they have given me is none the less great.

From Professor Sheffield, however, I have had a kind of help which should receive special mention, for Mr. Sheffield has conceived his own particular subject of study, that of discussion,[4] so broadly, the technique he is working out is so valuable for all students of social conflict, that my talks with him have been most helpful to me. He has also read the whole of my manuscript and made many suggestions and additions.

With Professor E. C. Lindeman my work has been still more closely connected. For two years Mr. Lindeman has engaged in a study of marketing coöperatives, not only for the purpose of investigating an aspect of the coöperative movement but also in order to observe an acute form of social conflict, that between farmers and middlemen. Mr. Lindeman and I shared the hope that from this investigation certain conclusions might be drawn which would be valuable for social conflict in general, and also that there might be developed some fruitful methods of social research in line with the general advance in sociological thinking. In recognition of much that was common in our aims, we decided that it would be advantageous to maintain a rather close working connection, and we have therefore had conferences from time to time from which I have learned much. Moreover, Mr. Lindeman has very kindly allowed me to use his material as freely as I wished, material which shows great discernment and which recognizes the difference between the dramatic moments and those more subtle and intangible workings that often reveal the real values of a situation. I have

[4] See Alfred Dwight Sheffield, *Joining in Discussion.*

used certain illustrations which he has given me and others which I have gained from going over a large amount of printed matter (coöperative news organs, propagandist pamphlets, contract forms, contested cases, etc.) which he has sent me. Mr. Lindeman's own forthcoming book, *Social Discovery, An Approach to the Study of Functional Groups,* seems to me a valuable contribution toward that new technique of social research which is so badly needed today.

To Mr. Herbert Croly I owe deep gratitude for the interest he has shown in my work, and for his generous encouragement which has not only stimulated my efforts but helped to give direction to them. To his books, *Progressive Democracy* and *The Promise of American Life,* my thinking is much indebted, for they greatly enlarged my vision and opened for me entirely new vistas of the possibilities of the development of democracy, of the meaning of citizenship.

It is impossible to express what I owe to my friend, Miss Isobel L. Briggs, for her untiring help, day by day, in considering with me difficult points both of thought and presentation, in preparing manuscript and in reading proof.

PART I

EXPERIENCE AS SELF-SUSTAINING AND SELF-RENEWING PROCESS

PART I

EXPERIENCE AS SELF-SUSTAINING AND SELF-RENEWING PROCESS

I

VICARIOUS EXPERIENCE: ARE EXPERTS THE REVEALERS OF TRUTH?

THE most striking characteristic of the thought of today is the trend toward objectivity: psychology has given us behaviorism, political scientists are emphasizing "accurate information" as the solution of all our difficulties, and jurists tell us that law must rest not on abstract principles but on social facts.

The present apotheosis of the expert, the ardent advocacy of "facts," needs some analysis. The question of democracy is often discussed on the assumption that we are obliged to choose between the rule of that modern beneficent despot, the expert, and a muddled, befogged "people." If the question were as simple as that, most of our troubles would be over; we should have only to get enough Intelligence Bureaus at Washington, enough scientific management into the factories, enough specialists (on hygiene, transportation, etc.) into the cities, enough formulæ from the agricultural colleges into the country, and all life would become fair and beautiful. For the people, it is assumed, will gladly agree to become automata when we show them all the things—nice, solid, objective *things*—they can have by abandoning their own experience in favor of a superior race of men called experts.

While I am sure that in the present appreciation of "facts" we have the most hopeful promise for our confessedly fumbling world, the most needed corrective for certain attitudes of mind into which we have fallen, while I know from experience that we often waste time in conference arguing about things that are ascertainable, still there are several points which must be remembered: it is of equal importance with the discovery of facts to know what to do with them; our job is to apportion, not usurp, function (the "people" have a place, what is it?); and also we must warn ourselves that a little of the ready reliance on the expert comes from the desire to waive responsibility, comes from the endless evasion of life instead of an honest facing of it. The expert is to many what the priest is, someone who knows absolutely and can tell us what to do. The king, the priest, the expert, have one after the other had our allegiance, but so far as we put any of them in the place of ourselves, we have not a sound society and neither individual nor general progress.

To overemphasize the importance of the expert would be impossible, but after we have fully recognized his value to society, there still remains to be considered the legitimate relation between expert and people. For a generation the slogan has been investigation, research, survey of cities, scientific management, social engineering, etc. Yet through all this steadily increasing appreciation of facts, the question that has recurred to us again and again has been: what is the relation of all this to the rank and file of the people? This is what is in the mind of the president of the industrial plant as he reads the report of his scientific manager; everyone who has taken part in any municipal reform finds this the crux of his problem.

I do not think that the solution of this problem is to be found in that doctrine known as "the consent of of the governed." To divide society on the one side into the expert and the governors basing their governing on his reports, and on the other the people consenting, is, I believe, a disaster-courting procedure. Yet this does not mean, on the other hand, that "the people" are to be unduly exalted. Formerly the supporters of democracy, concerned with the machinery of government, aimed to find those forms which should give voice to "the people," but for some time now we have not given much thought to this consideration: the thinkers certainly have not, and the community centre movement, the workmen's education movement, the coöperative movement, to mention only two or three, are not based on the assumption that the will of the people is "instinctively" good, and that our institutions exist merely to get at this will, to give it voice, etc. The essential aim of these, the most democratic movements we have, is to train ourselves, to learn how to use the work of experts, to find our will, to educate our will, to integrate our wills.

The greatest flaw in the form the theory of consent sometimes takes today is the assumption that the automatic result of scientific investigation is the overcoming of difference. This view both fails to see the importance of diversity, and also ignores the fact that the accumulation of information does not overcome diversity. This seems to me a point sufficiently important to warrant some consideration. Daily, hourly I might say, we see the failure of facts to produce unanimity of opinion. Our Supreme Courts try honestly to get the facts of each case, but the result is not unanimous decision. Boards are constantly sitting which employ experts and then view and discuss the facts obtained; those who have sat on such Boards know that difference of opinion has not been overcome. It is always the inexperienced man on the Board who brings in his "facts" and expects that the *impasse* of the previous meeting will be removed. Can you not see him in your various memories, smiling round at his companions in this happy expectation? And can you not see that smile gradually fade as the expectation fails?

We need experts, we need accurate information, but the object is not to do away with *difference* but to do away with *muddle.* When for lack of facts you and I are responding to a different situation—you to the situation as you imagine it, I to the situation as I imagine it—we cannot of course come to agreement. What accurate information does is to clear the ground for genuine difference and therefore make possible, I do not say make sure, agreement. The object of accurate information is not to overcome difference but to give legitimate play to difference. If I think I am looking at a black snake and you think it is a fallen branch, our talk will be merely chaotic. But after we have decided that it is a snake, we do not then automatically agree what to do with it. You and I may respond quite differently to "black snake": shall we run away, or kill it, or take it home and make a pet of it to kill the mice? There is now some basis for significant difference. Difference based on inaccuracy is meaningless. We have not done away with difference, but we have provided the possibility for fruitful difference.

To be sure, we need certain scientific information to help us make this decision. We shall have less tendency to run away when we learn that black snakes are not poisonous; but then we learn that they belong to the constrictor class, and some of us do not like even harmless snakes wound round our throats; still the risk of that is slight and my house is overrun with mice and another scientist tells me both that you can make pets of black snakes and that they are our best mice-hunters. And so on and so on. I am dwelling on this point because I want to make it clear that I think the possibility of a wise decision depends on just as much scientific information as we can acquire. I wholly agree that the number of decisions people are willing to make daily without such information is amazing, and yet I think that after we have obtained the greatest amount possible, there will still be difference, and that dealing with difference is the main part of the social process. President Lowell, in his recent book *Public Opinion in Peace and War*, says: "It might be supposed that men of equal intelligence without prejudice or bias would on the same evidence reach the same conclusion, but this is by no means always true."[1] The effect of the impact of facts upon us is not automatic, instantaneous and idea-levelling.

Moreover, the difficulty of securing accurate information is very great as evidenced by the frequency with which experts disagree. Two experts talking together do not always impress us with their unanimity. We have most of us listened to the "facts" produced at

[1] P. 15. Mr. Lowell then gives illustrations of this and adds, "Divergences of opinion result in a large part from attaching different weight to various factors in a problem." Mr. Lowell's discussion of the relation of opinion to facts throws interesting lights on this question.

legislative hearings by the experts on both sides. And the whole history of our courts gives multitudinous evidence in regard to the expert. Recall the testimony in negligence cases. In a suit brought a few months ago on accout of an elevator accident, of two experts called in to judge the tensile strength of the cable, the expert on one side testified, after examination of the strands, that the condition of the cable was such as to make it reasonable to expect that the cable would not break; the other testified exactly the opposite. Again, a large molasses tank owned by the United States Industrial Alcohol Company exploded, doing much damage to life and property in the neighborhood. In the cases which resulted, testimony was taken from Harvard and Technology experts. The expert on one side testified that the fragments of steel plates of which the tank was composed showed that the force causing the explosion came from within; the expert on the other side, that it came from without, as, it might be, from a bomb. Of course the question of liability depended largely on this testimony. In the case of medical experts, the fact of two doctors of equal reputation giving directly opposed testimony makes many cases arising from accidents difficult to adjudicate. But we need not enlarge on the diverse testimony of experts in the courts, it is a matter of almost daily experience for every lawyer and judge.[2] Fact-finding bristles with difficulties. Let us look at some of the practical difficulties involved.[3]

Many seem to imagine the expert as completely denatured: one who has no emotions, no interests, no

[2] See what Kohler, one of the greatest of continental jurists, has written on "the philosophy of testimony" in *The Philosophy of Law*.

[3] Fact-finding as a generic term includes fact-gathering, fact-analysis, fact-interpretation, fact-handling, fact-presentation, etc.

memories and associations. Is there an island where such a race dwells?[4] But waiving for the moment that different experts report quite differently on a situation, that they may have *their* prejudices, interests, stereotypes, that they too often seem mortal and find what they expect to find, or what "the habits of their eyes" lead them to see, or what fits in with their philosophy or moral code; waiving for the moment too that we have all known Commissions where the experts chosen to collect the information required were very carefully picked beforehand according to their probable or known leanings—waiving all this, still some difficulties arise.

First, facts do not remain stationary. A situation changes faster than anyone can report on it. The developing possibilities of certain factors must be so keenly perceived that we get the report of a process not a picture, and when it is necessary to present to us a stage in the process, it should be presented in such a way that we see the hints it contains of successive stages. Dean Pound, in speaking of the writing of legal history in the last part of the nineteenth century, says: "The details of legal and political institutions were described . . . so faithfully as they stood in detail on a given day that they had ceased so to stand before the book was off the press."[5]

Moreover, names remain the same when what they stand for has changed. It often takes a nimble mind to perceive this.

[4] Mr. Lippmann's brilliant chapter on stereotypes would completely dispel such an illusion. See *Public Opinion* by Walter Lippmann for a penetrating analysis of public opinion founded on inadequate information, on tradition, on emotion and "stereotypes."

[5] *Interpretations of Legal History*, p. 70.

Then of great importance is the danger of the expert's labels. When we are told of the accurate pictures of the expert, we remember that there are people who take their cameras to séances and then show us their photographs as conclusive proof of spirit faces! But these are accurate pictures, for "the camera does not lie." The retina of your eye, too, may not lie, but if you see a man strike his friend on the face, it is better to restrain your indignation until you find out whether he was perhaps killing a mosquito. An unprejudiced investigator says: "I am showing you a picture of men fighting for an eight-hour day." But perhaps the men were struggling for something else, such as higher wages or self-direction. You may say that the expert need not label his pictures. He is hardly ever known not to do so; our very language, overlaid with the ideas and emotions of the race, prevents it.

We must remember also that expert or official can choose which fact, of two, he will present to us. To say nothing of partisan assortment of facts, experts emphasize the one which fits into present needs or interests. For instance, when there is a scarcity of white flour, we are told that brown is much more nourishing; when white flour is plentiful, we are told that as it is more easily assimilated we really get more nourishment out of it.

We could carry this thought much further, for it is, from one point of view, the thing most necessary to remember in any analysis of fact-finding, namely, that the interpretation of facts depends on needs. The interpretation of existence has always and will always serve our needs. The perception of facts, our "attention," is determined by our needs or desires. The amoeba feels the internal drive of hunger and wraps itself round something which stills the hunger and this henceforth becomes "food" for him. He has discriminated between food and the acid in the upper part of the pool. In our own life, while the process is infinitely more complex, it is still the same: discrimination always goes on *pari passu* with needs. The satisfaction of human needs is the fundamental law of human existence. Since Freud, the importance of the "wish" has been before everyone's eyes, but many advocates of fact-finding have not seen the significance of the Freudian "wish" in its relation to the interpretation of facts.

As this is of great importance, let me state it again a little differently. Facts become such for us when we attend to them. Our attending to them is bound up in the situation. The kind of objectivity which some of the fact-worshippers are endlessly seeking will be endlessly hidden from them. We want, we say, "impartial," "impersonal" investigation of a fact, but the significance of that fact, by all the yet-known laws of the universe, must be part of the "wish" which demanded the "disinterested" (!) investigation. The implications of a psychology based on the "wish" are many and far-reaching.

Moreover, we often see the confusing of part of the facts with all the facts. No matter how accurate information is, if it is partial, decisions based upon it will be disastrous. In a book on business education containing problems for the student, his answer to one problem is expected to depend on the "fact," explicitly stated in the text as a "fact," that you can sell more soap at six cents than at seven. A business man I know was much amused at this; it assumed, he said, that the other firms died meanwhile. What happens as a matter of "fact" when you reduce your soap from seven to six cents is that your competitors reduce it to five and three-fourths, and the question arises as to what you are going to do then. One activity leads to another, and the "fact" is sometimes as elusive as the button in the children's game. As ardent an advocate of fact-finding as anyone, I want merely to insist that we must know what we mean by "fact" in any given situation, that we must not base our action on too narrow an outlook on the field of facts. Perhaps this point could best be summed up by saying that to view facts in relation to one another is of the utmost importance, and that fact-finding and fact-presentation must take this very seriously into account.

One might go further and say that the value of every fact depends on its position in the whole world-process, is bound up in its multitudinous relations. One might go further still and say that a fact out of relation is not a fact. Yet not all experts can see the relation. What has made the great decisions of the American bench great is that their authors have seen the relation of the facts before them to the whole structure of our social life, including its present stage of development and its ideals. As Mr. Justice Holmes says, "[it is not] the acquisition of facts [which is important] but learning how to make facts live . . . leap into an organic order, live and bear fruit."

I might connect with this point a crude use of facts which misrelates them to the situation, for things to be "facts" must be facts within the same field. That fire consumes is a fact, but it is not a fact for this book. Thus statistics and facts are not necessarily synonymous, but subtle estimates, comprehensive boundaries of vision will be required in order to decide what is a fact for the situation.

Moreover, those who wish conclusions to be drawn always from precise measurements, forget that many of our problems defy the possibility of precise measurement. For instance, what is the minimum a girl can live on "in health and decency?"—the phrase used in the Massachusetts Minimum Wage Law.

Another difficulty which should be taken into account in fact-finding is the limited opportunity of the mere observer; different facts are usually elicited by the participant-observer. That is, experiment rather than *mere* observation often illumines facts, or is the best way of getting at facts. As an illustration of the participant-observer I might cite Prof. William Z. Ripley who, as chairman of the National Adjustment Commission during the war, elicited facts, handled facts and created facts.

The following warning it would perhaps seem superfluous to give if I had not several times recognized its necessity while reading certain expert reports which seemed to be based on the notion that the scaffolding of a situation constitutes the facts. Facts must be understood as the whole situation with whatever sentiments, beliefs, ideals enter into it. The facts of the trade union are not the external organization, its constitution and by-laws, nor yet the strike, in its external features; these are the mere scaffolding of the facts of trade unionism. That this has not always been fully appreciated by investigators is the cause of some of our misunderstanding in regard to trade unionism.

Another very real danger in fact-finding is that

while you or I may both be responding to fact, we may be responding to quite different *kinds* of fact. For instance, I sat on a Board last winter where employers, employees and public coöperated to fix a wage scale to be based on the cost of living, taking into consideration what that particular industry could stand. It soon developed, however, that to a number on the Board cost of living and the condition of the industry were by no means the main facts of the situation, but the relative strength at that moment of labor and capital. When those members brought in a demand for a minimum wage of $21.40, these figures did not represent the cost of living in Boston in 1922, they represented an estimate of labor strength in Boston in 1922. But this also was certainly a fact. Let us not be too naïve about facts.

Facts have intimate connection with the whole question of power. Parallel to the history of the use of facts must be written the history of the use of power. Think of the cave-man standing over his fallen foe. The prostrate savage might say, if he were a passionate fact-finder, "Let us look at the facts: it's a big bear, we can divide it and there will be enough for both of us; moreover, if you will study the scientific tables for the nutritive qualities of bear-meat, you will find that you need less of this creature than you thought." But the cave-man would surely reply, "If you want to consider facts, the most important one for you to give your attention to is that I can kill you in another minute; that is the fact that gives me the whole of the bear." As this is the way our international conferences and many others are conducted at the present moment, it seems to me indisputable that the last word has not yet been said about fact-finding, or at least about facts producing unity. The integrating of facts and power is possible, but it would mean a different code from that by which we are at present living. Nations are at present power-organizations; trade unions are power-organizations; manufacturers' associations are power-organizations. They must be made into something else before "facts" can have their full value for us. It is interesting to watch in any controversy, particularly when it extends over a rather long period, the change in "facts" with the shift in power. Observation of various conflicts with this in mind would, I believe, be fruitful.

Another point sometimes overlooked is that there is a time and place for fact-finding. And I mean more by this than merely that facts should be produced at strategic moments. The trouble with Lloyd George was often that he got a quantity of facts and went into conference with them. But France did the same. Then they pitted their facts over against each other. These facts did not agree. Of course they did not, as they were not the facts of the case as the case had developed in conference. From my experience on Minimum Wage Boards I see that there is possible a coöperative gathering of facts which is more useful to the resolution of conflict than for each side to get them separately and then try to integrate them, for when each side gets them separately there is a tendency for each to stick rigidly to its own particular facts. On one occasion when the employees were bringing in figures for a certain item, that of clothing, in the cost-of-living budget, and the employers another set, and the representatives of the public still another set, a sub-committee of three was appointed, one from each of these groups, to collect the facts jointly. The figures brought in at the next meeting, thus coöperatively gathered, were accepted by the Board and the rest of the discussion based upon them.

Thus can facts be properly used in conference, not marshalled to bolster up partisanship. Moreover, since far more than honesty, disinterestedness, etc., is required in the gathering of facts and reporting of situations; since the greatest delicacy of perception, the ear to hear overtones, the sensitiveness to impressions as well as a certain imperviousness to impressions, are indispensable, our accurate information will probably always have to be gathered by a number of people. We must recognize also that the facts on two sides of a controversy are in part different, and will remain so except in those cases where the fact-finding can be a joint activity. It is true that even if we could have a coöperative gathering of facts we should still interpret them differently, but the initial difficulty would be avoided—we should at any rate be looking at the same facts. When the attention of each side is riveted on *its* facts, discussion becomes rather hopeless. When the middleman tells the farmer one thing and the Farm Bureau another, the farmer is puzzled even although both sets of information may be "facts."

The use of statistics to suit one's purpose has been too frequently noticed to need any elaboration here, but an unusually interesting case has just come to my attention which has a bearing on this point of a coöperative gathering of facts. The research department of a tobacco coöperative association was asked for figures on the price of tobacco before the time of the formation of the coöperative. They began at 1866, taking five-year periods for their averages, and showed that the average price was under 11 cents. Then an independent investigator made the same analysis, on the basis also of five-year periods, but began with 1868. The result was much higher. Of course it was in the interest of the coöperative to make the discrepancy before and since its organization as great as possible, yet this was not calculated manipulation to deceive, it was a tendency merely to make the best showing possible—the aim of both sides in every controversy. The result was two sets of figures confronting each other. This could have been avoided by making the investigation a joint affair; then it could have been decided what year it was fair to begin with, not fair to both "sides," but a fair estimate of tobacco prices irrespective of "sides."

One of the principal difficulties in fact-finding seems too obvious to mention: the deliberate withholding of facts. The chief weapon of the speculators is to keep facts from the public. If they can induce the public to think there is a shortage, so much the better for them. Much might be written on this question, for we have abundant material both for and against the advisability of opening business records to the public. The withholding of facts must be connected with the question of the seeking for power. Consider the attitude of the coöperatives on this point. They are trying to stand in two places at once in regard to open business: open for members, shut for the public—a difficult position to maintain. One of the leading principles emphasized by many different speakers at the National Milk Producers' Federation at Springfield, was the need for every coöperative organization to keep its members fully informed as to all its policies and all the details of its business. It was urged that while it is characteristic of big corporations and of business in general to be secretive for fear of putting information into the hands of competitors, the coöperatives ought to adopt a different policy. But one of the southern coöperative associations refuses to publish individual warehouse receipts for fear of their effect on prices, or to give information as to their solvency, or to publish prices until the end of the year (the payments are made in instalments); they have not yet told the overhead cost, the number of members, the number of contract violations or the amount of available credit. Any of this information, they consider, will give power into the hands of their opponents.

But above every consideration in the gathering of facts we must notice that the findings of experts can often be divided into the facts which are indisputable and those which can be looked at differently by different people. To illustrate. Experts from various agricultural colleges meeting in conference decide on the best balanced ration for milch cows. In that formula are two different *kinds* of information: (1) the analysis of the different grains showing the percentage in each of protein, carbohydrate, fat and fibre; (2) what proportion of each grain in combination furnishes the best mixture for milch cows. It is of the utmost importance to make this distinction. The farmer can have no opinion about the first: if two farmers should disagree in regard to the percentage of protein in oats, discussion would be futile; the only thing they could do would be to consult a chemical expert. But a farmer can watch the effect of the formula on his cattle; he can vary the mixture and keep a record of results; a number of farmers doing this can compare results and report to the agricultural colleges. Thus each man's share in the matter would not be merely getting the best feed for his own cattle, but also contributing to the formula. Thus the formula may change with the experience (happily, or I should say significantly, a word from the same root as expert) of all. This is all that democracy means, that the experience of all is necessary. There is no innate urge or abstract right which assures us the knowledge of how to feed our cattle, we find merely that the plus-idea is the best thing man has yet fallen on. This is as true in politics as anywhere else. Democracy is not "idealism" but plain common sense.

In this matter of cattle-feeding there has been a change in the last two or three decades parallel with our change in political ideas. Some years ago the farmer's attitude was, "I guess I know how to feed my own cattle." This reminds us of the every-man-can-govern species of democracy. The present aim of many agricultural experts—to get the farmer to follow their formulæ blindly—is in line with all the over-emphasis today on the expert. But the better way is to find out how to combine the experience of the agricultural colleges and that of the farmers. The intelligent farmer does not take the formulæ of the colleges as revealed truth, but as a basis from which to begin his own observations. He knows that the expert is not one who has access to the secrets of the All-wise, but one who has a particular kind of experience which must be added to his own particular kind of experience, that both have their parts to play.

To carry this illustration a little further, let us note three parts in the process: the first entirely a matter for the expert (percentage of protein, etc.); the second a matter for expert plus farmer (the best mixture); the third entirely a matter for the farmer, that is, of two formulæ with equal proportions of protein, etc., but different ingredients, it is for him to decide which to use.

I have allowed myself this long illustration because of its significant suggestion for politics and industry. In politics we do not keep these different kinds of information apart; there we are always trying to change the proportion of protein and carbohydrate. To reduce this practice should be our aim. And our aim in the so-called democratic organization of industry should be, not to give the workmen a vote on things they know nothing about, but so to organize the plant that the workmen's experience can be added to that of the expert; we must see just where their experience will be a plus matter, and we must plan to have the workmen learn more and more of the industry as a whole. To think that a man can come from his particular machine and vote intelligently on the running of the business is exactly the mistake we have made in politics. The problem of most managers of industry is how to use their "objective measurements" after they get them; how to ensure that they will keep as much of their objectivity as possible, and how to make them operative through, not in spite of, the will of the workmen.

Every increase of technical knowledge and mechanical invention, as President Lowell has so well pointed out, increases our dependence on the expert.

The indispensability of the expert is accepted; what we need is a clearer understanding of his relation to ourselves.

Of all the many difficulties which arise in trying to connect the findings of the expert with the will of the people, perhaps the greatest is caused by the methods the expert is often willing to use in the presentation of facts. Secure in the belief that he is "right," he does not hesitate to stampede the general public into acceptance of his opinions, for in spite of our wish to think of the expert as an unprejudiced observer who has no opinion, we see little caffein-less information presented to the public. And I ought to add, in justice to the expert, that the public on its side has shown little inclination for nourishment without stimulant. But the fact remains, whether it is due more to the zeal of the expert or to the demand of the people, that there is a pernicious tendency to make the opinions of the expert prevail by crowd methods, to rush the people instead of educating them.[6] Indeed there is often more of this in the select circle of experts than elsewhere, for those of us who are not experts are occasionally a little humble about our opinions and somewhat reluctant about forcing them on others. Not so with the expert. I have seen the method used subtly, insinuatingly, most cleverly, by one of the foremost economists of America, one who has done the best kind of research work, speaking before a meeting of the Amalgamated Clothing Workers at one of their national conventions. And after the war when the propaganda for the League of Nations

[6] I am not forgetting the educational methods of the Red Cross and other societies, as well as of settlements and social workers in general.

began, there was in one city a committee composed largely of trained thinkers, one of them at least an "expert" in international matters, who had as part of their programme what they called a "whirlwind campaign" of the School Centres in various parts of the city where citizens' meetings were being held. "All we want," they said when asking for permission, "is for the people to stand up and be counted." But as one of the friends of the Centres remarked, "The Centres were not opened for men to stand up and be counted but to sit down and think." When the expert in international affairs is trying to "whirlwind" an audience into voting for the League of Nations, he is using exactly the same method as the demagogue.

There is much more in this point than appears on the surface: it is by no means enough to persuade the expert to give up crowd methods; he has to understand what the difference is between the crowd method and the non-crowd method. The essential difference is that the former creates wholes and the latter breaks up wholes. Let me explain. The object of the crowd-speaker is to get unanimity: the way he does this is to take all the different aspects of a situation, about which men might and do differ, and either combine them into something so vague that all can easily agree, or else get them under the roof of a single emotion. One emotion will cover a multitude of ideas. This point is delightfully made by Mr. Lippmann. The non-crowd method, as I shall show in Chapter IX, is just the opposite: it proceeds by analysis, differentiation, discrimination. And this matter of discrimination is concerned as much with the expert's investigation as with the process by which he communicates his results. Generalization is often implicit interpretation. For any scientific accuracy we must use interpretative terms guardedly. Words should not be used which imply a judgment, which award praise or blame. We must seek a language without emotional content. For fact-finding we must invent a fact-language. To keep strictly to the observation of behavior, and to force our language to record that behavior, is what is necessary. Someone tells us that this workman "stubbornly" continued to do so and so; this is an interpretative term, not the language of scientific accuracy. If situations could be reported with scientific accuracy, I believe it would have a very marked refluent effect on the expert's observation; it could not fail to make him observe more keenly, it could not fail to sharpen his perceptions, if he deliberately separated facts from interpretation and made his language correspond exactly to the facts. Few experts are alive to this.

And we on our part, we like the crowd-words they give us; they have taken on so many consecrated ideas and approved-of emotions that we feel reinforced, unconsciously, by what they have gathered to them. Also the acceptance of crowd-words is enormously encouraged by our inertia; they save us the trouble of analysis.

I have been watching the presentation of facts in the farmer-middleman controversy in the South. In reading the literature of the coöperative movement in the South during the last two years, as found in newspapers, trade journals, propagandist pamphlets, etc., one notices on the one hand the "facts" presented to the farmers by the promoters of the tobacco and cotton coöperative associations, and on the other hand the different "facts" given by those opposed to these associations, the warehouse men, speculators and bankers, who wish to maintain the old system. The official organ of one of these marketing coöperative associations boldly contradicts the "facts" of the middlemen. It sometimes does this with an emotional appeal, sometimes with a logical appeal, but there is no effort to convince the readers that the facts which are being used to controvert those of the other side have been gathered in such a way that one could be sure they were facts. As many academic controversies consist, alas, in statement and counter-statement of opinion, so here we have statement and counter-statement of fact. A method of presenting facts which should first establish the validity of their claim to be facts would both help in the resolution of the conflict and be educational.

This chapter must not be considered as showing any scepticism in regard to the value of facts. I know that much of our muddle today comes from a willingness to base our decisions and our actions on inaccurate information or mere assumptions. We see this daily. Any example that might be given seems too commonplace to mention. I recently served on a subcommittee to look into the matter of inexpensive boarding-houses in Boston, that way of living which most people consider the menace of the working girl in the large city. We found to our surprise that the working girls of Boston lived chiefly with their families or the family of a friend. There were exceptions, but these were taken care of by Brooks House, Franklin Square House and homes of that description, well conducted and carefully supervised houses. The welfare worker at Jordan & Marsh's department store told me that of their two thousand women employees practically none boarded; they commuted from about sixty-three towns. She too had been much surprised at this, as she had supposed one of her chief tasks would be the boarding-house problem. My sub-committee reported these facts to the main committee, but for weeks afterwards that committee in its discussions assumed, as they had done all their lives, that working girls in a city lived chiefly in boarding-houses and ran all the dangers involved. We quietly hit that assumption every time it reared its head, but never killed it entirely. The mere fact, however, of a sub-committee being appointed to investigate this subject was a step towards "accurate information."

Another thing is interesting: we are advancing the boundary-line of ascertainable facts; while insisting that we shall not discuss as matters of opinion what are matters of fact, we are finding that more and more subjects can be taken from the field of mere opinion. In a meeting of the manufacturing committee in a large industrial plant the members were considering the advertising for the Christmas trade, and the discussion was over the question whether a three-line advertisement for six weeks attracted more attention than a longer advertisement for a shorter period. As the advertising was to cover the whole country, the cost was of some importance. The discussion went on, sides were taken, until the President of the company walked in, heard what was going on and said, "Why discuss what we ought to be able to find out? I will ask the department of psychology at Columbia to take up this question. By getting their students to read magazine advertisements over an extended period and make careful notes of what attracts them, we may be able to get some information on the subject. Meanwhile let us not go through the farce of taking a vote on something we know nothing about; let us go on as we have done in previous years until we get something on which to base our opinions."

I give my full adherence to the doctrine of "accurate information." We see every day how necessary are warnings to us on this point. For instance, "applied psychology," of which we hear so much just now, means to many business men the consideration of the influence of personalities on each other rather than the responsibility of individuals to the situation—that is, to the facts. And when the politician relies on what he too calls "psychology," he means the handling of men instead of the facing of a situation—that is, the facts. And it is only too apparent that the weakness of diplomacy is that it puts a disproportionate emphasis on the understanding of the "psychology" of one's fellow diplomats as against an understanding of all the facts involved. The "psychology" of the individuals concerned is of course also a fact, and an important fact, of any situation; I am criticizing here merely the too exclusive use of this particular kind of fact.

We have been speaking of experts and people, and have neglected the middleman in government, the administrative official, and there are several things here to bear in mind.

First, administrative purpose usually outruns the

facts. Indeed the administrative official's ardor for facts usually begins when he wants to change the facts!

Then the overemphasis of investigation draws a line between the gathering of material and the interpreting of material: the expert is to gather and the official to interpret. No such sharpness of division is possible; the gathering is always in itself an interpreting. Interpreting is part of the vision, not something done with the vision. Where indeed can we look for the separation of fact and opinion? The Federated Press began its career by telling us that the Associated Press was partisan, but that it (the Federated Press) was going to be nonpartisan; that the Associated Press gave us opinions, but that it was going to give us facts. We can see how far they have been able to keep that promise.

Moreover, facts are not poured in on the administrative official in helter-skelter fashion, they undergo a certain process first, and fact-analysis is to some extent fact-interpretation. Condensation is implicit interpretation. Yet the official necessarily calls upon the expert to provide him with the facts of the case in condensed form.

Those who give us the trinity of accurate information, administrative policy and assent of people as the political process sometimes forget that their glorification of facts would tend to reduce the administrative officials to a shadow, would tend to make them mere mechanical appendages of the organized intelligence departments. And thus policy becomes as foreordained as consent. There must be a place for experts *and* administrative officials *and* people.

And I wish those who advocate a more extensive system of fact-gathering would tell us more of the subsequent fact-handling. Since the war, Washington as a store-house of steadily accumulating research-reports has become a joke. Consider the vast sums spent by the Shipping Board alone and the material gathered; if the administrative officials are making use of this, they have kept it a secret from the rest of us.

I have left to the last what seems to me the most serious flaw in any exposition which makes a chasm between the expert and the people to be bridged only by the frail plank of consent. But I wish here merely to state, what cannot be elaborated until a later chapter, that the "will of the people" is already in the situation which the expert investigates; that the investigation of the expert often changes the situation (an investigation of the standard of living often raises the standard of living); and that the people help to create and to develop, by their response, the situation to which they are responding. The expert's opinion, the administrative official's opinion, the people's opinion, all affect the situation, so that before the expert has finished reporting and the administrative official deciding and the people "willing," the situation has changed. In short, my argument against acquiescence as the people's part in the political process depends first on the fact, in my opinion basic and all-important, that different kinds of accurate information are required, that of the expert and that of the people; secondly on the changing character of the fact-situation; third on the activities of the people as integral with the changing situation.

The expert must find his place within the social process; he can never be made a substitute for it. Technical experience must be made a part of all the available experience. When we see expert and administrative official, legislator and judge, *and* the people, all integral parts of the social process, all learning how to make facts, how to view facts, how to develop criteria by which to judge facts, then only have we a vision of a genuine democracy. We have not to choose between becoming an expert on every subject ourselves and swallowing whole the reports of experts. The training of the citizen must include both how to form opinion on expert testimony and how to watch one's own experience and draw conclusions from it.

I should like to say, as an indirect summing up of this chapter, that I wish we could understand the word expert as expressing an attitude of mind which we can all acquire, rather than the collecting of information by a special caste. While appreciating fully the necessity of more scientific observation, what we chiefly need I believe is not so much to increase the expertness of the expert in the hope that thereby we shall automatically increase the consensus of the consent, but for all of us to acquire the scientific attitude of mind, to base our life on actual experience, of my own plus that of others, rather than on preconceived notions. Much of our present clamor for the expert is, I fear, a "defence reaction," a confession of our own weakness. Many of us are calling for experts because, acutely conscious of the mess we are in, we want someone to pull us out. What we really wish for is a "beneficent" despot, but we are ashamed to call him that and so we say scientific investigator, social engineer, etc. Many of us are like the little girl who goes to her mother with her tangled knitting: she goes, often, not to learn to knit, but to be got out of a scrape. What we have to do is to learn how to use the findings of the expert: it is not by a blind acceptance; neither by balancing them against our own "innate" ideas; it is by learning how to unite experience with experience.

The social process is not, first, scientific investigation, then some method of persuading the people to abandon their own experience and thought, and lastly an acclaiming populace. The social process is a process of coöperating experience. But for this every one of us must first acquire the scientific attitude of mind. This will not make us professional experts; it will enable us to work with professional experts and to find our place in a society which needs the experience of all, to build up a society which shall embody the experience of all.

II

VICARIOUS EXPERIENCE: IS THE LEGAL ORDER THE GUARDIAN OF TRUTH?

THERE is no such thing as vicarious experience. The expert alone is not the revealer of truth. The judge alone is not the guardian of truth. Neither expert nor judge can be offered as the remedy for "the failure of democracy."

I spoke above of the present-day seeking for reality in facts, in the "objective situation," as only half our quest. We have, however, one great current of intelligence which is consciously striving to weld together into a reciprocally enriching unity principles and the objective situation. The legal order today is telling us that precedents are to be interpreted in the light of events always in flux. The philosophy of law today, in the hands of such men as Dean Pound, is contributing not only to jurisprudence but to the study of every aspect of human relations.

The founder of the modern theory of jurisprudence, Jhering, insisted that law is not a system of abstract principles, but rests on the objective purpose to be served. The acceptance of this view marked an important step in juristical thinking. Another step is now being taken, for that "objective purpose" is understood today as a purpose which is never static but which changes as rapidly as life changes. One activity sets in motion many others; in the interweaving of these lies at any one moment the sought-for purpose. Innumerable examples spring to mind of the way in which purpose develops. Take the aims of English labor a few years ago: the eight-hour day, union-recognition, safety devices for machinery, general health regulations, and the nationalization of mines and railroads. These were the interests labor wished secured. But now the eight-hour is changing to a six-hour demand, the demand for union recognition is changing to the demand for union control, health regulations are being brought about indirectly through insurance laws, and the wish for the nationalization of mines and railroads is giving way to the wish for guild control. Wherever one turns one sees examples of the evolving purpose. Credit Unions, begun in protest to bankers' contracts, became the sources for coöperative enterprise. Lockouts, begun as a weapon against strikes, became a way of breaking the union. Farmers coöperated to raise prices and then began to work for better schools. A capital illustration is the way shop-committees often develop. I asked the head of a big electrical plant where I went to learn something of its shop-committees what his purpose had been in starting them. He replied instantly: "To get the managerial policy across." But as I looked further into these committees, I found that the purposes they were serving—the purposes disclosed by their activities—were quite different from the one given me. This evolving purpose, rather than a preconceived purpose, is what the legal order has always to take into account, for while you are "securing" ends, life goes on to make ends of its own very different perhaps from the original ones.

A telelogical psychology sees an anticipatory purpose—the individual does so and so because it anticipates certain results; a teleological sociology is founded on anticipatory purposes; a teleological jurisprudence conceives the function of law as comparison of present activity with a preconceived purpose. But what the legal order has to do is not to hug its blueprints, but to recognize the purpose which the activity discloses. Yet while the judge can have no charted purpose, no architect's plan, by which to construct his decisions, still we must remember, in considering what the evolving situation means for jurisprudence, that the decisions of the judge do far more than take note of its developing character—they contribute towards it. While the power of the legal order as something outside the social process imposing patterns upon it has been greatly exaggerated, its place within that process has often been underestimated. This will be referred to again in a later chapter.

But if one accepts the notion of an evolving purpose, the next question is one of valuation: who is to decide between the values of various purposes? I think here the function of the legal order is not always conceived with entire accuracy. One writer tells us that the validity of law "is determined by the ends which the law seeks to realize." But who is to judge the validity of ends? We do not "decide" on ends, a word which occurs in much juristical writing today; ends appear from out our concrete activities. Again we hear that law is to meet real needs; many writers use this expression. But who knows what "real" needs are? Still another jurist tells us that the question always to be asked in law is "Does it serve a *useful* purpose?" Who is to have the decision as to what is useful? Is not that just where our difficulty, our perfectly genuine puzzlement, usually lies? And when we hear that there is now to be a conscious attempt to make law conform to ideals, we are still left inquiring, Whose ideals? It is said: "The State secures those interests which it thinks most worth while to protect." How does it know which are most worth while? Cardozo, thinking that "the interest that is better founded in reason and more worthy of protection should be helped to achieve victory," asks specifically, "How is the judge to know when one interest outweighs another?" And we are told that he must learn it from the practice of his art, "from tradition, other judges, the collective judgment of the profession, the pervading spirit of the law."[1] But the judge cannot learn how to weigh interests from legal tradition, legal reason, legal activity alone—as of course Cardozo knew.

In short, when we are now told that the problem has become one of valuing—of finding criteria of the relative value of interests—our first thought is: How is this valuing to be done, who is to do it? Mr. Justice Holmes brings in the word social. He speaks of establishing the postulates of law on "accurately measured social desires." He tells us that it is because of the estimated relative worth of our different social ends that we extend the sphere of one principle and allow another gradually to dwindle into atrophy. Here again the question we naturally ask is, Who is to "accurately measure"? Who is to "estimate relative worth"? But

[1] Benjamin N. Cardozo, *The Nature of the Judicial Process.*

Mr. Holmes gives us some hint of a process by which, in his opinion, these desires receive measurement when he says that the justification of a law must be found in some help which it "brings towards reaching a social end which the governing power of the community has made up its mind that it wants."[2] But law is far more than either the weapon of the strong or the protector of the weak, as no one has better shown us than Mr. Holmes. Social interests are not exclusively the interests of the governing power, nor can they be declared by the legal order alone. The evaluation of interests involves the psychological development of an interacting people; it depends not on "the wisdom of the judge" except as he is part of that development.

Moreover, the distinction between individual and social interests needs careful analysis. The phrase social interest is, to be sure, now defined with precision by modern jurisprudence, but the legal meaning has not yet found its way into general usage, hence arises some confusion of thought. Moreover, while the word interest is today employed by jurists in its psychological sense, until recently that word has been used by the legal order as well as by economists not in its psychological meaning, but as connoting economic advantage. Many jurists have thought, as Pound has pointed out, that they could dispense with the most pressing human claims by demonstrating that no economic advantage was involved in them. The interest involved was what that particular jurist thought the people concerned *ought* to need, what they ought to want, what ought to be their economic advantage considering them in the abstract. Today, however, the

[2] *Law in Science—Science in Law* in *Collected Legal Papers*.

"interests" of the legal order are merely the de facto claims and desires of concrete individuals; "social interests" are such claims generalized. Yet even if interest is no longer employed by jurists in the sense of economic advantage, even if one of the contributions of contemporary jurisprudence to all the social sciences is the getting away from the "individual in vacuo" (as from those absolute rights which can never conflict), still I think that because the word social is used so loosely in general speech and writing, it would be well if either it could be avoided in legal literature, when possible, or else the sense in which it is employed more fully explained. In general literature the word social is often used as a pure abstraction; or it is used to express a personal estimate—what a man himself thinks the best way of acting he dignifies by calling it the social way; it is used as a blanket expression by all of us when we feel too lazy to think out what we really mean; it is used emotionally times without number. Therefore, while the jurists of today are not using the word social either sentimentally or subjectively, are not using it either as an abstraction or a rationalization, but merely, as I said above, in the sense of a concrete claim or desire generalized, still it seems to me that a distinction which is thought of by many people so vaguely and inaccurately as the distinction between individual and social interest might well be replaced by something else, as perhaps by the difference involved in the long and the short view.

One point I think is very necessary to note in this discussion, and that is that we sometimes go astray in our use of the word social because different uses of that word merge so imperceptibly one into the other; they merge so imperceptibly that two sets of people dealing with the same situation may employ this word in different ways without its being noticed. It is often used as a "rationalization" when all the time there *is* a genuine social interest if it be employed in another sense. For instance, we are told that the organization of winter sports is a social interest because winter sports are good for the health, yet we all know that they are being encouraged in New England towns because they bring trade to the local stores and hotels. But this also is a "social interest" without any rationalization at all, for it is a concrete claim generalized. Again, when town-planning is presented to the general public, it is presented as an æsthetic policy with an appeal to local pride based on a comparison with what other towns are doing. Yet the boards of trade in our small cities, most of the members of which are interested in local real estate development, accept town-planning after they have been convinced that it pays. After that we have town-planning bills in the legislature. When two of our state courts declared that such legislation should stand, had they recognized "social" or individual values? Social values, to be sure, in the sense in which jurists use that term—individual values generalized—but not in the sense in which that term was used when the social reformers or the architects or the legislators supporting the measure addressed the voters. These speakers used it with its emotional appeal, with its moralistic appeal of "sacrificing" your individual interests to the "general good." I think, therefore, a term unfortunate which has this objection of double usage; it seems to me that often it would be well to substitute for individual and social interests, the idea of the short and the long view. Whenever we are informed, as we often are in juristical writing, that the court has made a particular decision not in the individual interest of plaintiff or defendant, but in the social interest of the security of acquisitions and security of transactions, we recognize that that is an accurate statement, and yet the layman who has suffered much and long from the crowd orators' use of the phrase, from promoters of all kinds, might prefer the notion of an *individual* interest in the security of acquisitions and security of transactions divided into the short and the long view. When we are told by jurists that the Germanic peace which played so large a part in building common law—the house peace, the peace of highways, the peace of festivals, the peace of markets—was a securing of social interests against individual self-assertion, it seems to me that here too we might prefer to make the distinction between what is to the interest of individuals for the moment, and in "the long run." When it was found difficult to enforce the Rivers' Pollution Act in some towns in England, the mill-owners, who were the chief offenders, were finally won over not by urging them to sacrifice their individual for the social interest, but by showing them that their interest in the long run was unpolluted rivers.

What I am objecting to chiefly is the self-deception which the notion of "social interest" allows or even encourages. I saw it stated in a description of the coöperative movement among the fruit growers of California, that Calfornia had bankers and merchants so socially minded, so public spirited, that they supported the coöperative movement because they saw that, however it might affect banker or merchant, it was better for the community as a whole, they saw that they had an "opportunity to render a great public service." But this was not the reason for their participation in the coöperative movement. It is obvious, and those merchants and bankers who went into the coöperative movement saw it, that the merchants will not do much business unless the growers are prosperous and have money to spend. It is equally true that the bankers' prosperity is in the long run bound up with the prosperity of the farmer: whatever increases bank deposits, develops the farming industry and stabilizes real values, helps the banker; orderly marketing means orderly financing and avoids peaks and dips in the credit situation.

The difference here is clearly between a short and a long view. It is true that the old "time-merchants" who charged exorbitant prices to cover bad debts and long accounts, being able to do so because they had the farmers in their power, made something out of the farmers' extremity, but in the long run it is obvious they stand to gain by the farmers' prosperity. The same is true of the bankers: temporary high rates of interest are not to the bankers' advantage in the long run because the conditions on which they are founded are to the advantage of no one in the community.

Examples could be multiplied indefinitely. Any plan made to initiate or stimulate joint effort in small towns is usually presented to the townspeople as an appeal to their sense of "social" values as against individual values, which they are told they must "sacrifice." How often we hear that *cliché!* But the difference between competition and joint effort is a difference between a short and a long view. When we become enlightened enough to realize that we individually get more out of joining with people than by competing with them, we do it. For instance, formerly the local stores in a small town competed sharply with one another. Now, in some places they are beginning to join in an effort to secure the trade of the outlying farming districts and of the summer residents who tend to buy from the city by mail order. They do this by saving capital through common store-houses, through dividing specialties and thus increasing stock without increasing expenditure, by improving local service through coöperative deliveries, etc.

I should like to say, too, in support of the suggestion that the short and the long interest is perhaps a conception fraught with less possibility of self-deception than that of individual and social interests, that I do not find the distinction between individual and social made anywhere in actual life. I telephoned to my bank this morning and asked what my balance was. They replied that they could not tell me unless there was someone there who could recognize my voice, and added, "This is to protect you." If I ask them in a shop to give me some article although I have not my charge coin with me, and they refuse, they always say, "We have this rule in order to protect you." In neither case do I hear anything of the social interest. In both cases, however, they show me that my immediate is against my long-run interest. Nowhere in actual practice do I find the categories of individual and social interest.

Another difficulty in the distinction between individual and social interest is that even after you have decided on the validity of social interests, it is not always possible to tell what the social interest is. For instance, is our law in regard to illegitimate children an illustration of the sacrificing of individual interests for the social interest in the security of domestic institutions? There are people who think the social interest better secured by laws which legitimatize the children of the unmarried mother. I am giving no consideration to this question; I mention it merely to point out that there would be a difference of opinion here in regard to the social interest. Agreements on such points will come not through accepting the wisdom of one man, the judge, or of the legal order, but through the interweaving of many desires and attitudes, emotions and ideas, through much trial and error.

There is one consideration alone which should show the undesirableness of the separation of social and individual. When society is given an interest, this tends with some writers to make an entity of the "social soul," the "group mind." "Social interests," "general security," "public safety," is it possible for these to be other than individual interests, individual security, individual safety? If we are looking to the future, social interest may be merely a synonym for the unborn—individuals. One of the ways in which Kohler allowed his conception of Hegel to influence him unduly was when he conceived the development of society as separate from the development of individuals "each trying to perfect itself." This very markedly influences his philosophy of law, but there should be no separation between development of individual and development of society.

Moreover, it seems to me that in some of the writing of today which tells us of "social ends," we are bound to a certain extent by deterministic assumptions. Do we see, as we should, that social ends are not pre-existing things but eventual things, to use an illuminating expression of Dr. Kallen's? Do we not run the risk of making the same error which Graham Wallas tends a little to make in *The Social Heritage*, where he sometimes seems to invoke the "Good Life" as an abstraction? The arbitrary determination of interests may lead us into as many errors as the doctrine of "rights." To declare that certain interests, aims, are "social," and therefore valid, and that some are not, is exactly as arbitrary as when any jurist of the past chose certain principles and declared them "right." The arbitrary choice of interests is no more legitimate than the arbitrary assumption of rights.

But if the expression social interest has seemed somewhat unsatisfactory of late, and if the distinction between the short and the long view given above is not adequate to cover all cases, or cannot be invoked when we are dealing with a sharply drawn conflict the immediate issues of which for the persons involved overshadow all other considerations, there seems to be some reason in the development of recent thinking for substituting the term integrating interests—the integrating of individual interests—for that of social interests, or to give the latter term this more concrete meaning. With English, American and German psychologists, physiologists, and physicists too, now employing the term integration, it may certainly be considered in good use, and the students of the social sciences may well ask if it is not exactly the word they need to describe what their own observations note. And as for some years now jurisprudence has seemed in advance of the other social sciences, so here too we find it in the forefront of thinking. We see a theory of law now emerging which goes as far beyond social interest in the looser usage of that phrase, as that conception was an advance on individual interests in the sense of private or personal interests. We see signs of this newer theory in our courts, in legislation, in juristic writing. This theory rests on a recognition of the fact that opposed interests are not necessarily incompatible interests.

In Massachusetts the judges of our Small Claims Court have the opportunity to show us law as not inevitably a struggle resulting in victory for one side and defeat for the other, but as a struggle which may show the way by which each side can attain its desire. The following shows the point. Smith brought suit against Panotti, a small fruit-dealer, for a debt of forty dollars and attached his business for that amount. Panotti claimed that the payment of that sum would ruin his business. The judge ruled (he could not have done it before the law which went into effect January, 1921) that the amount be paid in instalments out of the defendant's earnings. What is the result? Smith gets his money; Panotti's business is not injured. Both are satisfied. I believe that in every conflict—beween persons or nations, classes or races—this method should be tried. We cannot always reach such happy conclusions as in the case of Smith vs. Panotti, but I think we should succeed much more often than we now think possible; at any rate it seems as if the method were worth a trial. I wish someone would make a study of recent decisions of the bench to see what evidence could be found of the recognition of the fact that cases brought to court, while showing apparently clashing desires, may at the same time reveal to a perceptive judge the way by which the desires on both sides can be fulfilled. Dicey says that the history of law has been the history of "rough compromises" between "conflicting rights." It does not seem now as if that need always be true. The illustration I have given was not a compromise; it would have been if Smith had had to be satisfied with twenty-five dollars. I believe that the legal order is now beginning to see that there may often be found by acute, fair-minded, and inventive judges ways of settling disputes which give to both sides what they really want. The increasing powers given to the judges in the municipal courts may give the opportunity for this.

There have been of recent years many integrations made by legislation; there seems happily to be a growing tendency in that direction. Take the Workmen's Compensation Act; the active coöperation between employers and workmen to carry out this law shows its value to both. The employer has the following advantages: he had formerly to pay much more when the employee's lawyer succeeded in winning the case than he pays now; and there was an uncertainty hanging over a business that might be wiped out if a serious accident occurred. On the other hand, the employees under the old system either did not get anything if the other side won, or even if they themselves won, they had to wait a long time for the award and payment, when it was at the moment of the injury or illness that they needed the money. Since the negligence of fellow-workmen has been included, the employee has been fully protected. This is a good example of the integrating of individual interests.

Moreover, the doctrine of integrating interests does away with that of the balance of interests which has so many advocates. And this modifies Adams' theory of law as the resultant of the struggle for power. When Adams points out that contradictory precedents register the points of dominant power he says, "You will find . . . that the law is regularly wrenched, more or less violently, from its logical path, to facilitate the rise of each new species of the competitive man, and that it is again dislocated to accelerate that species' fall." And since lawyers "may be assured that that party will prevail before courts of justice whose cause embodies power rather than logic," his advice to them is "to measure intelligently the relative energy of the forces locked in the controversies" in which they may participate.[3] While I am sure that there is much truth in this, I do not think it is wholly true. In fact, observation of industrial controversy for the last ten years leads me to think that those disputes which are "settled" merely by the balance of power are not really settled at all. The slightest shift of power brings the matter up again with accumulated rancor and hard feeling. The balance theory gets us nowhere in law or politics or international relations.

The illustration just given of the Workmen's Compensation Act shows the important thing about integration. The moment you try to integrate loss, you reduce loss; as when you try to integrate gain, you increase gain. This is the whole claim of integration over either domination or compromise, the three ways of dealing

[3] Brooks Adams, 19 *Green Bag,* 32–33.

with conflict. In either of the latter you rearrange existing material, you make quantitative not qualitative adjustments, you adjust but do not create. In the case of the Workmen's Compensation Act, you have done more than distribute loss, you have prevented loss. This is creating. You have not balanced or weighed interests, those of industry, workers and community. By integrating these interests you get the increment of the unifying.[4]

A further aspect of such legislation is of great significance in showing one of the essential functions of legislation to be adjusting conflicts in advance of the conflicts by providing the means of integrating before the conflict has taken place. It would take another book to unfold the implications of this thought. We are now given a conception of politics which can so vitalize our political life that it may yet emerge from the slough of greed and strife in which it is so largely immersed at present.

We have been considering legislation which tries to integrate interests instead of choosing between them. From this point of view do we want "labor legislation"? It is at any rate an unfortunate term. Labor legislation is called social legislation. It cannot be both. If it were truly labor legislation it would be class legislation, and class legislation does not become social by legislature or court so declaring it. Of course the interdependence of society is recognized in most labor legislation; it is not therefore labor but social legislation. This is however a good illustration of one of the dangers of this word; it shows the temptation to call what *we* think good "social." "Social behavior" usu-

[4] This is taken up at length in Chaps. III and IX.

ally means the behavior of which the person using the expression approves.

I have said that we now see the theory of integrating interests emerging in legal writing as well as in legislation and legal decision. I refer chiefly to what Pound has written of relation. All that he says of relation implies that we must seek and bring into use those modes of association which will reveal joint interests: those between employer and employee, landlord and tenant, master and servant. Law, he tells us, must find the essential nature of the relation; this seems to me a more profound truth than some of the vaguer theories of social interests. Moreover, Pound defines social interests as "the claims or demands involved in the existence of society," and here we have nothing vague or abstract. "The social interest in the individual," "the individual interest in the social," must become coördinate expressions. Thus does the individual preserve his integrity through all our "social" theories. Thus also we do not discard the abstract man of the nineteenth century only to put in his place an abstract society; social interests are the interests of men in their multitudinous and every-varying *relations*.

Pound tells us also that relation is taking the place of contract in modern law, that the duties of public service corporations are not contractual, flowing from agreement, but quasi-contractual, flowing from the calling in which the public servant is engaged. Social in its doubly concrete significance—in the sense of interdependence, and as the authority derived from the activity involved—is happily a conception which is gaining ground. Much remedial legislation rests on the growing realization of the interdependence of community life. When certain bankers and welfare agencies in Massachusetts decided a few years ago that the loan shark was a social evil which ought to be curbed, and banded together to secure the passage of the Small Loan Act, it resulted not in benefit to themselves directly but to the group of workingmen who were the borrowers. Yet it was felt that the community life as a whole was more sound. Pound gives a number of examples of the recognition of community of interests, such as the limitations on building laws, limitations on the part of creditors to exact satisfaction, limitation on water rights, etc.[5] A community of interests understood as a unifying of interests benefiting and developing individuals, benefiting and developing society, is the true social interest. In this sense the conceptions of the social function of property, the social functions of industry, have been very valuable ones in the progress of the last twenty years because they acted against "special" and "private" interests.

Perhaps, indeed, the prejudice against individual interests has come from the fact that they are often associated with the bad meaning we give to "special" interests, but this is unfortunate. If some years ago we began to use social as a blanket word which meant anything that was not "private" or "personal" or "special," if then and therefore it came unhappily to be considered the opposite of individual also, surely the time has come now for a closer analysis, and for us to realize that the opposite of all particularity may yet keep its oneness with everything individual, that in fact its authority is derived from nothing else but interweaving *individual* activity.

[5] *Harv. Law Rev.*, 28, 195–234.

The greatest objection perhaps to the word social has not yet been touched on. We live today in a power-society; therefore social interest by its very wording *might* mean the interest of the most powerful class or individuals. What we sometimes hear called "the social recognition of an individual interest" may be merely the legalizing of a particularly private interest. When we abandon our power-society, we can perhaps use the expression social interest without ambiguity; it can then mean the interest involved in, evolved by, relation.

Moreover, if we should substitute the conception of integrating individual interests for that of social interests, I think we should avoid the fallacy involved in the idea of "as many interests as possible to be secured." For here we come dangerously near involving ourselves in regard to social and individual interests in Rousseau's distinction between the general will and the will of all. Society flourishes through the satisfaction of individual human desire, yet not through as many as possible, but through interweaving human desires.

To sum up this section. The chief objections to the term social interests are: with too zealous advocates it may mean the abandonment of the individual; with some it opens too easily the gates of the ever-ready stream of sentimentality in us all—it has been vitiated or at any rate weakened by platform and propagandist use; and especially, it is very difficult not to connect the social interest with the interest of the governing class. It seems to me that the phrase integrating individual interests, as referring both to the possible outcome of conflict and the anticipation of conflict, both to the measure of value and the developing of value, is a more fruitful and more legitimate expression than that of social interests, and one supported by both recent legal and psychological thinking as well as by our most profound philosophy. The gravest danger in the word social is that society tends too readily with all of us to become an abstraction. Social interests are often either an abstraction or a "rationalization"; integrating interests are both concrete and genuine.

Yet I realize that both philosophically and practically there may be advantages in the word social: philosophically because we need a word to indicate that integration is not mere coördination, practically because it is sometimes better to re-define an old term than to invent a new one. What we must be careful about, if we do use it, is that we do define it carefully. Perhaps we shall be rid of some of the objections I have noted to the term social when there has been time for those two doctrines of contemporary psychology—the *Gestalt* theory and what I have called the theory of circular behavior—to penetrate our thinking in the social sciences. For the implications of these doctrines confirm our philosophical thinking, our empirical observations in the social field, in regard to the unity of individual and society. Many people who embrace the doctrine of social interests advocate the "sacrificing" of the individual to the social, but these can never be sufficiently opposed for one to be "sacrificed" to the other, since the social interest is not merely an interweaving of individual interests, it is an interweaving *with* the parts as well as an interweaving *of* the parts. This makes it impossible to pit individual and society against each other. This at the same time saves us from the suggestion of atomism in the word individual and from the suggestion of abstraction in the word social.

We can now answer the questions asked at the beginning of this chapter. We see now at the same time the function of the legal order and in what way that function is limited. Social interests, as now defined, emerge *as* social interests through a certain process; the inestimable service of the judges is to open the way for and to promote this process. They can never take a step beyond; they can never substitute themselves for the process. The judge must understand the life of his day, but he can live life for no one. Not in the wisdom of the judge nor the facts of the expert nor the "will of the people," but in life itself do we put our trust. A more penetrating analysis of the interactivities of men in their daily lives is what is needed today.

To be sure the judge must know and consider all three essentials: (1) the principles, (2) the precedents, which include both the application of principle and the emergence of principle—it is important to notice this double aspect of precedent—and (3) the particular case in hand. The interpretation of the Anti-Trust Act is an example of the emergence of principle from legal enactment. In applying the statute, the first cases appeared to prevent certain useful forms of combination. The court therefore resorted to what has been termed the rule of reason, and decided in particular cases that the monopoly was beneficial and should be allowed to continue. The wiser the judge the more ability he shows in uniting principle, precedent and case in hand. Any reading of legal history shows us that when the legal order is not able to do this, the principle tends to become choked by the precedents. Thus our view of the origin of law does not reduce the obligation of judges to be very closely in touch with the social facts of their day—on the contrary it increases many times that obligation—but we must also remember, what is often forgotten, that the integrating of principles and facts has taken place to some extent before the matter comes to court. Law has its origin in the concrete daily activities of us all.

We need not commit ourselves to *laissez-faire* doctrine, nor, on the other hand, entrust to the legal order a too exclusive guardianship of our "rights" or interests. Another doctrine is emerging. The social agency of the law is not something *outside* the democratic process, an apparatus of safeguards provided as a check upon misdirections of "will." Still less can we think that there are patterns of what is socially valid which can be invoked from time to time to be superimposed upon the changing order in order to correct its aberrations. Law must be integral with the social order.

And yet this does not take away from the function of the legal profession, but rather adds to it. The legal order by helping to integrate purposes is helping to produce larger purposes. The judicial decision must anticipate this process, it must meet the larger purpose even although the larger purpose does not exist until the contribution of that very decision has been made. Thus the difference between declared and de facto purpose is more subtle than is always seen: the judge is working for an end which does not exist as an end, wholly, until he begins working for it.

III

EXPERIENCE IN THE LIGHT OF RECENT PSYCHOLOGY: CIRCULAR RESPONSE

THE principle of integrating *interests* is not yet sufficiently recognized and acted on by jurists and economists, the principle of integrating *power* is not sufficiently acknowledged by political scientists. But while many political scientists and economists as well as statesmen and labor arbitrators have stuck to the theory of the balance of power, of the equilibrium of interests, yet life continually escapes them, for whenever we advance we slip from the bondage of equilibrium.

This view, which springs so insistently to the eye with every fresh study of social situations, is supported by our recent psychology which is giving us more than hints of a truth that may mean large changes for politics, economics and law. The heart of the truth about integration is the connection between the relating of two activities, their interactive influence, and the values thereby created. This chapter will be devoted to a consideration of that point, or rather to the contribution of psychology on this point; a separate chapter (IX) will take up, chiefly by illustration, what the study of social situations yields on the subject of integration as the creative principle.

Progressive experience, I say, depends on the relating. The ardent search for objectivity, the primary task of the fact worshippers, cannot be the whole task of life, for objectivity alone is not reality. The crux of philosophical controversy we have seen mirrored everywhere. As the subjective idealists have overemphasized the subject, and the realists, the object, so there are the historians who deny "economic determinism" and those who give it more than its place; there are the political scientists who talk of "the will of the people" and those who, in reaction to "empty will," give us the "objective situation" as always our ruler; there are the jurists who exaggerate abstract conceptions and those who see all truth in "social facts." In the arts, especially in painting, the swing of the pendulum between "subjectivity" and "objectivity" is most interestingly apparent. In psychology we have the introspectionists and the behaviorists.

I do not see how such opposing tendencies can be avoided while we see reality either in subject or in object; I do not see how we can run fast enough from one to the other to keep ourselves within the region of truth. But our latest psychology is taking a step beyond this and putting itself in line with the oldest philosophy. Holt,[1] more clearly perhaps than any other recent writer, has shown us that reality is in the relating, in the activity-between.[2] He shows us

[1] Edwin B. Holt: *The Freudian Wish, The Place of Illusory Experience in a Realistic World* (one of the studies in *The New Realism*), *The Concept of Consciousness.* I have also had the privilege of reading some of Dr. Holt's unpublished lectures as taken down by students. There are undoubtedly many things in this book with which Dr. Holt would not agree, some inferences which he might think mistaken, but I have given what for me are the implications of his thought.

[2] In *The New Realism*, p. 366, he defines reality as "some very comprehensive system of terms in relation." He expresses this more

how in the "behavior-process" subject and object are equally important and that reality is in the relating of these, is in the endless evolving of these relatings. This has been the grain of gold of the profoundest thinkers from Aristotle to the present day. Of course the object is not created by the percipient; of course the subject is no more "a mere reflex arc" than it is an evangelical soul; nor are subject and object "products" of a vital force. For a century, roughly speaking, objective idealism has given us—its innermost truth—existence as unitary experience which upon analysis resolves itself into the two great generic differings which have been called subject and object. Now physiologists and psychologists in their treatment of response are approaching this view.

The present psychological treatment of response, by emphasizing "the total situation," happy phrase showing the importance of the outer object or situation as constituent of the behavior process, is extraordinarily interesting to students of social research. Add to the total situation what might be called the evolving situation, as hinted in Holt's formula and clarified by him in other places, and you have an important contribution to the social sciences. This formula defines behavior as a function of environment and identifies thought (purpose, will) with that function. The use of the mathematical term function has many suggestive implications. For instance, this definition of behavior, taken with the rest of this writer's teaching, implies the possible reciprocal influence of subject and object, or to keep to the language of the mathematical analogy,

actively later, although nowhere explicitly as a definition of reality. In fact the word reality is now very little used; it does not fit in with our present mode of thinking.

implies that the variables of this formula *may* be interdependent, either being a function of the other.[3] He does, it is true, in one place speak of environment as if it were always an *in*dependent variable,[4] and that would make his formula inapplicable for what we see in most social situations; industrial conditions are influencing the behavior of trade unions while the behavior of trade unions is influencing industrial conditions. But while Holt uses the words "object" or "object of environment" continually, he often uses also "situation," "event," "process," and with these words it becomes more obvious that the "object" is being influenced by the "subject" while the "subject" is being influenced by the "object." Moreover, in the illustration he gives of the girl discriminating between different plays, he says that her choice influences "the sound moral development of the institution itself."[5] Here the theatre is not an independent but one of two interdependent variables. When we are employing this formula, therefore, we have to decide in the case

[3] Perhaps an illustration, although it may be only roughly accurate, would make this clearer. Take the European situation and a gold mine in America. The European situation and the amount of gold taken out of the mine are two interdependent variables either one of which may be taken as a function of the other. The European situation will vary according to the amount of gold taken out, that is, it "depends" on it, and it is equally true the other way around, for the total amount of gold taken out will depend somewhat on the European situation. Increase the birth-rate in Europe and more gold will be taken out at Nome. If, however, we should be speaking not of the actual amount of gold taken from the mine, but of the percentage per ton of gold in quartz in a mine, the matter is quite different. The European situation is affected by the variation in this percentage, but the percentage varies quite independently of the European situation; increase the birth-rate in Europe and you do not increase the percentage per ton. We have no longer two interdependent variables; the percentage of gold per ton is an independent variable of which the European situation is a function.

[4] *The Freudian Wish*, p. 95.

[5] *Op cit.*, p. 124.

in hand whether environment is an independent or one of two interdependent variables—it is in each case a question of observed fact.

The interweaving of the different factors of the evolving situation sometimes takes place so rapidly before our eyes as to make the process very plain. On a Wage Board, one year, we were up against an interesting objective situation: a drop in prices, indications of unemployment, and at the same time a demand for higher wages in that particular industry. In anticipation of the proposed heightened wage scale which our Board was to effect, some employers were turning off their less efficient workers. We had to ask each week the changes in that respect in the objective situation; those changes had been brought about by the trend of our deliberations, but also our deliberations were very much affected by these changes. We saw that it would be a disadvantage to the employees as well as to employers to have the minimum wage too high, since we had evidence in the actual situation, not mere threats, that that would mean a certain amount of unemployment.

This reciprocal influence, this evolving situation, fundamental for politics, economics and jurisprudence, is made clearer if for the words thought, purpose, will in a description of the behavior process, we substitute thinking, purposing, willing. It is not thought which Watson is writing about, but thinking, for surely Watson if anyone gives us thinking as a process. As long as we use the word thought there is a tendency to think that bodily mechanisms are the expression, the organs, of thought, whereas they *are* thought, or rather, they are thinking. Again, there is a tendency to conceive of thought as the thing we have left over when we have finished thinking, the thing which thinking produces. All static expressions should be avoided. Integrated organism (one psychologist speaks of "the completely integrated organism") is unfortunate, for the organism is the continuing activity of self-organizing, self-maintaining. We must be careful of the "eds" because they lead to "wholes," the wrong kind of wholes, the "influence of the whole on the parts," etc.[6] Such expressions as "coördinated wholes" are seen in the writings of some of the behaviorists, but, unless explained, seem against the very truth which behaviorism is trying to stand for. An "-ed" becomes a stopping place to thought, and when man cannot think any further it is dangerous. God has been to many races and to many individuals the place where thinking stops, as mind is often "the sanctuary of ignorance."

To return to our consideration of the behavior process, Holt has made his formula clear by a description of the working of two laws: one from physiology, one from physics. First he has shown us the importance of the physiological law that when a muscle contracts,[7] the sense-organ in that muscle is stimulated so that there is an almost simultaneous afferent nerve impulse from the muscle back to the centre, and thus a circular reflex is established. Hence the contraction of the muscle is only in a certain sense "caused" by the stimulus; that

[6] I have tried to show in Chap. V when and how I think it is legitimate to use this expression.

[7] A sense organ has been stimulated, the energy of stimulation has been transformed into nervous energy, this nervous energy has passed along an afferent nerve to the central nervous system and has passed through this and out by an efferent or motor nerve to a muscle where the energy is again transformed and the muscle contracts.

very muscular activity is itself in part producing the stimulus which "causes" the muscular activity. Holt's estimate of the value of the circular reflex appeared in his Harvard lectures in 1917, perhaps earlier also, but as they have not been published I quote from Bok, although Bok's article came out at a later date. I quote at some length because I wish in a later chapter, in speaking of the political process, to recall the circular reflex as a law which observation shows us as operating on infra-personal, personal and social levels.

"The reflex arc is the path of the stimulations received in consequence of a function of the individual itself. . . ." "This view does not start from the function of the receptor, but just from the action of the effector, which sounds strange at first, since we are accustomed to look upon the action of the effector as a result only of irritation in the receptor. . . ." "On a visual stimulation the animal must react with a movement which alters the visual stimulations . . . in other words, so that the attitude very specifically changes with regard to the stimulation given. Thus the reflex-reaction must alter the perception of the reflex-stimulus: in other words, it must very specifically alter the relation of the animal towards that specific stimulus, it must 'respond' to that stimulus."[8]

This will throw much light on the interdependent variables of the formula given above when we come to use that formula for social psychology, whether one thinks of it only as an analogy or as the operation of

[8] S. T. Bok, *The Reflex-Circle*, in *Psychiatrische en Neurologische Bladen, Amsterdam, Juli-Augustus*, 1917. See also James, *Principles of Psychology*, II, 582, and Baldwin's *Mental Development in the Child and the Race*, 2nd ed., pp. 133, 263 ff., 374 ff.

the same law on different levels. We shall see that the activity of the individual is only in a certain sense caused by the stimulus of the situation because that activity is itself helping to produce the situation which causes the activity of the individual. In other words behavior is a relating not of "subject" and "object" as such, but of two activities. In talking of the behavior process we have to give up the expression act "on" (subject acts on object, object acts on subject);[9] in that process the central fact is the meeting and interpenetrating of activities. What physiology and psychology now teach us is that part of the *nature* of response is the change it makes in the activity which caused so-to-speak the response, that is, we shall never catch the stimulus stimulating or the response responding. The importance of this cannot be overestimated. Stimulus is not cause and response the effect. Some writers, while speaking otherwise accurately of the behavior process, yet use the word result—the result of the process—whereas there is no result *of* process but only a moment *in* process. Response is not merely the activity resulting from a certain stimulus and that response in turn influencing the activity; it is *because* it is response that it influences that activity, that is part of what response means. Cause and effect, subject and object, stimulus and response: these are now given new meanings. All the possibilities of connections in the neural pathways which we are now beginning to suspect, or rather to have evidence of through the work

[9] This has important consequences for psychology, for as long as we thought of matter as something "acted on" we inevitably thought of "sensory experimentation," etc., in a certain way. A truly dynamic psychology, by giving us both environment and ourselves as activity, has implications which have not begun to be unfolded yet.

of Pawlov, Bechterew, etc., have new light thrown on them by this approach to response. On the social level, cause and effect are ways of describing certain moments in the situation when we look at those moments apart from the total process.

In the behavior process then we see the interlocking of stimulus and response, a self-sufficing process. Here there is no taint of the psychological fallacy which held the results of mere abstraction as primary *Dinge an sich.* We get completely away from the fallacy which dissected experience and took the dead products, subject and object, and made them the generating elements. The most valuable part of this teaching is that the reflex arc is the path of stimuli *received in consequence of* an activity of the individual. Thus experience is given us as self-creating coherence.

What we may now call circular response or circular behavior we see every day as we observe and analyze human relations, social situations.[10] We see it clearly in the European conferences because there it is evident that there is no static European situation; moreover, it is evident that we can never understand the European situation by watching stimulus and response as mere stimulus and response. We have another example in labor conflict which would be much simplified if employer's purpose and workmen's purpose would remain stationary while the situation developed, but they never do. We see the same thing in our own lives:

[10] I believe physiologists have not decided yet how far the sensory side of circular response is necessary to its continued functioning even although necessary to its formation, and if I were trying to establish any exact parallel between the physiological circular reflex and circular response as seen by the students of social research, such questions would be important for us, but I hope it is understood that no such exact parallel is intended.

as we perform a certain action our thought towards it changes and that changes our activity. Or we do something which requires courage and we become more courageous and do a braver thing. The relation between leaders and group is an excellent example of the reflex circle. All amicable discussion is another. The state and individual another.[11] Or "the man and the hour." But we need not go further afield for the working of this law than the meeting of two individuals. You say, "When I talk with Mr. X he always stimulates me." Now it may not be true that Mr. X stimulates everyone; it may be that something in you has called forth something in him. That is why I said above that we must give up the expression "act on," object acts on subject, etc. Do we not see here, to quote Bok, "the path of the stimulations which are caused, actualized or altered by the future reflex-reaction?" Through circular response we are creating each other all the time. This seems too obvious to mention, and yet where is it taken account of sufficiently? Le Bon, one of the most penetrating of sociologists, tells us much of crowds, much of individuals, but does not reveal the process of a creative meeting of individuals.

To sum up this point: the most fundamental thought about all this is that reaction is always reaction to a relating. Bok finds it in the neuro-muscular system. Integrative psychology shows us organism reacting to environment plus organism. In human relations, as I have said, this is obvious: I never react to you but to you-plus-me; or to be more accurate, it is I-plus-you reacting to you-plus-me. "I" can never influence "you" because you have already influenced me; that is,

[11] See Chap. XI.

in the very process of meeting, by the very process of meeting, we both become something different. It begins even before we meet, in the anticipation of meeting. We see this clearly in conferences. Does anyone wish to find the point where the change begins? He never will. Every movement we make is made up of a thousand reflex arcs and the organization of those arcs began before our birth. On physiological, psychological and social levels the law holds good: response is always to a relating. Accurately speaking the matter cannot be expressed even by the phrase used above, I-plus-you meeting you-plus-me. It is I plus the-interweaving-between-you-and-me meeting you plus the-interweaving-between-you-and-me, etc., etc. If we were doing it mathematically we should work it out to the *n*th power.[12]

This pregnant truth—that response is always to a relation, the relation between the response and that to which the response is being made—needs further consideration, for it is the basic truth for all the social sciences. Let us consider the implications of this statement, even although this will necessitate some repetition. First, my changing activity is a response to an activity which is also changing; and the changes in my activity are in part caused by the changes in the activity of that to which I am in relation and vice versa. My response is not to a crystallized product of the past, static for the moment of meeting; *while* I am behaving, the environment is changing because of my behaving, and my behavior is a response to the new situation

[12] I mean by this that if we could formulate the process mathematically, we should obtain a differential equation or a set of differential equations to be solved by integration.

which I, in part, have created. Thus we see involved the third point, namely, that the responding is not merely to another activity but to the relating between the self-activity and the other activity. The psychologists who are using the language of calculus have opened up whole reaches of thought for us, for the principles of relation as given by differential calculus help us to a clear understanding of this fundamental principle of life. Let us take an illustration—we can take one from our simplest, everyday experience—and see what help mathematical thought gives us. Think of the boy going to school. He is not responding to school merely, but also to his own response to school. That is, the going to school may so stimulate him that he works much better than at home with his mother; his activity is a function of the activity that is set up between him and school. And the school too is affected by the activity-between; through either his or his parents' demand upon it, it may improve its methods. And so the interweaving goes on: the more the school alters the boy, the more chance is there of the boy altering the school. This is a situation which suggests the calculus, for if the child's going to school so stimulates him that he works harder, his performance is continuously changed by that very performance. Hence the functional relation between the two cannot be expressed in terms merely of the boy and the school, there must always be included the activity-between.

Thus the relating involves an increment that can be measured only by compound interest. In compound interest part of the activity of the growing is the adding of the growing. This is the same with all organic growth. Simple response, if there were such a thing, would be like simple interest—if there were such a thing. There is no such thing as simple interest in the organic world; the law of organic growth is the law of compound interest. Organic growth is by geometrical progression. This is the law of social relations. France and Germany have surely not been "influencing" each other by simple, but by compound interest. We have always the increment of the increment.

Before considering social phenomena from this point of view, let us note two points that we shall have to keep in mind: first, the objective situation as constituent part of the behavior process; secondly, that internal conditioning is of equal importance with external conditioning. Both these points are very important for social research. Often, for instance, we see the head of an industrial plant trying to solve a situation by studying his men rather than by considering men and situation, and the reciprocal effect of one on the other. In regard to the second point, as the psychologist notes the neuro-muscular interplay, using every possible instrumentation to make it apparent, as he takes into consideration the factors contained in the mechanisms which are maintaining the functions he is studying, which are modifying these functions, so the sociologist must note as carefully, must see as integral part of the causal process, internal as well as external conditioning. Of course we shall remember that what is internal in the mechanism has also come from integration. When the organism experiences certain lacks, there arises a disturbed nervous system which causes the animal to make movements to supply these lacks from its environment. These responses to external environment caused by general motor restlessness integrate with the internal stimuli and the general motor restlessness becomes specific conduct. Thus "behavior" emerges, always from the activity-plus. In one of his lectures Holt put it this way, "If driven by metabolism, we have a disturbed nervous system, that system will so act toward environment as to put environment in that state which will make it send to the nervous system what it needs."[13] In this sentence the efficacy of the interrelating becomes still more apparent. Much of our older psychology failed to note sufficiently the interlacing of external stimulus and the conditions of neural, muscular and glandular response. Only recently I was surprised to see the question asked by a psychologist: "Is behavior internally or externally conditioned?" The factors of intra and extra-organic stimulation are not only equally important but are bound up together. They must be considered simultaneously. We have now a wholly dynamic psychology. The neuro-muscular mechanisms of the behaviorists tend in the hands of some writers (only in some) to become as static as the old "mental states." Behavior "pattern" is a figure of speech and not altogether a good one. We shall have, if we are not careful, as much trouble with the "patterns" of the behaviorists as the behaviorists have felt they had with the "minds" of the older psychologists.

[13] See also Kempf. "Whenever the autonomic . . . apparatus is disturbed . . . it compels the projicient sensori-motor apparatus to so adjust the receptors in the environment as to acquire stimuli having the capacity to produce adequate postural readjustments in the autonomic apparatus." Edward J. Kempf, *The Autonomic Functions and the Personality*, p. 1.

The matter of internal and external conditioning has an exact parallel in the social sciences. No one can understand the labor movement, the farmer movement, international situations, unless he is watching the integrating of internal stimuli, the lacks felt, with the responses to environment caused by these lacks. Moreover, the so-called stored-stimuli are exactly as important for sociologist as for psychologist; the sociologist has to consider in each case how far the person or persons are acting from present stimuli and how far from action patterns already existing. Let us take an illustration which involves all the points so far given:

The workman responds to	1. Employer: wages, share in profits or management, conditions of factory, etc. 2. General conditions: cost of living, etc. 3. His own desires, aspirations, standards of living, etc. 4. The relation between his responding and the above.

The important things to notice here are: first, that the workman is responding to something in himself as well as to something outside; for instance, we have now to add to the factors which made the internal conditioning of the workmen of 1914, the restlessness caused in many by the varied life and experiences (including even foreign travel) afforded by the war, the change in his desires caused by the lavish expenditure of war profits which he sees about him, etc., etc. Secondly, he is responding to the relating between his responding and the environment. Finally, all the factors involved are varying factors and must be studied in their varying relations. By the use of the language of calculus in the definition of behavior which we are considering, we are brought at once to the heart of every situation: the relating of things that are varying, which makes the relating vary. The Checker Taxi Company announced this week a cut in rates because of an increased volume of business; it thus makes volume of business the independent variable. Mr. Ford, on the other hand, when he reduced the price of his cars *in order to* increase volume of business, made the rate the independent variable. But both did the same thing: they measured a varying thing in relation to a varying thing, taking into account that these were affecting each other simultaneously.

We must therefore in the social sciences develop methods for watching varying activities in their relatings to other varying activities. We cannot watch the strikers and *then* the mill-owners. We cannot watch France and *then* Germany. We all know that the action of the mill-owners is changing daily the action of the strikers, that the action of the strikers is affecting daily that of the mill-owners; but beyond this is the more subtle point I am trying to emphasize here, that the activity between mill-owners and strikers is changing the activity of mill-owners, of strikers. We have to study not only a changing France in relation to a changing Germany, but also a changing France whose changes have been partly caused by the relation between its variations and Germany's variations. That is, France is not responding to Germany, but to the relation between France and Germany. To return to the language of our formula: the behavior of France is not a function of the behavior of Germany, but of the interweaving between France and Germany. The interweaving which is changing both factors and creating constantly new situations should be the study of the student of the social sciences. Trade unionism is not today a response to capitalism; it is a response to the relation between itself and capitalism. It is of the utmost importance to bear this constantly in mind. The concept of responsibility takes on entirely new meaning with the introduction of the notion of circular response into the social sciences. The farmers are not responding to the middlemen or to middlemen plus economic conditions or even to middlemen plus economic conditions plus their own desires, but to the relation between themselves and the whole total environment, or rather the relating becomes another element of total environment.

Much light is now thrown on the subject of Chapter I, the relation of "facts" to the social process. We cannot study the "psychology" of the workman, the "psychology" of the employer, and then the "facts" of the situation, as so often seems to be the process of investigation. We must study the workman and the employer in their relation to the facts—and then the facts themselves become as active as any other part of the "total situation." We can never understand the total situation without taking into account the evolving situation. And when a situation changes we have not a new variation under the old fact, but a new fact.

A professor of philosophy told me that it made him dizzy to talk with me because, he says, he wishes always to compare varying things with something stationary. But this philosopher could not go to Europe most economically in his summer vacations unless someone were watching for him the relation of speed to fuel consumption and from this determining rates of change that are themselves functions involving variables. Suppose a school-boy should say to his instructor in calculus: "You are making my head swim; I cannot compare unless you give me something stationary to compare with." The only thing his instructor could reply would be: "You will have then to leave this universe; in this one we so often have variations in relation to other variations that we are obliged to learn to think in the terms of those conditions." That is, if in calculus we measure a changing activity by an activity which is also changing, if there is involved rate of change, and also rate of change of rate of change, this is only the same as in all life. But psychology sometimes abstracts from life. For instance, a behaviorist tells us that if a man disregards the red flag at a railroad crossing and crosses in front of the train, he will be fined or imprisoned, and the red flag will thus acquire that much more "meaning" for him. If he suffers from loss of limb or kills the occupants of his car, the red flag acquires still more "meaning" for him. True as an abstraction, true on the supposition that this is all that happens. What is forgotten in this illustration is that the railroad company is not slumbering meanwhile, and the second time the man may not meet red-flag-plus-meaning, but gates, at the railroad crossing.

Take again the classical illustration of the child and the candle. It is a capital illustration supposing the candle to be stationary, in other words, to be a nucleus for "meaning," but it is not always. The child burns its hand. The mother may say, "We must put electricity into the nursery," or, "We must have no uncovered flames in the nursery." This possibility is not ignored by those psychologists who use this illustration, for it is the same kind of thing that is indicated when they speak of the mother holding the child's hand away from the flame instead of teaching him something about it. I am not, therefore, quarrelling with the illustration, but only pointing out that the process of education would be easier for all of us if red flags and candles merely rolled themselves into bigger balls of "meaning"; we should in that case learn how to behave toward first one object and then another until our education was completed. And this is, indeed, a large part of education, particularly in infancy and youth, but it becomes a smaller and smaller part as we get older. We usually cannot apply what we learn from one experience to the next because the next will be different. Moreover, it is usually we ourselves who have made the next experience different. It is the child's burning himself, perhaps, which makes him find something different the next time he puts his hand out. And when we remember all that the child has to learn about flame—to discriminate between flame bare and flame enclosed, between flame enclosed with a conducting and a non-conducting substance, to distinguish between the lighting, heating and burning qualities of flame—we see how complex the matter becomes. But however you enlarge the equation with more brackets, etc., the conditioning equation expressing the relation of the variables remains the same. That is why I think the formula I have cited so useful for the social sciences if we understand and accept what is implicit in it, namely, that behavior is not a function of environment but a function of the relating of behavior and environment.

This seems to me the most illuminating thought that

has been given us of recent years for the study of social phenomena. Holt's formula does not give it to us explicitly, but his treatment of circular response does, his emphasis on the significance of the *organization* of reflex arcs and of the functional reference of behavior, the something "new" of his "critical" moments of evolution, his insistence on the fact that behavior is not a function of immediate stimulus, and his use of the functional theory of causation. The last two points will be taken up in the next chapter. We now see behavior not as a function of environment, but as a function of the relation between self and environment. The activity is a function of itself interweaving with the activity of which it is a function. In the illustration given above of the cut in rates by the Checker Taxi Company, the rate was not really a function of volume of business, but, since the rate increased the volume of business, the rate was a function of the relation, the interlacing relation, between rates and volume of business. We must be sure that our formula will fit an evolving situation.

It will perhaps be thought that I am rather forcing the use of mathematical language in this chapter, but I am using this language deliberately for several reasons. First, in order to unfold the implications in the words function and variables used in the definition of behavior which I have been employing; secondly, because I find the language of calculus so stimulating to my own thought on this subject that I hope others will too; in the third place, because the word function is used so widely, and often carelessly, nowadays, that I think we had better look into its origin and make sure that we use it accurately.

We have now, to repeat in summary, three fundamental principles to guide us in our study of social situations: (1) that my response is not to a rigid, static environment, but to a changing environment; (2) to an environment which is changing because of the activity between it and me; (3) that function may be continuously modified by itself, that is, the activity of the boy going to school may change the activity of the boy going to school. Or it might be put thus: that response is always to a relating, that things which are varying must be compared with things that are varying, that the law of geometrical progression is the law of organic growth, that functional relating has always a plus value. The social sciences must learn to deal with that plus, to reckon literally with it. A dynamic psychology gives us instead of equivalents, plusvalents. It is those which we must look for in every situation. These are the "novelties" in the psychologist's "critical" moments of evolution. It is impossible to overemphasize this point; it means a new approach to the social sciences. In the farmer-middleman controversy, find the plusvalent. In the France-Germany situation, find the plusvalent. Let every statesman and diplomat, every legislator and judge find the plusvalent; it is the only approach possible to politics or industry or international relations or our own smallest everyday problems. *Progressive* experience on every level means the creating of plusvalents.

In the physical sciences, we have some interesting, although not wholly exact, parallels of the plus value of the relating. In chemistry we find a chemical substance X decomposing into another Y at a rate proportional to the amount of X undecomposed; at the same time by a reverse reaction Y is decomposing into X at a rate proportional to the amount of Y present. X is continuously influencing Y at the same time that Y is continuously influencing X.

In engineering we have what is called "regeneration." A radio receiving set takes in only a small amount of energy from the electromagnetic waves that reach it, but this is made to control the output of a source of considerable energy located in the set. In some sets a part of the latter energy is carried back to the former, so that the former is now intensified and effects an increased output; and the process repeats itself, building up the power of the set perhaps a thousandfold. This "regenerative" action occurs in many physical and chemical processes and is used by engineers in devising mechanical apparatus, electrical and other.

A dynamic physics studies activity rather than mass; it defines things in terms of activity, not in terms of mass. Present-day physics tells us that the rate of change of the activity may not be proportional to the mass of what is active but to the activity of the mass. We had not a dynamic physics until this was seen. It used to be said that in organic growth the increment of the organism in a given time is proportional to the magnitude of the organism itself. Now, looking at the "organism" as an activity, we should have to use some word which would include magnitude and intensity of the activity.

To conclude this chapter: the most significant thing in recent thinking is, I think, the correspondence of thought in different fields and on different levels. Philosophy has long taught us the unity of experience. You can tear it to pieces if you will and find subject and object, stimulus and response, or—you can refuse to; you can claim the right to see it as a rational interplay of forces, as the functioning of a self-creating coherence. Consciousness is the living interplay of a self-generating activity. Or, consciousness is the living interplay of myriads of self-generating activities which all generate themselves as a moment of the interplay. The most fundamental idea of philosophy is, I think, the recognition that there is no *Denkform* in which as mould all thought is cast, but rather a constant mode of self-generating as thought, a perpetual law of unifying to which the free activity submits itself, law and freedom each the entelechy of the other. Study of social situations reveals the working of this principle. In psychology and physiology, also, we find certain conclusions which lead us to think that experience on every level may be found to be an interrelating in which the activity of the relating alters the terms of the relating and also the relating itself. Politics, industry and law need the impetus of this thought. Our older social philosophy gave us the pernicious theories of the balance of power between nations, of adjustment between capital and labor. It gave us always equivalents; our more recent thinking shows us how to create plusvalents. This will be developed further in the chapter on Experience as Creating.[14]

[14] It has been pointed out to me that the term plus-value does not express my idea since the very thing I am opposed to is the plus-relation, the one-by-one connection rather than the integration. But I am certainly opposed to the word super, which has been suggested in its place, for the "something new" of integration is not "over" or "more than" or "greater than" the parts, as often erroneously claimed for "wholes." I think plus-value *is* what I mean, for I am not referring to a plus-plus relation of the parts, but expressing the fact that integration gives an additional value, one more value, but not necessarily a greater or super value. See pp. 98–102 for further

Because the word function is being increasingly used to express relation, there are certain warnings necessary. First, we should not use the word function to excuse us from studying each situation; this I have seen done several times recently. A phrase may be a legitimate short-cut in exposition, but it is inexcusable to let it be a short-cut in investigation. Secondly, we must not confuse function as relation and function as quantity. For us function is not a quantity left over when the activity of relating is completed; function is the activity of relating, it is the operation, not what results. A function is always functioning; our interest in it is on that very account. In the third place, the independent variable is independent only within a certain equation and our equations are constantly changing. We must not confuse a variable which is constant from moment to moment in the same statement, and varies only from statement to statement, with one that varies in the same statement. This is very important to remember in social psychology. The constant of one situation may not be, probably will not be, the constant of the next situation. In studying any one situation we look on this quantity as constant while the mutual effects of varying quantities are studied; two facts or individuals, let us say two activities, adapt themselves to each other in a certain way for any given situation; change the situation and they will probably adapt themselves in a different way.

Take the economic "law of supply and demand." According to that law price is a constant function of demand: as demand increases, price increases; as de-

consideration of this point which is perhaps the most important in the whole range of discussion on human relations.

mand decreases price decreases. But this law is true only on a certain assumption: that supply is fixed, that there is a certain amount of the commodity in existence which stays fixed. This is an assumption which speculators are always trying to make true, but in ordinary, legitimate, economic operations it is seldom a possible assumption *except for one situation.* Probably demand is increasing the volume of business which, in most cases—in the case of manufactured articles the materials for which can be got in practically unlimited quantities—lowers the cost of production. As a matter of fact, therefore, increased demand means, other things being equal, eventually decreased prices. Thus the function assumed for one situation cannot be carried over into another. Price is a developing situation; it depends on an interweaving; it is a function not of an independent variable alone but of the relation between it and the independent variable. Thus to say that demand raises price is wrong except in regard to a given situation. To put this into mathematical language (which seems to respond more readily than any other to our present thinking on this subject), the error would be to take a variable constant for an absolute constant. Given the amount of commodities at any minute and taking demand as an independent variable, the price will be the function of that, but from situation to situation the supply changes. The economist makes no mistake here; I am giving this as an illustration of the *kind* of error in thinking sometimes made by those who use the word function nowadays rather carelessly. In the use of the word function, the thing to be kept constantly in mind is the developing situation.

IV

EXPERIENCE IN THE LIGHT OF RECENT PSYCHOLOGY: INTEGRATIVE BEHAVIOR

I SAID above that Holt has shown the dynamic nature of his thought most clearly by his use of the reflex circle and the functional theory of causation. This theory, that "every physical law is in the last analysis the statement of a constant function between one process or thing and some other process or thing," Holt makes one of the basic principles of his psychology. The "bead" theory of causation which once prevailed in physics, and "which tried to describe causal process in terms of successive 'states,' the 'state' of a body at one moment being the *cause* of its 'state' and position at the next,"[1] is as fatal for psychology, he tells us, as for physics. It is equally fatal for sociology. It is the theory by which statesmen and diplomats so often try to solve national and world problems and fail. Behavior on neither level is governed by immediate stimulus. Both psychologist and sociologist note that as the number of integral reflexes involved in behavior increases, the immediate stimulus recedes further and further from view as the significant factor.[2] The stimulus becomes the total situation of

[1] *Op. cit.*, p. 157.

[2] " . . . the development from reflex action to highly organized

which the total behavior is a function. As the psychologist finds that what the bee is *really* doing is laying up honey in its home, that it is only incidental that it sips from this flower or that, so in studying social relations we find that a situation of which behavior is a constant function is usually very complex. We must observe every case of behavior as a whole; this must never be forgotten in the study of social situations. The next chapter will be taken up with the *Gestalt* concept, which is a concept of wholes, and which some psychologists think will have more influence on all our thinking than any single concept has for long exercised. In Chapter VI behavior as response to a complex stimulus will be again considered in connection with the importance of total environment in the conception of adjustment.

This appreciation of "total behavior" brings us back again to our formula: the will or purpose of a man or group is to be found in that activity which is a constant function, or a combination of such functions, of some aspect of his environment. I said in the last chapter that this formula, with its implied definition of behavior as a function of the interweaving between the activity of organism and activity of environment, gives us a new approach to the social sciences. In saying that, I do not ignore the many signs we already see of this approach. Mr. Earl Howard, labor manager for Hart, Schaffner & Marx, told me that the first question he always asks himself in regard to any complaint or request of the workman is, "What in the

behavior is one in which the correlation between stimulus and organism becomes less and less direct, while that between the organism and the object of response becomes more and more prominent." *Op. cit.*, p. 169.

conditions of this plant or industry, or in general living conditions, has caused this attitude on the part of the workman?" This is very different from the manufacturer who told me that when a workman came to him with a complaint, he always set someone to study the psychology of that man. We can hardly estimate the difference Mr. Howard's method would make in industrial relations. The similarity between this method and that advocated by our present psychology seems to me significant. Mr. Howard studies variations in their relation to other variations; also he takes into account all the elements of "the total situation." The rule for politics or industry, for trade unions or manufacturers' associations, should be exactly Holt's rule for man: "study his movements until we have discovered . . . that object, situation, process (or perhaps merely that relation) of which his behavior is a *constant function.*"[3] The American workman today is responding neither to high post-war prices nor to his accumulated rancor against capital; he is reacting to a situation of which these and other factors form component parts.

It must be remembered, however, that when I speak of a "new" approach to the social sciences, I am thinking of conscious approach; success in human relations has always meant if not the conscious, at any rate the unconscious, use of this principle of present psychological thought, but today we have an increasing amount of deliberate social analysis and conscious use of certain fundamental principles.

It now seems clear that we must look for purpose within the process itself. We see experience as an

[3] *Op. cit.*, p. 163.

interplay of forces, as the activity of relating leading through fresh relatings to a new activity, not from purpose to deed and deed to purpose with a fatal gap between, as if life moved like the jerks of mechanical toys with only an external wire-puller to account for the jerks, or a too mysterious psychic energy. What we possess always creates the possibilities of fresh satisfactions. The need comes as need only when the possible satisfaction of need is already there. There is no gap in the process. The automobile does not satisfy wants only, it creates wants; this is the meaning of our formula for sociology. The automobile was not invented to solve the farmers' problems. The purpose in front will always mislead us. Psychology now gives us end as moment *in* process.[4]

Sociologists, too, look for purpose in "so far" integrated behavior. We are urged by whips, not rewards. Our aims are in the motor-mechanisms of our neuromuscular apparatus. No magic wand will change these, it is a process. Many psychologists use the expression "striving towards some goal," but we can see in our own lives that the urge is always the lack; the goal changes as we try one means after another of meeting that lack. With the workman the urge is inadequate conditions for normal living. The goal changes from year to year as he conceives, for the bettering of those conditions, one method after another: shorter hours,

[4] "It is not true that we do something in order to attain a dead and static 'end'; we do something as the necessary but subordinate moment in the *doing* of something more comprehensive. The true comparison then is not between deed or means and thought or end, but between part deed and whole deed."

"The doctrine of the wish shows us that life is not lived *for ends*. Life is a process. . . . Its motion is forward; yet its motive power comes not from in front (from 'ends') but from behind, from the wishes which are in ourselves." *Op. cit.*, pp. 93–94, 132.

higher wages, share in profits, share in control, nationalization of industry, etc. The relation of preconceived end to growing end must be carefully watched, with all that contributes to the change, with all that happens because of the change. You cannot coördinate purpose without developing purpose, it is part of the same process. Some people want to give the workmen a share in carrying out the purpose of the plant and do not see that that involves a share in creating the purpose of the plant. A noted teacher of ethics tells us, "A citizen is one who helps to realize the purpose for which this nation exists." The citizen must also help to *make* the purpose.

It could be put this way. Purpose is always the appearing of the power of unifying, the ranging of multiplicity into that which is both means and ends, the One holding Many.

I have given examples in an earlier chapter of the difference between preconceived and actual purpose. We can find those differences for ourselves every day in what we see and what we read. There are no static purposes for us to lay our hands on; put salt on the tail of the European purpose today—if you can. We make two mistakes in regard to purpose when we are considering social process: we try to substitute an intellectualistic purpose for that involved in the situation, or, when the purpose appears from out the activity, we think, by some strange mental legerdemain, that that was the purpose which had been actuating us all along. But our dealings with our fellowmen should not be so different from those with our natural environment. Last summer I noticed a strange plant in our pasture. I did not know what it was, I had no picture in my mind of what flower or fruit it would bear, but I freed it. That is, I dug around it and opened the soil that the rain might fall on its roots, I cleared out the thistles with which it was entangled so that it might have room to spread, I cut down the undergrowth of small maples near so that it could get the sun. In other words, I simply freed it. Every friendship which is not treated in this way will surely suffer; no human relation should serve an anticipatory purpose. Every relation should be a freeing relation with the "purpose" evolving. This is the truth underneath the admonition that we should not pray for specific things.

But the great mistake people often make is to say, when the flower and the fruit appear, "This [the particular flower or fruit] was what I was working for." We must be ever on our guard against post facto purposes. We have all had experience of the modifications which take place in a policy when we begin to carry it out. When legislation establishes what is called a general policy, and a commission is appointed to form specific regulations and provisions to see that that policy is carried out, it often happens that the commission finds a different purpose developing from that on which the legislation was founded, and has then to try to get the law changed in such a way as to embody the new or the actual purpose. Activity always does more than embody purpose, it evolves purpose. With the general acceptance of this fact, part of our political and legal science will have to be rewritten. All history which jumps from one dramatic moment to another falsifies the situation; history must be viewed as continuously evolving relations, just as the steam in the boiler, no matter how rapidly it increases, yet always increases gradually.

We must remember, moreover, in any analysis of ends, that what we call ends are often means. Take the formation of a stock company for the building of a railroad. Of all those who buy stock perhaps no one is interested in the "purpose" of that company: the opening of a new route of communication. Some wish an investment for their money, others wish to speculate, others to control the direction of the traffic, others to influence the selection of the route in order that real estate values in which they are interested shall be increased.[5]

The matter of purpose, interests, needs, requires much more empirical study, and certainly a volume to itself; I can give here only the briefest indications of the way recent psychology has illumined one of the most important conceptions of the social sciences.

I said above that we are to look for purpose in the so-far integrated behavior of the organism. I shall recall this later in the chapters on law and politics. Political leaders cannot persuade people to adopt purposes, the legal order cannot assign purposes; they are found in the so-far integrated behavior of people. Moreover, when we see end as involved in the process, not in contentless will, we see that we cannot "choose" our ends as some would have us "choose" a cause to be loyal to. Life is richer than this: we have now a far greater responsibility, a nobler ethics, not less but a larger freedom. Choice is not given up but is put further back in the process. When we do not understand this, it may mean disaster for us, for as we cannot make arbitrary choices, so we cannot postpone

[5] See Jhering, *Law as Means to an End*, p. 32.

choice; we cannot make up later for the lost moment, that is, not directly. Choice has a place in the process, we must learn exactly where the place is and act on that knowledge. If we try to make a choice with our "minds" when another already exists in our neuromuscular apparatus, we only come up against a dead-wall of impossibility. Or rather we have to attack our problem differently; we have to set to work to change our motor mechanisms.

Through our observation of human relations, through the teachings of psychology, we learn then that from our concrete activities spring both the power and the guide for those activities. Experience is the dynamo station; here are generated will and purpose. Further, and of the utmost importance, here too arise the standards with which to judge that same will and purpose. Men used to say that they relied on their wives' intuitions, but wives today are more apt to be out viewing facts for themselves than staying at home intuiting. I think that for some time we have been a little astray in regard to the relation of standards to the social process. We have, for instance, long thought of ourselves as a nation of idealists who have wonderful ideas and struggle to carry them out. But take the average New England town: it is sunk in the apathy of accepted routine; someone comes along and proposes that it shall do something. The citizens, being Americans, have the genius for doing; they *do* and then they have the ideas involved in the doing. Someone told a certain New England village that it ought to have a social welfare department; the inhabitants did not know what it was or what it was for, but they organized it and did it well too, and then they told themselves and the neighboring towns what their purpose *had been* (notice tense) and one would have thought that all their lives they had been longing for a social service department.

Our ideals are involved in our activities. Take for instance all the talk of "getting together" which has filled our press and public halls for the last fifteen or twenty years. It has been assumed that our lives were growing too isolated and that we ought to correct this. Not at all. After we had begun to live together, crowded in cities and factories and mines, after our whole organism had got set and attuned to living together, then we heard that we must cease (!) our separate lives and "get together." But we never heard of this duty of getting together until it was a *fait accompli,* then behold it became an aspiration—after the event! Herd instinct? Christian brotherhood? No, it is the inevitable tendency to make an ideal of the fact. Here we are, our whole industry and business system based on credit, on faith and coöperation, and then we cry out, heads in sand, "Let us take example from the little loving ants and bees and bring association and coöperation into our daily lives." But they are *in* our daily lives all the time and that is the reason we are thinking of them. Coöperation in the business world did not come about by emulating the bees and the beavers, as some of the biologists exhort us to do. One by one the integrations are made, as environment changes, and the behavior patterns constructed.

We do not adapt our activities to ends in front or to principles behind.

I am not implying that I wish this were different. To get our ideals and our culture from our daily life means that they have a vital energy which can be used refluently on that life. Many of us are ashamed of our "mechanical age" and deck it out with trimmings which are like the buttons of dresses which don't button, put there for ornament only; but we must realize that our daily living may itself become an art, that in commerce we may find culture, in industry idealism, in our business system beauty, in mechanics morals—the ethics of the lathe are of a pretty fundamental kind. People tell us that "when the spirit of art spreads far enough down we shall redeem the sordidness of our present civilization," but grown-up people cannot tie apples on the trees and then pick them. Only when the spirit of art rises from the roots of our mechanical age will it "redeem our civilization." The divorce of our so-called spiritual life from our daily activities is a fatal dualism. We are not to ignore our industry, commerce, etc., and seek spiritual development elsewhere; on the other hand we shall never find it in these, but only by an eternal influence and refluence. If we point with satisfaction to our material progress, it is only because of its evidence of a virility, a robustness, which is capable of fruitful interweavings. There is energy flowing from it which, uniting with other energies, will create new men and new environment.

In many of the arguments for shorter working hours this is forgotten, and we have a kind of time-theory of salvation: keep the debasing influences of industry to certain hours of the day, employ the others in some educational way, and if the race is keenly enough run the spiritualizing influences will win out. But we cannot split ourselves up like this, the eight-hour influences will continue into the leisure period;

it is the eight-hour influences themselves that we must reckon with.

Yet we see many signs that we are not unappreciative of the relation of all our doing to all our thinking. Why are we getting engineers as presidents of colleges? Why is the very word becoming one to conjure with, "social engineering," etc.? It is because we have made up our minds that we want the doer-thinkers.

To sum up this chapter: one of the chief contributions to sociology of the psychology I am trying to indicate is the *continuing* activity of the specific-response relation, the relatings and then the evolving of these relatings. The essence of this psychology is that the "release" and the integrating are one process: this is as important for ethics as for physiology or psychology; for sociology its value is inestimable.

When some of the behaviorists tell us that "knowledge lives in the muscles" they seem to leave out the deeper truth of the continuing activity. I am objecting here merely to the word "knowledge." I think it better when practicable to keep to verbs; the value of nouns is chiefly for post mortems. It is just here that Holt gives us, in *Response and Cognition,*[6] a fundamental part of his teaching: the activity of knowing including the knower and the known. After all what *Response and Cognition* does is not so much to explain knowledge as to abolish it—to abolish it in favor of knowing, of an activity, of a process which involves knower and known but which never looks from the windows of either. The knower knows (an active verb) the known; reality is in the knowing.

The profound truth we have now recognized we

[6] Supplement to *The Freudian Wish.*

could express differently by saying that you can define the actors only in terms of the process. Modern playwrights are beginning to see this. And we ourselves are beginning to appreciate more and more plays and novels written by those who have this understanding. The old-fashioned hero dominated the situation and came out alone to bow before the curtain, and we did not care very much *what* he had conquered, we were "thrilled" by the act of conquest. And we certainly did not analyze the difference between conquest and defeat, a subtle matter indeed and often hidden far beneath the surface. But nowadays we do not think of the hero alone or with his feet upon the fallen foe—in fact we may have to look among the prostrate foes for the hero—we see him in the multitudinous relations of life, we see him in his significance to some of the meanings of his age.

I think we can now go back to our formula and its definition of behavior as a function of environment, and bring to it a larger understanding. I should like, for social psychology, to express it as follows: Thinking (willing, purposing) is *specific* relating of the interdependent variables, individual and situation, each thereby creating itself anew, relating themselves anew, and thus giving us the evolving situation.

The important points to bear in mind are:

1. Behavior is both internally and externally conditioned.
2. Behavior is a function of the interweaving between activity of organism and activity of environment, that is, response is to a relating.
3. By this interlocking activity individual and situation each is creating itself anew.
4. Thus relating themselves anew.
5. Thus giving us the evolving situation.

These two chapters are obviously not a wholesale endorsement of what has been called behaviorism,[7] for the behaviorists as belated mechanists leave much to be desired. But Holt's thought seems to me to go further and to be more discriminating. It is pregnant and important for the social sciences because it makes us think of our problems in terms of process and not of "pictures." The self-sustaining process which this writer gives us is the fundamental law of human activity. And this psychology is both a challenge and a reward: it carries in one hand the compass for the journey, and in the other the only gift we can ever hope for for all our pains, the opportunity for greater pains, for harder things. We give ourselves to our task and our task not only becomes larger but at the same time it becomes deeper and higher. The reward for all activity is greater activity.

The full acceptance of life as process gets us further and further away from the old controversies. The thought I have been trying to indicate is neither conventional idealism nor realism. It is neither mechanism nor vitalism: we see mechanism as true within its own barriers; we see the *élan vitale* (still a thing-in-itself) as a somewhat crude foreshadowing of a profound truth. It is now possible to rid ourselves of the limitations of these more partial points of view; we have now given to us new modes of thinking, new ways of acting.

[7] Although I wish to acknowledge fully my indebtedness to Watson.

V

EXPERIENCE IN THE LIGHT OF RECENT PSYCHOLOGY: THE *GESTALT* CONCEPT

IT is hardly possible to consider recent developments in psychological thinking without mentioning that outstanding feature of contemporary German psychology known as the *Gestalt* doctrine, a doctrine which is having a marked influence on American psychology. While the novelty of this doctrine has been, it seems to me, much overrated, for it has long had a place in philosophical thinking, and in the psychological field itself it has had many anticipations, yet I am considering it here for several reasons. First, because the experimental verification it brings to the doctrine of integrative unity, of functional wholes, is certainly valuable, also because there are aspects of this doctrine which can help correct certain tendencies today which are seriously, disastrously, against our progress, and finally because I am trying in this book to show certain parallel developments in thinking, in quite different fields, which seem to me significant. And none is more significant, none is more valuable, than the present trend away from atomistic conceptions. Let us therefore look briefly at the *Gestalt* concept which has been called a doctrine of wholes.[1]

[1] I am much indebted for my knowledge of the *Gestalt* school of

Köhler has expressed the central idea of this school succinctly when he tells us of psychical states and processes whose characteristic properties and activities differ from the properties and activities of their so-called parts. Such psychical states and properties, he says, may justly be regarded as units (*Einheiten*), and following von Ehrenfels he gives the name *Gestalten* to these units.[2] This view denies that physical, psychical or social situations are made up of elements in a plus-plus relation, a mere "*Und-verbindung*" or "*Und-summe.*"

It should be noted that Köhler believes that the environment as well as subjective experience is composed of *Gestalten,* that the *Gestalten* are both objectively real and experientially real.

By far the most valuable approach to this doctrine has been made, I think, in the field of perception; indeed the conception originated with workers in this field. The conclusions of these workers deny the existence of "a sensation" as a fact of experience. Many experiments seem to show that perceptions have a quality in addition to the sum of the single sensory excitations. This quality represents the essence of the perception. Split it into its parts and the essence of the experience vanishes. "What we find," says Koffka, "is an undivided, articulate whole. Let us call these wholes 'structures,' and we can assert that an unprejudiced description finds such structures in the cases

psychology to Dr. Gordon W. Allport who has kindly allowed me to read his paper on Contemporary German Psychology in advance of its publication, and also to make use of his letters to me on the subject. I would not, however, thus make him responsible in any degree for the views I have expressed in regard to this school.

[2] Wolfgang Köhler, *Die physischen Gestalten in Ruhe und ein stätionaren Zustand,* p. ix.

underlying all psychological experience. . . ."[3] All Koffka's experiments lead him to the conclusion that perception is not composed of mere elements of sensation. In other words, his conclusion is that perception and not sensation is the psychological unit.

One of Köhler's simpler experiments with apes and chickens shows plainly the meaning of "structure." The animal is confronted with two stimuli: one a light gray *b*, the other a darker gray *c*. Food is concealed behind *b*, but not behind *c*. The animal is trained by repeated trials to get his food from *b*. Then the conditions of the experiment are changed and the stimuli now used are *b* and another still lighter *a*. According to the traditional theory the animal would be expected to associate his food with *b*, but Köhler found that in most cases (and he has explanation for the exceptions) he did not do this, he chose the lighter gray *a* as he had formerly chosen the lighter gray which was then *b*, This means that he had not perceived *b*, but *b* in relation to a field. His perception is of a complex, of a field of relationships. He is reacting to a perceptual total.

In showing us that *Gestalt* is not a simple function of stimulus, Koffka tells us that the process is one depending not on stimulus alone, but also on the "attitude" of the organism which has in readiness certain modes of response, these physiological processes which underlie the structural phenomena having themselves the character of structures. *Gestalt*, he tells us, is a relating of the "movement-structure" of the organism

[3] *Perception, An Introduction to the Gestalt-Theorie, The Psychological Bulletin,* Oct., 1922. To this article is appended a list of references.

to the stimulus. Often the strength of the movement-structure is such that it can be touched off by what would seem totally inadequate stimuli. This point should be carefully noted, for when we see that sensation is not the simple function of the stimulus, and that perception, the unit of experience, is not the simple function of sensation, we have grasped one of the most essential features of this theory. Koffka remarks on the specific, concrete nature of this "attitude" as compared with the old attention, but the traditional view of attention has largely disappeared in this country.

The main features of this school are then: first, it gives us "so-functioning" properties of phenomena rather than "so-being" properties, to use the expressions of the school itself; secondly, the definite and specific character of the wholes—every psychical situation has a specific character different from the "absolute" nature of the component parts; in the third place, the physiological correlates of these wholes, that is, the physiological structures which underlie the *Gestalt* phenomena, are themselves *Gestalten*. Thus in all our study, from that of the simplest perceptual experience, or the physiological structures underlying that experience, up to the work in the field of personality, the same thing is found, the necessity of studying wholes because the nature of the whole is different from that of the parts and could not be deduced from the parts.

None of this is new, yet stripped of its claim to "novelty," this theory is, I think, interesting. Or rather what I find interesting is not so much the doctrine itself as the enthusiasm with which it has been acclaimed, which is hardly less than the fervor with which it has been promulgated. Thus we see plainly the need it meets. Köhler tells us that this idea seems to have greater scientific possibilities than those conceptions which have hitherto been regarded as fundamental for psychic life. Koffka says, "Wherever this new method of thinking and working has come in touch with concrete problems, it has not only showed its efficiency, but has also brought to light startling and important facts which without the guidance of this theory could not so easily have been discovered."

A significant thing about this school of psychology is that it has gathered its forces from quite different fields of research. Köhler speaks of "all those researches which at present from different sides and in different realms lead always to this central idea. . . ." Kruger, in opening the Leipsig Congress of Psychology last April,[4] gave an account of the central doctrine of this psychology and said that the concept had been developed within the past decade simultaneously from four directions, the psychologists of each direction working quite independently of the others.[5]

A very interesting approach to this doctrine has been made in the studies of personality. Much psychological study of personality has been concerned with separate "traits," and the fact has been rather astonishingly ignored that personality can never be revealed to us by a study of its constituent traits;

[4] Both at the Leipsig Congress and at the Congress of Experimental Psychology which met at Marburg in 1922 there was a marked divergence from the Wundtian school.

[5] For a brief characterization of these four approaches—the approach through perception, the approach through *Geisteswissenschaft*, the genetic approach, and the approach through *Personalismus*—see Dr. Gordon Allport's account of the Leipsig Congress in the *American Journal of Psychology*, Oct., 1923.

moreover, that it is not disclosed merely by adding together these separate traits. No single characteristic of a man has much meaning until it is understood in its relation to his other characteristics. Or, more accurately, it is the total interactions and the something being brought into existence by these which make the whole personality.

Many psychologists, as Stern, are now insisting on the study of personality as a whole. It seems to some of us a little late in the day. Our daily problems in home or office, factory or store, have already insisted on this. I had for a few years something to do with engaging people for the staff of a Vocational Guidance Department. A man just out of the university asked for a position with us as psychologist. In describing to me his methods, he told me the tests he would give to our boys and girls, and the conclusions he would draw from them. I remember that he apparently attached great importance to what seemed his pet test, that of introducing snakes suddenly to unsuspecting young people, and he told me what estimates he would form of those who jumped or screamed at their appearance. But I did not consider his estimates worth anything because he isolated this test and drew his conclusions within that isolation. We decided therefore not to have an "applied" psychologist on our staff. Since then, indeed, large strides have been made in this department of psychology, but the weakness that still persists to some degree is that of not giving sufficient attention to the whole man, the whole boy or girl.

Yet it has been preached with clarion clearness by some of our psychologists. The emphasis of the German school on an undivided complex as the psychological object is no more insistent than that of our American psychologists who tell us to "keep the man whole," to find out what he is "really doing," not to describe his behavior in terms of the thousand separate gestures he is making. Moreover, when we are told to study the movements of a man until we have discovered "the object, situation, process (or perhaps merely the relation) of which his behavior is a constant function," we are being shown that man reacts to a total.

When the behaviorists say that the way to find out what the man is really doing is by watching his behavior, I should add to that: Be sure to remember that his behavior always includes, (1) what he is doing, (2) what he thinks he is doing, (3) what he says he is doing. In the study of group behavior we have many interesting examples of occasions where all these three enter vitally into the situation. To discover the "purpose" of an association we have always to consider these three. When psychologists become willing to join hands with the students of the social sciences, it will be a day of prophecy and hope for the solving of human problems.

We have in the social sciences innumerable examples of that error of atomism which the *Gestalt* theory is combating on the psychological level. Perhaps none is more interesting than the recent treatment of instincts by a number of economists. When these economists discovered instincts a few years ago, their first tendency was to consider the workings of separate instincts, but the instincts do not work apart from one another. The relation of the instincts to one another, the interlacing of instincts and their total effect, were almost wholly ignored, hence many erroneous conclusions drawn from the so-called "instinct theory." The economists' instincts simply do not exist. Experience is not a matter of instincts or sensations or reflexes or—of anything else atomistic. And we must not only study instincts acting together but also the relation of the organism as a whole to the separate instinctive tendencies.

But the nature of the whole is open to different interpretations. Many writers of the *Gestalt* school say that the whole is "more" than its constituent parts. I think this word dangerous; the whole may be *different* from the parts without being *more*. Some writers have called the *Gestalt* a super or over phenomenon. These words are equally objectionable. We should not give the names super or over to that which is itself so entirely, so vitally, so actively a part of the total process. The quarrel over the word *more* is due, I think, to a confusion of thought in regard to a quantitative more and a qualitative more. It is true that quantitatively the one is more than the many, that is, we do have "something else," but when we go on from this to attribute greater value to the one than the many, we are making a serious mistake. It would certainly lead us far astray in the social sciences. In politics or economics it would be very dangerous to think of the whole as more or greater than the parts. If we could analyze the mental make-up of some of the people who are opposed to the League of Nations, we should probably find that it is because they think a "whole" must necessarily be "more" than its parts that they have a horror, and in my opinion justly if this were true, of a League of Nations which is "greater" than America. Is the United States greater than the states? No, but it is different, and the nature of such difference is the fundamental thing for us to determine in every department of thought, every department of life. It is the cardinal question for all human activity.

And those who give a super character to the whole often give it a static character. I think that we get a better idea of the true nature of a whole from the theory of circular behavior given in the last two chapters, for the relation between whole and parts is one of circular response. A number of writers on the *Gestalt* theory come to a stopping place, or at any rate a gap, in their exposition; they realize indeed that if they would give us a full explanation of their doctrine they must explain the relation of whole to parts as well as of parts to one another, but this they cannot do satisfactorily, I think, without including some description of circular behavior. In other words, these writers seem to me to need a fuller understanding of the dynamic nature of their wholes, for with some the whole seems to be a moment of rest between activities. To no doctrine must we make swifter or more emphatic denial; the whole is itself as much a part of the entire process, is itself interweaving with the parts at the same time that the parts are interweaving to make the whole. An understanding of this on the personal and social level is of inestimable value. Our educational methods must accept this doctrine, for its connection with any theory of the formation of habits is obvious. While habits are being formed the whole organism is affecting the formation of each separate habit. That is, that organization of action systems which we call the organism is influencing each separate action system even while the action systems are making the organism. In our personality studies we find that the total personality affects each "trait" (not a good word and happily now being abandoned) while the traits are making the total personality. Again, the probation officer who is trying to "adjust" the boy to society does so by dealing with separate activities of the boy—finds him a suitable job, gets him to go to night school, suggests his joining the boy scouts—but it is obvious that the "whole" adjustment which is thus being made is influencing each one of these activities. The "whole" adjustment of capital and labor influences each separate adjustment of wages or hours or working conditions. But such instances might be indefinitely extended.

The dangers of both a super whole and a static whole are seen in a certain treatment of the doctrine of values. We could find in the *Gestalt* psychology a more penetrating doctrine of value (both as psychologically and socially considered) than we have yet had, if the super-nature of the whole were not insisted on. This is of the utmost importance for students of the social sciences. For in any social situation, however necessary it is to analyze it into its component activities, a part of our task is to discover value-units, that is, to quote the definition of *Gestalt* given above, a whole-value which is different from the sum of the value of the parts, and which cannot be dealt with in the same manner as the values of the parts. To watch for the emergence of the value-unit, the interest-unit, the desire-unit, must be the valid method for the social sciences. To further this emergence, to accept and act on the validity of these units, is the fundamental task of any adjuster of industrial or international controversy. When statesmen and managers of industry do this, when students apply this doctrine to the method of social research, we shall have a better chance of solving our social and political problems. And these whole-units, which take us away from atomistic values, are neither super-values nor static-values, for they gain their very existence by their continuous interknitting with individual values.[6] In my chapters on government I have connected the federal principle in political science with what I have called a federalistic ethics. On lower planes too the federalistic principle holds; it is the essence of the theory of integration, the heart of biological and personal as well as of social development. Creative experience is a federalistic growth.

In order to rid ourselves of the temptation to think there is such a thing possible as a static whole, we had better always ask, What is the whole doing? It is not a quiet Beneficence watching benignly over its busy children. It does not live vicariously *in* its "parts" any more than it lives vicariously *for* its "parts." The parts are neither its progenitors nor its offspring. There is no influence of whole on parts in a vague, mystical sense, neither by a "rationalization" of autocrats, but only through circular behavior. When we say "keep the man whole," "keep the experience whole," "always study the whole," we must bear in mind just what we mean by that, for we certainly do not

[6] There is an interesting parallel here to recent developments in both legal thinking and legal practice.

mean that we are not to study parts; analysis is as important a branch of psychological or social study as integration. What the psychologist must do in his field and the social scientist in his is to study the whole a-making; this involves a study of whole and parts in their active and *continuous* relation to each other. A psychology which studies integrative processes is a dynamic psychology, that is, is concerned with activities; when we are watching an activity we are watching not parts in relation to a whole or whole in relation to parts, we are watching a whole a-making.[7]

But there is an additional point to be considered: environment too is a whole a-making,[8] and the interknitting of these two wholes a-making creates the total situation—also a-making. "The psychological situation" is always a total situation. No penetrating psychological study, no penetrating study of social conditions, is possible without a study of these three wholes a-making. If we wish an example from the social level, think of the relation of trade unionists to one another on the one hand, of employers on the other, and of these two bodies to each other and to the conditions which they are meeting. The recent split among the telephone girls in Boston would be an interesting subject for study from this point of view. But it is unnecessary to pick out illustrations, for in every

[7] I think that some of the psychologists of the *Gestalt* school, as Koffka, do not describe accurately what they call the "member character" of the part as contrasted with its "absolute character," but any consideration of this question would take us too far into philosophical discussion for our present purpose.

[8] Köhler says the response is to "actual life conditions as a whole." *Op. cit.*, p. xiii.

psychological experience, on individual or social level, these three activities are always present.

Köhler touches on the question whether "the peculiarly characteristic happening in a totality" is the result of the interactions of the parts or whether it is the response of the *unit* to "its actual life conditions." Of course it is both and it is both simultaneously. The interactions are going on at the same time that the unit is responding as a whole to "life conditions." This is the most interesting part of the study of groups; we see that the interactions between the individuals of a group are being constantly influenced by "life conditions" and also by the interactions between group and "life conditions."

The direction which the *Gestalt* movement is taking is somewhat unfortunate as it seems to imply more interest in the whole than in the constitution of the whole—a fatal mistake wherever it exists. The attention of the *Gestalt* school seems riveted on the product to the neglect somewhat of the process. In drawing attention so constantly to the uniqueness of the whole, the moreness of the whole, they seem rather to discourage interest in the making of the whole. Moreover, each product of the integrative process engages their attention to the neglect, to a certain extent, of that continuity of process which is the essence of the psychology I have tried to give in this book. We have seen that process must be emphasized rather than product, that the process is continuous, and that the making of wholes and the breaking of wholes are equally important.

Yet the conclusions and still more the implications of this school of psychology are of value to the students of the social sciences, for over and over again we note in our own work that the problem before us is one of discovering a technique for unifying. One of the difficulties about using experts is often the lack of technique for uniting the knowledge of different experts. The following example was recently brought to my attention. In a certain county in California a celery disease specialist went from farm to farm to examine the celery and look for heart-rot. On his rounds one farmer said to him that he had some evidence that the disease had something to do with the way the crop was cultivated, the process of irrigation, etc., and he asked the specialist if that were true. The specialist replied that he didn't know, that he knew nothing of cultivation, he was a specialist on disease!

Social work suffers often from too great specialization. In a Child's Guidance Clinic, reports on a certain child were brought in by a doctor in regard to the child's health, by a social worker in regard to the family conditions, and by a psychologist who had made certain tests. But there seemed to be no technique for uniting these approaches. The chairman simply drove through what he considered each one should next do, and they went out again as specialists, again to work on the child separately.

Yet it is in the field of social work that we find some very interesting parallels to recent psychological conclusions in regard to wholes. As in contradistinction to traditional psychology which gave us experience as composed of sensations, images, affections, one of the principal features of present psychological teaching is that experience is always a complex, that experience is always a unity, so this is exactly what some students of the social sciences have felt to be the most illuminating part of their observations, namely, that the very essence of experience evaporates in analysis. The case-studies of Mrs. Ada E. Sheffield—the result of a scientific method of observation, of an insight which penetrates beyond surface values, and a synthetic handling of masses of material—are a valuable contribution to social psychology. I find in her last one, "What is the Case Worker really doing?"[9] an interesting illustration of the theory of circular behavior given in Chapter III and of the *Gestalt* theory of this chapter. I give a rather free interpretation of her material. The social worker takes a young person whose mal-adjustment to his environment has brought him to her care and does one thing after another for him: takes him to the dentist, sees that he has proper eye-glasses, finds a suitable job for him, suggests certain wholesome forms of recreation. Yet these things, one after the other, are not what she is "really doing." All these things, taken together, will have an effect on his life which one after the other they would not have. Still even this total effect is not all that the social worker is doing. What she is doing is to make possible the child's adjustment to his social environment. But, and this is the fact so often forgotten, not to a static environment. The various and varying activities of the child relate themselves to the various and varying activities around him which constitute his social environment. This interacting is the "total situation" of recent psychology. This "total situation" is often looked at as a total *picture;* it is thought that you can get all the

[9] *The Journal of Social Forces*, May, 1923. Mrs. Sheffield is Director of Research Bureau on Social Case Work.

factors if you examine the picture in sufficient detail. But a total situation is never a total picture; it is a total activity in which the activity of individual and activity of environment constantly interweave. What the social worker tries to do is to bring about the *kind* of interweaving from which it follows that further responses from environment, further responses from individual, will mean a *progressive* experience.

This all implies that the social worker is concerned not merely with the child's responses to environment; she must understand that the child's behavior is not, to speak exactly, a function of social environment, but a function of the continuous relating of child and environment. The value of the worker with children depends largely, not on her understanding of children, ("She is charming with young people" is no longer looked on as the chief praise we can give a social worker), neither on her understanding of social conditions as a student of sociology, but on her ability to do her part in so freeing the life of the child that possibilities of child and possibilities of social environment may form a "whole," or working-unit, which shall make the child's life more happy and fruitful, and also make the social environment contain more possibilities for all young people. Thus the next response of the child will necessarily be a more comprehensive one (taking that word intensively rather than extensively); that is, to use the expression I have already employed, his life will be one of *progressive* experience. Integrative experience is always progressive experience.

We have now a conception which must have large influence on our thinking, a conception which we might call psychological continuity. Integrative behavior means circular behavior which implies the continuity of experience—an important psychological conception. This view necessarily pays much attention to the external stimulus. I have said that the social worker must keep the child whole; she must also keep the environment whole. But analysis is, as we have seen, as important as integration, or rather it is a necessary step in integration. In all social research we see that we cannot dismiss "social environment" with the mere phrase and let it go at that. There is an illustration in the article of which I have just spoken which is a capital example of this. In the case in question, that of an unmarried mother, Mrs. Sheffield looks at the complex of conditions which influenced the conduct of the girl and breaks that complex into six parts: "First, the economic independence of working girls, which permits them to be free from home restraint at will; second, the dependence of girls upon men for their pleasures; third, the sex standards and conventions among men in general, especially perhaps among the smaller business men; fourth, this girl's own sex standards as compared not only with those of the ladies of the committee, but also with those of girls more depraved than she; fifth, the social effect of this manifestation of the social evil as compared with the effect of commercialized forms of vice; and sixth, the effects—known and probable—of the girl's behavior upon acquaintances, friends, and her family—including the child."

Then, after this careful analysis of environment, Mrs. Sheffield, I take it for granted from the implications in her article, tried to find what we are calling here the "whole" character of that environment. This dual method is necessary for all students of human life. In labor conferences the trouble often is that the trade-union delegate does not succeed in explaining the demands of the trade unionists in their "whole" significance, and one by one his arguments are demolished by the representatives of capital. The real demand is often in that whole demand which lies hidden. The man who has a genius for leadership is the one who can make articulate the whole demand. Elsewhere I have spoken of the necessity of breaking up the whole demand of the workman in order to discover what he "really wants." I hope it is apparent that these statements are not contradictory. We can find an illustration of this dual method in our everyday experience. Someone asks us, "Why did you do so and so?" And we are a little puzzled to give a satisfactory reply. We give a certain answer, and then seeing a look of surprise on our friend's face we recognize how inadequate that must seem as an explanation of our behavior, and we give another, and yet another, and we are aware that they all sound trivial as we state them, and indeed unless we can find the "whole" reason, we shall not be able either ourselves to understand completely, or to explain to our friend satisfactorily, why we acted in that particular way. But the whole reason is surely there all the time waiting to be recognized, and it is all the time influencing the separate reasons. Yet woe befalls the man who cannot differentiate his reason and discriminate.

Again, many more students of history are able to tell us of the different causes which are supposed to have led to a certain event than there are those who can estimate these as a multiple cause, that is, as a whole with a different character from the mere sum of these causes. All of us who are studying social situations and watching individual and group response see every day that we cannot understand behavior by noting only response to the various stimuli; we must see the multiple-stimulus as a whole and watch response to that. Any technique for a study of human relations must include this very important point. It is to be sure also true that in social situations, as in biological situations, reactions may be, as a biologist puts it, "to phases or parts or elements of a total situation," that is, this may be true to an extent, but obviously what we have to do is to be able to discriminate when it is one and when it is the other.

It should be noted that when we say total environment we of course do not mean total "total environment," but that which is in such immediate relation to the individual that its forces can be reckoned with both as cause of and effect of his activity, that is, that much of environment which comes within the appreciable range of circular behavior.

This all means that the social worker must work with the idea of circular behavior in mind. She studies, not individual, not environment—these can never be studied separately and then brought together—she studies a whole situation as it develops, as the factors interknit to make the whole developing situation.[10]

In what the *Gestalt* school tells us of "figure and ground," we might find a rough analogy to individual

[10] A Freudian might speak of the social worker's rationalization in the illustration given. I shall try to tell in Chap. VIII how far, or rather in what way, I think he would be making a mistake in so doing, and also what I think the Freudian himself might learn from the *Gestalt* concept.

and situation. In describing the "figure and ground," which writers of this school think the most important part of their doctrine, the illustration often given is that of the musical melody, which remains the same when transposed from one key to another. The *Gestalt* psychology seems somewhat confusing on this point, however, because of contradictory statements of different authors in regard to "meaning," yet as I am not making any estimate of different writers, but merely noting certain affinities between this school of psychology and other fields of thinking, there is a general correspondence here which it might be interesting to notice. Those of this school who are working on personality tell us that the personality in action cannot be studied apart from that general setting within which it acts. This is exactly what students of social research are finding every day so important for their work. The *Gestalt* school throughout, not only in the personality studies, emphasizes the inseparable union of "figure and ground": the isolated figure is nothing, it must be set off against a background of some sort else it is nonexistent. Here is the "unique," the "indivisible" unit. Of course this is exactly where philosophy makes one of its richest contributions to us. Any consideration of the *Gestalt* concept must necessarily be superficial which does not enter into the philosophical question of relation, but I have attempted here only to give certain aspects of this doctrine which might be immediately useful to students of the social sciences.

It is certainly of large significance that the most thoughtful students of social research agree with the conclusion of contemporary psychology that the elements of experience are not susceptible of isolation. How reiteratingly philosophy has told us this. How emphatically our everyday experience confirms it. Moreover, the relation of whole to parts is the core of many of our present political problems. In questions of government this is, on the theoretical side, the central battle ground for the political pluralists and their opponents, on the practical side, for the supporters of the League of Nations and their antagonists, for the advocates of increased or decreased federal legislation, etc. Federalism can never be fully understood until we see that it is not a governmental form alone but the most fundamental principle of life, expressing in the field of politics wisdom gathered from many sources. To use the language of this chapter (technical language if you will but language it seems to me full of suggestion for all our thinking) federalism is the embodiment of the theory of circular response and the *Gestalt* doctrine. Although I must add to that that probably most of the *Gestalt* school would be interested in the state of federalism, so to speak, rather than in federalization, that is, they would show a lack of interest in the process.

In Chapters XI and XII I shall try to show that we ought no longer to give adherence to the doctrine of the "consent of the governed," because the relation between governors and governed, between experts and people, must follow what seems to be the law of all relation, that of circular response. Also, the very essence of any legitimate theory of wholes is a relation of the one and the many which makes it impossible to give to the many the mere rôle of consent. Democratic thinking, or "the will of the people," in order to be democratic thinking, in order to be truly the will of the people, must have the character of integrating wholeness.

In Chapter XIII the necessary integrations suggested of representatives in representative assembly, and of each representative with his constituents, is an example of both these psychological doctrines. Many conceptions of political science will have new light shed on them when considered from the point of view now given us. For instance, to give one example out of many that spring to mind, the weakness of occupational representation is that it does not recognize the psychological doctrine of integration. Resting on its theory of "functionalism," it says that each man should represent his function, forgetting that man is an interplay of many functions, and that the "whole" man—this interplay of many functions—must go into his citizenship.[11] The "function" of a man is no more the political unit than sensation is the psychological unit; the question of unit is as important for politics as for psychology. Again, the doctrine of political "rights" must obviously be reshaped, but this is not the place to speak of that or to continue these illustrations; the whole field of political science will show before long the effects of this recent development of thought.

In the field of ethics we are coming to see the ethical unit, or determining wish, as a true whole, that is, it is not the arithmetical sum of desires, nor one which has wiped out "minor" desires, but an integrating desire which is continuously interweaving with the separate desires. That is, the ethical unit gets its char-

[11] See M. P. Follett, *The New State*, Chap. XXX, *Political Pluralism and Functionalism.*

acter of "wholeness" by an interweaving *with* the parts as well as by an interweaving *of* the parts. This is the characteristic of wholeness which has often been disastrously overlooked, but which the doctrine of circular response so illuminatingly gives.[12]

As social workers, psychiatrists, students of politics, economics and ethics, of law and international law, thinkers in many fields, are more and more recognizing and working on the principle of circular or integrative behavior, its importance becomes increasingly evident; it may be that we shall find it the cardinal principle in every department of thought.

In summary: any individual psychology which has not recognized the unifying nature of experience, any social psychology which has failed to see this, has dealt not with life but with abstractions from life. As we have found that a sensation never exists in experience but is a psychological abstraction, that a "trait" of personality is also a psychological abstraction, so many times our studies reveal to us that the meaning of a social situation is to be found not in its elements viewed separately but only in the total situation, or to use the still more suggestive word of the *Gestalt* school, a *Gesammtsituation.* Our perceptual experience, our personal experience, our social experience, is a complex structure, a unity. But it must be remembered that the *Gesammtsituation* cannot be comprehended by thinking of it as a matter of mere interaction. Integration is more than "mere coördination," as was pointed out by Watt when he spoke of the tendency to emphasize the process of coördination of sensations

[12] This seems to me a very interesting part of Dr. Richard C. Cabot's teaching of ethics.

with one another and to ignore what he calls integration.[13] For some years we have been approaching this point of view. It has often enough been questioned whether there is such a thing as "pure sensation" in experience. James recognized this in his chapter on *Sensation* where he stated that a pure sensation is an abstraction, and in *The Stream of Thought* (*Principles of Psychology,* 1890) we find plainly an anticipation of the *Gestalt* doctrine. In *The Compounding of Consciousness* (*A Pluralistic Universe,* 1909) he gives us the view of this chapter as corrected by his studies in the years intervening between the two publications. Ward in 1918 tells us that perception is not a sum of properties which can be taken to pieces and distributed like type.[14] Of recent years the doctrine of functional unity has had many adherents. J. S. Haldane points out that the metabolic activity within the organism is a "whole" activity. "Such processes as secretion, absorption, growth, nervous excitation, muscular contraction, were treated formerly as if each was an isolable physical or chemical process, instead of being what it is, one side of a many-sided metabolic activity of which the different sides are indissolubly associated."[15] A number of biologists have dealt with a whole organism and another whole the constitutive elements of which

[13] "An intimacy of connection between nerve-paths or impulses emanating from different sense organs is, of course, recognized in many forms. But this connection has been somewhat exclusively considered to consist in a *mere coördination* or association of afferent and efferent impulses with one another. Sufficient attention has hardly been paid to the possibility that upon these afferent impulses an afferent structure might be raised which is dependent upon but is essentially an addition to these. To distinguish it from mere coördination such a structure might well be called integration." H. J. Watt, *Some Problems of Sensory Integration, Brit. Journal of Psy.*, 1910, 3, 323 ff.

[14] James Ward, *Psychological Principles*, p. 303.

[15] *Mechanism, Life and Personality,* p. 79.

are organism and environment. But perhaps the most suggestive treatment of wholes, in the fields we are looking at, has come from those who have been working at the integrative action of the nervous system. Sherrington as early as 1906 gave us his view of mental life as the progressive creation of new and higher functions through integrative processes.[16] Holt in 1915 insisted on the difference between organic and mechanical response and made *organization* the central point of his psychology. He used the term integration clarifyingly and suggestively, and indicated its implications. Watson in 1919 said explicitly, "The behaviorist is interested in integrations and total activities of the individual."[17] The whole behaviorist school tends more and more to see the organism not as a mere *collection* of reflexes or instincts or habits. Psychobiologists are dealing with "whole personalities." When Kempf, in a book which I have found very helpful, describes "the dynamic nature of the personality," he tells us of an integrative unity, of a functional whole.[18] If dissection has been the method of traditional psy-

[16] Charles S. Sherrington, *The Integrative Action of the Nervous System.* He uses in the course of his book the phrases compounding together of reflexes, the combination, the alliance, the coalition, the coördination, of reflexes, but his meaning is clear, and he expresses it briefly in the following passage: "The unit mechanism in integration by the nervous system is the reflex. . . . We have hitherto dealt with reflex reactions under the guise of a convenient but artificial abstraction —the simple reflex. That is to say, we have fixed our attention on the reaction of the reflex-arc as if it were that of an isolable and isolated mechanism, for whose function the presence of other parts of the nervous system and of other arcs might be negligible and wholly different. This is improbable. The nervous system functions as a whole. Physiological and histological analogy finds it connected throughout its whole extent. . . ." P. 114.

[17] John B. Watson, *Psychology from the Standpoint of a Behaviorist,* p. 40.

[18] Edward J. Kempf, *The Autonomic Functions and the Personality,* pp. ix–xiv, 1–2, 77–78.

chology, the study of integrative processes is surely the chief characteristic of contemporary psychology. Ogden has written recently of what he expressly calls "the psychology of integration."[19] And—the thesis of this book—any psychology of integration, of whatever school,[20] shows us that kind of relating which creates. The psychology of the specific response did not give us the creating relation; the doctrine of circular response involved in the theory of integration gives us creative experience.

Circular response is the psychological term for the deepest truth of life. We move always within a larger life than we are directly cognizant of. But many men have deliberately shut their eyes to that larger life because they felt that any view must be false which made the individual seem to "transcend" what we know he can never transcend. But the theory of creative experience given to us by the most profound philosophy throughout the ages, and now so happily strengthened by recent research in several fields, shows that the individual can create without "transcending." He expresses, brings into manifestation, powers which are the powers of the universe, and thereby those forces which he is himself helping to create, those which exist in and by and through him, are ever more ready to respond, and so Life expands and deepens; fulfils and at the same moment makes possible larger fulfilment.

[19] Robert M. Ogden, *Are there Any Sensations? The Am. J. of Psy.*, April, 1922.

[20] The *Gestalt* psychology cannot strictly be called a psychology of integration, since a circle is a *Gestalt*, yet it is true that in much of their writing the psychologists of this school are describing integrative processes.

VI

EXPERIENCE NOT A PROCESS OF ADJUSTMENT

THE word most often used in biology, law and economics is adjustment. In biology we have the adjustment of organism and environment; in law the adjustment of rights or, in more modern language, of interests or desires; in industrial controversies too the avowed aim is adjustment.

But are we perhaps ready now to take a step beyond "adjustment," or rather, does not adjustment take on a somewhat different meaning in the light of our theory of circular response and of the doctrine of wholes given us by the *Gestalt* theory? The following items I consider of great significance. A jurist who has made valuable contributions to the problems of labor controversy has said to me that the secret of arbitration in labor disputes is not adjustment but invention. The head of a big industrial plant which has joint committees of management and workmen said to me, "I find that we come to agreement not by adjustment but by invention, not by reconciling our ideas but by finding the new idea which is always something different from the addition of the previous ideas." Compare this language with that used in *Response and Cognition.* It is here that the break from the old psychology is so illuminating for all conflict. This psychology supports the jurist and the manufacturer, for the whole matter of adjustment was carried a step forward with the use made here of the term "progressive integration," and with the emphasis placed upon the "novelty" in the moment of synthesis, the "critical" moment of evolution. We have now a scientific explanation of the "new." This does away with Huxley's "mystery moments," or else every "critical moment" is a mystery moment because there is the incalculable increment of the unifying.

This very striking coincidence in the language of jurist, manufacturer and psychologist, men of wholly different types and different experience, seems to me significant. Let us therefore examine the concept of adjustment further. Every advance in physics, physiology and psychology shows us life as process. Our still imperfect understanding of this is evident in our discussion of adjustment. In this discussion we see on the one hand an implied rigidity of environment and on the other an environment which can and must be "mastered." We are told by hundreds of writers that man must conquer environment; we are told by just as many that man must submit to "the iron laws of nature." Neither is true. The psychology which we have been considering shows us that we are neither the master nor the slave of our environment. We cannot command and the environment obey, but also we cannot, if we would speak with the greatest accuracy, say that the organism adjusts itself *to* environment, because that is only part of a larger truth. My farmer neighbors know this: we prune and graft and fertilize certain trees, and as our behavior becomes increasingly that of behavior towards apple-bearing trees, these become increasingly apple-bearing trees. The tree releases energy in me and I in it; it makes me think and plan and work, and I make it bear edible fruit. It is a process of freeing on both sides. And this is a creating process. As we have seen, the release and the integrating are the same process: this is one of the profoundest truths which psychology has given us.

Whether the popularity of the conception of conquering nature has come from "the urge to power" or not, it is certain that we do often like to think of our surroundings as "adverse"; we like to "wrest from nature" because that enhances the ego which is able to do that; we love to be the conquering hero whether it is in relation to nature or anything else. But the idea of mastering environment is unfortunate because we have carried it over into social relations; it becomes our duty to conquer all external circumstances, nature and other men too. In America we first "subdued the forests" and then turned our attention to our fellow-creatures.

Let us consider for a moment the phrase "resistance of environment," used repeatedly by both scientists and laymen. Kempf defines behavior as wishes (manifest, later repressed, adolescent and preadolescent) opposed by the resistance of environment.[1] In spite of the fact that resistance of environment is a technical term in psychoanalysis, I venture to suggest a slight change, not perhaps a change for the psychoanalysts, but for those who take this term over into other fields. Significant for much that the psychoanalyst sees, it seems to me that it should not be used

[1] E. J. Kempf, *Psychopathology*, p. 75.

by social psychologists as a definition to cover the behavior process in general. I should like for Kempf's opposed by the resistance of environment to substitute *confronting the activity of environment.* Thus we need not make anticipatory judgment; there may be opposition, there may be resistance, but this definition leaves it possible for us to wait until we find them. This would make a great change in the social sciences. Here we should have not necessarily the opposing, but the confronting, of interests. This confronting would make apparent many incompatibilities of interests, but does not judge the case beforehand as to what shall be done about it. Confront does not mean combat. In other words, it leaves the possibility of integrating as the method of the meeting of difference. Moreover, to use the language of Chapter III, Kempf's definition of behavior does not consider the increment of the growing. It is difficult, in social situations, to see the wish confronted with environment because the interweaving between them is a continuous process: the wish confronts an environment as altered by the wish; the environment confronts a wish as altered by the environment. Further than this, as has been shown, each is altered not only by the other but by the activity between them. The ignoring of this is why we find in some psychoanalysts an over-simplification.

I am not forgetting, as a psychoanalyst might think on reading this, that unconscious wishes are not so easily changed as conscious, and that we have many more unconscious than conscious wishes. Certainly as a student of social research I should not want it to be supposed that I confused the superficial, surface wish with the fundamental wish, for the distinction between these is the first step in the analysis of any social situation. I am also aware that the kind of activity which I have been trying to indicate between wish and environment is far more apparent in the case of the conscious than of the unconscious wish. Yet the therapeutics of the psychoanalyst would contradict his theory if he regarded unconscious wishes as unchangeable.

In Chapter III the point most emphasized was that response is to a relating. This shows us the limitations of the word adjustment for the behavior process by giving us an enlarged conception of environment. In viewing the total situation we found that we were not watching simple reactions correlated serially with external events; we found that we were watching exceedingly complex reactions to a complex environment, that complex sets of reflexes resulting in unitary acts respond to complex combinations of stimuli. In other words, we saw the integrating of motor mechanisms as more than simple receptor-effector response. We saw too, in considering response as two-fold, to internal and to external stimuli, that all stored-stimuli are themselves the result of previous responses, that every internal mechanism has incorporated environment. Those who define behavior as the integrated response of muscles and glands do not always emphasize this sufficiently. We have to study total response to total environment and to a developing environment or situation. The very phrase "functional" adjustment shows the inaccuracy of the statement "acting in harmony with environmental demands" because it shows how environment enters into every fresh response, shows what part environment has in response to environment,[2] and that each response or "functional adjustment" makes the organism capable of response to a more comprehensive environment. Of course the mechanism of each adjustment is the integrating of reflexes connecting the receptors with muscles or glands, of course we adjust ourselves by means of our habit equipment, but every habit system is organized by, is being organized by, interaction between movements and external situations. It seems as if there ought to be a different word for "first" response, and those later responses which more and more incorporate the environment or stimulus which produced them. Could we perhaps say response and developing response? Moreover, for social psychology we cannot keep physiological and social adjustment in different compartments. If I am hungry and eat, my organism becomes adjusted in the sense of that particular internal stimulus disappearing, but if I have stolen the food I am not adjusted to my total environment and that non-adjustment may also affect my body very soon.

We should notice, too, what is sometimes forgotten, that in the social situation two processes always go on together: the adjustment of man and man, and the adjustment of man and the situation; in social psychology objective reference is always two-fold. The southern marketing coöperatives, organized during the last two or three years, came into existence in reaction to tobacco and cotton speculators *and* to the period of

[2] Kempf brings out a very interesting point: that when environment cannot be changed, we tend to build a controllable environment within the greater one.

depression after the war. One should of course add here the internal conditioning which makes our study as much more interesting as it makes it more accurate. Thus we see the necessity, in observing social behavior, of taking into consideration total environment and total response. We can understand this by watching our own lives. We are always adjusting ourselves to our total environment which brings about an evolving of all the circumstances of our life in such a way that our wishes toward a particular circumstance will be changed, or, more probably, will create such different total circumstances for us that life will no longer present itself to us in the bare form of shall or shall not that particular wish be fulfilled. For just as the organism is responding to many stimuli at the same moment (through sight, hearing, touch, etc.), so man is responding to many people, many duties, many demands, many aspects of the life around him. The integrating of the former responses makes the normal physiological life; the integrating of the latter, the "balanced" individual.

The ignoring of the total situation is the weakness of many discussions on adjustment. The illustration given above of the defiance of the red flag at a railroad crossing ignored the fact that the railroad company may take a hand in the situation, may respond as well as stimulate, may respond to an accident by deciding to have gates at this crossing instead of the red flag. And so on, and so on. Stimulus and response interweave at every instant. A friend of mine says she always writes notes instead of telephoning because then she does not have to hear any back-talk; she makes her statement and that is the end of it. But life, alas, is more like the telephone than our writing desks; it is full of "back-talk." Some of the behaviorists tend to ignore this point, to look merely at stimulus and response, and not to appreciate that elaborate, complex process which makes it difficult at any one moment to know which to call stimulus and which response. Behaviorism declares itself as concerned with environmental adjustment, and the more superficial of its supporters conceive this in terms of adjusting ourselves to a rigid environment, disregarding the very obvious fact that my response changes the environment or rather that environment-plus-my-response changes the environment. It was red flag plus man's defiance of it which produced the gates, to put the matter rather crudely. It should be noted, in short, how far our doctrine of circular response takes us beyond reciprocal relating as this is often understood. Beyond the effect of organism on environment and environment on organism, the organism responds to the relation between itself and environment. Any analysis of behavior which does not take into account that response is to a relating, will be inadequate. Any analysis of society which does not take into account that response is to a relating, gives us the determinism of the last century.

But if the doctrine of circular behavior is changing our conception of adjustment, the *Gestalt* theory also might have some influence on that conception, for that too, it seems to me, must necessarily help to abolish the idea of one "acting on" another. Biology has made large contributions on this point, for biologists have for some time shown us the interactive influence of organism and environment as a "whole" activity, as I noted in the last chapter. Biologists have seen that biological experience cannot be defined in terms of organism and environment "acting on" each other; they have recognized that organism and environment together form a working-unit or functional whole. Moreover, biologists have shown us in regard to organism and environment what psysiologists have shown us in regard to the organism. Physiologists tell us that a response to an afferent impulse through a sense organ is not determined by that impulse alone, but is affected by the impulses which are coincidently coming into other parts of the body, as well as by the whole functional activity of the rest of the organism (nutrition, respiration) and the chemical stimuli thereby produced. Likewise biologists tell us that any activity between environment and a part of an organism is affected by the rest of the organism. There is one weakness however seen sometimes in the biological notion of wholes which should be corrected. The biological conception of experience which indicates that organism and environment "express a whole" (I have seen that phrase used recently by a biologist), sometimes ignores the subtler implications in the notion of a whole a-making. What remnant of intellectualism is this? Organism and environment do not "express" but make wholes.

In the matter of total environment, moreover, we are sometimes misled by the way some of the biologists express themselves. In the case of the flatfish we are told that the flatfish adapts itself to environment, meaning the sea bottom, when it forms the pattern of the sea bottom on its back. But what is really happening is that there is taking place in the flatfish a change such that its back looks like the sea bottom to an observer, that is, it is adapting itself to a larger environment than the biologist always takes account of. In the biological discussion of adjustment we see several limitations. It often neglects adjustment to total environment, that is, it does not take sufficient account of the comprehensiveness of environment. Again it often confuses purpose and teleology, and to those who think of "organism adjusting itself to environment" as a teleological notion, external environment becomes overemphasized at the expense of internal desire or stimulus. Moreover, some biologists blur the whole matter by not keeping to the same plane during the discussion; at one moment they are on the perceptual plane talking of cells, and the next they are talking of direction and distance which are on the conceptual plane of mathematics. Finally, biologists do not always see the truth that that which you call organism and that which you call environment is usually a purely subjective matter. While some writers write of individual and environment as if the individual were always man, and the environment were always "nature," whatever that may mean—a too-inclusive term on the one hand and far too limited on the other—as a matter of fact the choice of point of view and appellation in regard to individual and environment is an entirely subjective matter. Le Dantec, the biological sociologist, shows that we decide which is the individual and that then all the rest is environment. This is obvious, often overlooked, and important.

The more comprehensive idea which we now have of the adjusting relation has many lessons for us. The definition of intelligence given by some psychologists is adaptability to new situations, that is, an individual possesses intelligence "in so far as he has learned or can learn to adjust himself to his environment." One would want to know, before one could accept this definition, what adjustment means here. The "invention" of our jurist and manufacturer shows more intelligence than *mere* adjustment.

We have only to look around us to find many examples of our meeting difficulties by invention, or what I should prefer to call progressive adjustment,[3] rather than by an adjustment which gives to one factor the office of dictator to the other. Take insurance: we cannot do away with accident, but we do not let it bring financial disaster to the individual, we distribute the loss over society. But *thereby* the number of accidents is reduced (greater effort is made to avoid them), and thus also total loss from accident is diminished. Both factors are affected, but neither affects the other directly, only through this new activity, the specific response of man to accident. This should always be our rule: progressive adjustment, not mere adjustment. Instead of "adjusting" the competition for markets among nations, we ought to get more markets by developing backward countries. Instead of "adjusting" the demands for the division of the products of industry, it is better when we can through scientific management increase production.

With the narrower idea of adjustment we should often be getting more than we bargain for; for instance, do we want a capitalistic society to "adjust" itself to our present trade unionism with its many weaknesses, with

[3] I like the term progressive adjustment better than invention, for invention might connote too much causeless spontaneity and too little specific response. See Chap. IX for a fuller treatment of this.

its organization based on outgrown political ideas? Must there not be found the way of fruitful uniting? Again, take the word "socialization" so often heard nowadays. It is used as a good word even when it means adaptation to the present social order. But socialization, which people speak of as a supreme virtue, is often a pure crowd idea, the crowd trying to preserve itself as it is. Harmony between the individual and the social order must mean changes in both individual and the social order, yet not arbitrary changes, but changes which will come about by a deeper understanding of that relation. The individual is not adjusted to society; there is a creating relation between them. The infant, to be sure, must adjust himself, for a time, to the family and the whole social milieu in which he finds himself, but as heresy is the coefficient of religion, and illegality the coefficient of law,[4] so this milieu will be changed only by the action of individuals; individual variation is the coefficient of social life. All that we call social has been built up by *individual* reaction. The individual by his responses to the social fabric contributes that which so enhances it that the stimuli proceeding from it to the individual enhance his reactions and he has more to contribute than before. Thus are built up the customs and conventions, rules and laws, we call society. We are making our environment anew all the time, but that new environment is at the same time recreating us. To use the language of Chapters III and IV adjustment is an aspect of circular behavior.

We considered in the last chapter the case of the social worker and what she did to help the child "ad-

[4] Jean Cruet, *La Vie du Droit.*

just" himself to society. We can see clearly now, what was implied then, that if we use such an ambiguous word we must be careful that there is no slackness in our thinking, for we do not wish to adjust the child in the sense of fitting him into certain social conditions. In the more comprehensive meaning we are now giving to that word, it includes always changes in environment as well as in child. Henceforth we should use the word adjustment in social situations only if we understand it as an aspect of circular behavior.

This conception of adjustment will necessarily mean large changes in all the social sciences. Take, for instance, the idea of conflict. If I am never fighting you but always you plus myself, that is, that "whole" which the interweaving between you and me has created, is creating, we shall have a very different idea of the way to deal with conflict. This will mean changes in both legal and political thinking.

To sum up. The conception of circular response, of integrative behavior, cuts under the meaning of adjustment in ordinary use and gives us adjustment as a creating relation. Thus submission and invention are not opposed; on our submission (of the right kind) depends the "something new" we can produce. It is in the light of this view of the specific-response relation that I wish in Part II to consider "obedience"—to state, to employers, to ethical rules, etc. Adjusting in the sense of integrating is the perfect union of submission and mastery. When we have really acquired the dynamic habit of mind which we boast of now, and think always in terms of process, we shall think of both organism and environment, individual and situation, as activities, and that will make it easier to understand the activity of functional relating which involves these two activities. "Opposition" then disappears under the more subtle interpretation of stimulus and response which is now given us.

Is it, then, ever legitimate for me either to conquer you or to submit to you? Both of them fail in the long run—and often in the short run. I can only free you and you me. This is the essence, the meaning, of all relation. As physiologists and psychologists talk of "the release of energy," so it is a fundamental idea for the social sciences. It should be the basis of every sociological concept. Economics must acknowledge its truth. Political science must see in it the foundation of all it may *thereafter* erect. The task for politics, economics and jurisprudence is to provide those contacts, find those relations, which free in each the spiritual energy which, uniting each with each, gives us, on no conceptual plane but in our daily lives, a "will of the people." This reciprocal freeing, this calling forth of one from the other, this constant evocation, is the truth of "stimulus and response." I object to calling physiological stimulus and response the "material" part of life. We find the same life-process—the self-yielding of organism and environment—on every plane; here in the concrete circumstance is the "living" truth. Where then is reality? In the objective situation, or in "the people"? In neither, but in that relating which frees and integrates and creates. Creates what? Always fresh possibilities for the human soul: expressed in new tariff laws or shorter hours of work or co-operative banks or whatever it may be. The political problem, then, is not how to obtain "consent," but how to open the way for the creating relation between man and man. This can be done by an adult education which shall deliberately try to find and teach those methods which shall make possible, encourage and develop this relation between men, by a journalism of insight, by coöperative movements, by the development of local units for discussion; but however furthered, it is the process of a self-creating will of the people through the release of energy. As in physiology and psychology, so in human relations, the release and the integrating are the same process. In the course of this chapter I have already made this statement, but it cannot be repeated too often.

The deeper truth of adjustment brings us this illumination: if the biological ideal is "adjustment," and the ethical "right," and the juristic "justice," and the political "freedom," and the economic "satisfaction of wants," the definition here given of the social process and of functional adjustment shows that there is no quarrel between these. They need not be considered even as registering different stages of thinking. They need not be classed, some as idealistic, some as materialistic, they are but different ways of viewing the same fundamental principle.

In considering the phrase "resistance of environment" it is patent that the whole philosophy of the person who tells us of resistance of environment is different from that of those who dislike the term. The latter believe that we are at home in our world, that we have not just happened on a cosmos that is alien to us, that we have not come where we do not belong. There seems to me a presumption that there is a fundamentally blessed relation between self and circumstance. It is the philosophy back of the resistance of environment notion that I do not agree with. Resistance implies the opposition of nature, suggests, "I am but a pilgrim here, Heaven is my home," gives you a pretty forlorn idea of a self that has strayed out of its orbit. The philosophy involved in "progressive integration" gives us a soul at home and it gives us the crescent self; it shows us that our greatest spiritual nourishment comes not from "inviting our soul," but in meeting the circumstance. There is only one way by which the spirit mounts, by that meeting which is the sacrament of life and needs no symbol because the self lives daily that sacrament from which it draws its sustenance.

VII

EXPERIENCE NOT A VERIFYING PROCESS

WE can now think of experience more as a creating than a verifying process. Experience is the power-house where purpose and will, thought and ideals, are being generated. I am not of course denying that the main process of life is that of testing, verifying, comparing. To compare and to select is always the process of education, beginning long before birth; in anatomical physiology we see the nervous system growing by a selection which is a creating. The fallacy in the notion of comparing does not lie with the idea of comparing but with the things compared. This is certainly true in social situations. When we go to a conference we have to compare the idea we bring to it not with the idea we "find" there, but with what is being developed there. The employer may meet his workmen expecting to find out what they have been thinking about things. He can never discover that! For as soon as he meets them, and partly by the very fact of his meeting them, a different situation has arisen. When you get to a situation it becomes what it was plus you; you are responding to the situation plus yourself, that is, to the relation between it and yourself. As in the physiological circular reflex you cannot compare stimulus and muscular activity because the muscular activity through the instantaneous movement back to the centre is included in the stimulus which is causing the muscular activity, so in social situations you cannot compare what you bring and what you find because these have already influenced each other. Not to understand this is the onlooker fallacy: you cannot see experience without being a part of it. Of course if we were always getting ladders and climbing up and peering into windows, and tapping wires, and getting dictaphones into people's cellars—but there seem to be too many practical difficulties about this. Life is not a movie for us; you can never watch life because you are always *in* life. (The old fairy stories recognized this difficulty and provided the cap of invisibility.) Does this make an *impasse* for us? On the contrary, the evolving situation, the "progressive integrations," the ceaseless interweavings of new specific respondings, is the whole forward movement of existence; there is no adventure for those who stand at the counters of life and match samples.

There is an investigation going on at the present moment of a certain institution. The committee which is paying for this investigation wished to find out how far the methods of the institution in question were in line with what they considered the best modern ideas. But they are not going to find out, exactly, because the committee and students are, by this very study, somewhat changing their ideas in regard to the best way of developing such institutions. It might, however, be replied to this, "But they can discover how far their remodelled standards are being carried out." No, they cannot even do that, for this very investigation has caused that institution to change its methods, in a degree, even while the study is going on. Testing in an exact sense is an impossibility; we can live and progress and create, and we must use all the conceptions we can get hold of to help us do this, but life never stops long enough for us to "test," or rather we cannot get outside life to view it. In the case I have just given, the moment the committee decided to make that study they placed themselves inside that bit of experience. Outside they could not observe, but the moment they began to observe they stepped inside, and then the interweaving between standards and institution began. The activity-between was at the same time moulding the institution and developing their own ideas. This again is like the circular reflex, where not stimulus and not response is the chief thing, but the functioning, what I am calling the activity-between. "According to the reflex-circle, reflex-reaction is a function [functioning] that actualizes and alters the perception of the stimulus."[1]

On the social level, self and circumstance, thought and concrete experience, are always interweaving; this, not comparing, is the life-process. We now see the life-process as that of creating through specific response. Observation is the most important part of the procedure of the social sciences, but we should have a more accurate understanding of observation—of observation, of comparison, of testing. I cannot test activity by previous thought because every activity carries within it its own tests. Yet we try to do so because it is so much easier; to take a foot-rule and measure is one thing, but it is quite another to live through an experience with stress and strain, to discover, with

[1] Bok, *op. cit.*, p. 296.

infinite pain perhaps, what is involved in that situation.

The people who "learn by experience" often make great messes of their lives, that is, if they apply what they have learned from a past incident to the present, deciding from certain appearances that the circumstances are the same, forgetting that no two situations can ever be the same. I know a man whose life has been seriously affected by his saying to himself at a rather crucial point in his career, "I cannot treat this man so and so because I did it some years ago to a man and it did not work." But this second man was one whom he might have treated in this way. Of course the first contact might have been of great value to him, but he did not learn how to use it; instead of integrating it with the rest of his experience, he kept it apart and generalized too hastily from that one episode. Part of my intellectual and spiritual integrity depends on an understanding of this. All that I am, all that life has made me, every past experience that I have had—woven into the tissue of my life—I must give to the new experience. The past experience has indeed not been useless, but its use is not in guiding present conduct by past situations. We must put everything we can into each fresh experience, but we shall not get the same things out which we put in if it is a fruitful experience, if it is part of our progressing life. A woman recently said to me: "The trouble with me is that I don't integrate my experience." I think she stated a very fundamental truth. We have the choice with each fresh experience, if we do not disregard it altogether, of either pigeon-holing it to take out at some future time when a similar circumstance arises (a similar circumstance never will arise), or of integrating it with all the rest of our experience. We integrate our experience, and then the richer human being that we are goes into the new experience; again we give ourself and always by the giving rise above the old self.

Thus when we integrate there is nothing left to pigeon-hole. Our great judges are those who do not pigeon-hole but integrate. It is the difference between a mechanical and a creating intelligence. Those who interpret mechanically are "robots." The "robots," made in factories to do man's work for him, had mechanical intelligence; they could have taken experience and put it into pigeon-holes, then when they needed principle or precedent they could have gone to the pigeon-holes and take out what "corresponded." But men who are exercising that kind of intelligence are not claiming their birth-right; what man is capable of is activity that creates.

There is a hint of the fallacy of preconceived purpose about the old idea of verifying, for you must decide on the purpose before you can decide on the validity of the verification. The psychology which destroys the doctrine of final ends corrects the two fallacies in the notion of verifying so often held: a tendency to divorce for the moment thinking and doing (if you separate thought and activity you can test by the criteria supplied by mind); and an ignoring of the self-evolving nature of the specific-response relation. We do not think, and do, and think again, but the thinking is bound up in the doing. There is one thing essential to understand: activity does not carry on the activity which produced it, it generates new energy.

No conception of democracy is sound which does not take this into account.

What is most intriguing in the theory of verifying is the fate of the rejected hypotheses. If principles are merely hypotheses with which to experiment, then they have no value when discarded; but they can never be discarded. They are, as I have said, thrown into the process and thus contribute to the new principles, or the way I should prefer to state it, to the new situation. We must remember too that discarding is in fact impossible according to the very psychology of those who most frequently use this word. If we "hold" a thought long enough to test it, it has become a part of the organism, of the internal mechanism. I am not saying that therefore we shall always have to "hold" it, but only that something has happened, a very complex process has gone on, so that we can never discard that thought in the sense of things being for us as if we had never held it. Our neuro-muscular arcs are not like slates on which we can write and then sponge out. There is no forgiveness for us in the sense of wiping out. We have to accept our behavior fully and go on—behavior in its technical sense, implicit as well as overt.

The impossibility of discarding is in a certain sense true even of scientific hypotheses. To be sure, when we are talking of, say, the space arrangement of atoms, we may test by an hypothesis which we then discard. Still even in science one hypothesis helps us in forming the next; scientific hypotheses are never chance guesses. But at any rate I do not think you can transfer to the field of the social sciences the simple sort of testing that takes place in physical science. For I do not see this discarding taking place anywhere in the life around me. I know of no dump yards where I can go to see the discarded hypotheses. Do you say history is full of them? I find traces in the present of all that history has seemed to give up. In our own individual lives this sometimes seems one of the hardest laws to reconcile ourselves to, and yet it is the very heart of the truth in regard to individual as well as social progress, and I suppose the degree in which we accept it indicates in large part our capacity for growth. That is, the measure in which we learn how to make that which we should like to discard (but we cannot because it is undiscardable) serve the larger truth, contribute to the bringing forth of that new life which will be for us a "critical moment in evolution."

Each period has its magic word par excellence. A few years ago when science was the word to conjure with, the idea of verifying appealed to us because we were told that it was "scientific," but the social sciences, while learning everything possible from physical science, must develop their own method. The best word on this subject has been spoken, I think, by Dr. Kallen: ". . . a fact is not a preëxisting thing to which a conception may conform, but an eventual thing. . . ." Dr. Kallen does not forget, what too ardent apostles of the verifying process do forget, namely, the compound interest, that creating includes the increment of the increment, that it is the activity-plus with which we are chiefly concerned.

Another thing which the idea of verifying does not take into account is this: what makes me test out a certain idea at a certain moment? There is some reason for it. I have a shoe-factory; out of the whole ramified activity of making and selling shoes, into which countless ideas and standards have gone, a certain situation arises. If I find myself then testing some idea, it is because the running of my factory has brought the necessity of doing so to the surface. There is no arbitrary testing, one might almost say there is no abstract testing; the whole process which has brought me to the moment of verifying affects also the process of verifying. Which shows again that testing in human situations can never be the same as testing in the laboratories of the physical sciences. In the illustration I gave above of the study being made of a municipal institution, the suggestion for that study arose out of the elaborations and complexities involved in the thought about that institution, the many activities of city life related to it. I have read recently, "We choose the truths which have vital consequences." But where do we go to find them, and does life ever give us time for choosing? In my own experience truths usually hit me in the face before I have time to "choose" them.

There is a point closely connected with this which is sometimes misunderstood. We often hear people talk of the "interpretation of experience" as if we first had an experience and then interpreted it, but there is a closer and a different connection between these two; my behavior in that experience is as much a part of my interpretation as my reflection upon it afterwards; my intellectual, post-facto, reflective interpretation is only part of the story. This is a very important point.

Moreover, it should be noticed that those people who take a thought to a situation to be confirmed or discarded, also do the converse and take the observed fact to an old principle and classify it. There is much that is intellectualistic about the notion of testing. Our "pigeon-holes" are our action tendencies to abstract logical construction, but those who live by logical systems are simply taking "a moral holiday."

I do not want of course to give up classification; that would be absurd, but I believe that the relation of observation to preëxisting classification has to be worked out on different lines from that which most of us are pursuing at present. To test and discard, to test and verify? Life is not as simple as that, or as "scientific" either. Life is an art. Life with its creating power, depending for man on the self-yielding of activity and thought, is an endless interplay. And at this moment when we are urged so constantly to look at facts, the objective situation, the concrete circumstance, the actual event, it is especially necessary that we learn how to connect the conceptual and perceptual planes, how to let every fact contribute to those principles which by use again in the factual world become again transformed, and thus man grows—always through his activity.

Classification as "conceptual short-hand" is of course necessary, but we must be ready to change our classification with every new contribution of experience. Is this too obvious to need stating? Judge Gray tells us that "the besetting sin of the analytical jurist is the conviction that his classifications and definitions are final." The way in which bacteriologists use classification, changing it readily with every new discovery, might be a lesson to us.

As this seems to me important, let me try to express it differently. Our later empiricism does not deny the importance of principles. We have not to choose between a moral atomism and general ethical laws; principles are immensely valuable—on the other side of the equation, as part of the stuff of the situation, as part of the warp and woof of our concrete life. A teacher of ethics says that we "adapt" our principles to the new conditions. Many jurists tell us the same. I do not think that this is the process. For instance, a man comes to a conference with a certain idea or principle; it should not be adapted, and also it should not be kept outside the interweaving of the conference to judge the conference by; it should be thrown into the situation in order that from all the intermingling a new thought may be evolved. The X of one situation should always be X′ in the next. I often see men meeting in conference who confuse X and X′ or are concerned only with X. The consent to meet should be a tacit agreement to the contrary, should imply that all are to be concerned with X′, that is, with what may come forth from this meeting. A man may say frankly that he prefers fighting to conferring, that is, he prefers to maintain his own ideas irrespective of another's; but if he accepts the method of conferring, that acceptance means that he is thereby bound to see what can come of the conferring. This is the only way that conference can ever be made a valid process.

When we try to adapt our principles to conditions, not only we forget that they are already in the conditions, but also we are not doing justice to them; they are worth far more to us than that. When we "adapt" principles we are false to one of the deepest truths of existence. Concepts are created by motor reactions. Then when these concepts come into contact with fresh conditions we have new motor reactions which means new concepts. The creating is always done through concrete activity, never, except very partially, through intellectual activity. The primitive tribes woo nature with incantations and ceremonies; we *do* things to her. Many Christians pray to God to change their characters; yet most of us learn gradually and painfully that the only way to change our characters is by *doing* things.

There is indeed truth in the doctrine of verifying, a basic truth, but it does not consist in comparing results with a preconceived idea, since thought and activity cannot be separated. Yet there is a test which we may always make, a legitimate question we may ask: Does this activity fit in? This is the deeper meaning of all our wish to "verify." This is the process which all biology discloses. In the progressive self-evolving of experience, from the tactile sensations of the amœba to the rational knowing of man, every activity which functions as a necessary activity in the whole a-making at that particular moment is "verified." We verify through the process of creating: no dualism, no *Dinge an sich,* no static moment.

VIII

FORMULATED EXPERIENCE: THE RELATION OF PERCEPT TO CONCEPT

I SPOKE in the last chapter of the place where conceptual and perceptual meet, in our concrete activities. Thus concepts are not formulated, but formulating, experience. Those who hurl diatribes against the conceptual simply do not understand its place. Concept-making is a long, slow process. It is all life working ceaselessly on itself, building itself up. Bergson describes as a mere abstraction this self-initiated, living activity of concept-building. When we are told of the dangers of the conceptual, the only warning we need take from that is that we must never allow the conceptual complex to be separated from the concrete field of activity, we must always understand what thought is perceptually. When we read the judge's decision, we should be able to see how much is empty words and how much is concrete activity condensed into his conceptual and inferential tissue. When the judge can convince us that his decision is kneaded out of concrete acts, when we feel the current of sensings pulsate in every "abstract" word, then we need not be afraid of his concepts.

When James, Bergson and others tell us of the emptiness of conceptual thinking, this reproach is based on a misunderstanding of conceptual thinking. Percept and concept are part of the same activity. Every experience is the binding together of past and present. Conceptions do not remain conceptions. They enter into the bone and blood of our daily activities and then from these, new conceptions arise. If we keep close to the earth-struggle, if we heed every moment the needs of man, we shall see every moment the passing of one concept into another but always through the perceptual. One concept is not discarded and another adopted; integration is the law on every plane, and it is the integrating of percepts and concepts that we must study if we would understand the history of thought. There is no antagonism between the two. Concepts are the grip of life. We tend to think of concepts as self-existent and they are not. All our concepts professedly stand for specific behavior to us; are we keeping them to that or do we become satisfied with words? We tend to become satisfied with words whenever we allow ourselves to use a word in relation to ourselves which does not correspond to the actual behavior in ourselves. The facile use of conceptual words is a serious danger.

Life is an organizing process, each complex is organized with others into a higher complex. Each organization simplifies, but it simplifies only to take its part in further complexity. The tissue of life is elaborating; the concept gives us unity, simplicity; we may make full use of its unity and simplicity if we understand the elaboration from which it has come, to which it is going. Life is enriched by collaboration with all the powers of the universe. Man lives on several planes and his development depends on the uniting of them; we can live as "thriving earthworms," or something more.

Thus we see that every single bit of life is part of experience. You cannot say that we will take this bit out and call it the conceptual side and this bit we will call the other side. You cannot arbitrarily keep distinct that which is not distinct. Experience is unitary.

I wish now to connect the thought of the last five chapters—that is, the psychology of the circular response and the evolving situation—with what I have said in Chapter I of experts and fact-gathering, for many writers do not show us that continuous integrating of percept and concept, of "fact" and principle, which is so important a part of the social process. Sometimes we even hear the static term "conceptual pictures." But the evolving situation is against conceptual pictures. There are not, as some systems of philosophy imply, two principles of the universe, that of fixity and that of flux, there are—"progressive integrations." The thought I have been giving shows the difference between stability and rigidity; its essence is stability through the laws of activity. Conceptual pictures are always pictures of the past; you proceed then to deduce principles, laws, rules, from the dead instead of from the living. And the only way to get new pictures would be to take down some and hang up others. Pictures do not evolve. Situations do. Situations evolve by the force within, by their own momentum. "Conceptual pictures" belong to the same order of thought as God creating the different species.

The heaviest blow at conceptual pictures is that thought alone does not govern activity; my pictures depend on my behavior. I do not conceive that object as a shade tree and go and lie under it. My lying under it is made up of a thousand reflex actions; then, because of the organization of these reflex arcs, that object becomes a shade tree for me. Thus all our pictures of the world are made by our specific responses to the world. These specific responses have depended on many things, on all the habits incorporated in the organism from birth and before. Many, ignoring this process, base all their hopes on conceptual pictures influencing us directly in some mysterious way, but there is no such thing in the universe as passive acceptance, no such thing, that is, as *mere* response; this is the profound truth of the psychology I am trying to indicate. Because of all that has been already incorporated in the organism, we shall respond in a certain way; it is the behavior of the organism which is influencing the organism through environment but not by means only of environment. It is exactly this which we must allow for in the situation between France and Germany. France and Germany respond to, behave towards, the same actual world, but in their behavior towards that world is involved thought, will, purpose (see formula). That thought involves pictures which change their behavior which again changes the pictures. What we have been trying to do with Germany has been to make her see shade-tree before all the preliminary integrations have been made which make her response to the tree convert it into "shade-tree." It is a sheer impossibility for her. We can convince Germany of nothing except through her own activities. We can, and must if we would solve in any degree the European problem, open the way for her to do certain things; the doing of those things will give her—shade-tree. Her response must come before what she is responding to, objectionably paradoxical as this may seem.[1] She will tell you what she is responding to *after* the response; she will discover what she is responding to after the response. No, it is more subtle even than that: she in part creates what she is responding to; if we want something to exist for her to respond to, we must first open the way for her to respond to it. Until we understand this, we cannot have the most temporary settlement of the European situation.

An ignoring of this is the weakness of European diplomacy today. All the different nations are presenting their pictures of the world: France and Germany each its own, England and Russia each its own, etc. They think that if they can only paint their pictures with sufficient skill and in vivid enough colors, the other nations will see them with their minds. They never will. Because we do not see with our minds.

Thus, far from minimizing the importance of the objective situation, I think it cannot be too strongly emphasized if it is understood as part of the total situation. The thing which changed the relation of France and England (among others not so dramatic or tangible) was coal; when France got control of coal in the Ruhr Valley it meant unemployment for England. Coal is certainly objective enough, but the interweaving here of picture and purpose has been apparent to us all. In the textile strikes we see the situation change with market conditions. It is not, however, always so apparent. For instance, the short versus the long view of self-interest has usually been analyzed

[1] This should not seem objectionably paradoxical in the light of the theory of circular response.

from a quantitative point of view: we say it is better to have a larger happiness or ease in the future than a smaller amount now; therefore we have developed maxims of foresight, etc. But we have not the conception of the interchange of influence between people sustaining a situation as a thing which requires time to show its potentialities. This is because we do not understand life as process; we posit static situations.

Of course we do not want to do what our State Department in Washington has been doing; it has been relying on time instead of what can be put into time. The damning effect of this is that it has blunted the American people to the European situation. We had in 1919 the beginnings of certain behavior patterns that could have been enlisted in coöperative enterprise. What the policy of our State Department has lost for us is the incipient motor sets of a coöperative activity; those we are now forming are against coöperative activities.

I have said that the chief argument against conceptual pictures is that thought alone does not govern activity. In our own lives we see sadly, and often tragically, our will (as we call it) and our actions at variance; we have wished to do so and so but we have done so and so. Our tendency is then to think that our "will" represents the ideal, the soul part of us, and our actions the way our will has been betrayed by circumstances. It is exactly the opposite: our actions represent our real will (or habits incorporated in the organism); our "better self" is still to be gained through fresh activity. The solving of our problem comes when we see that the only alchemy by which we can get our gold is the process of creating will through activity; all our disaster comes when we try to interfere with this process. What we have to learn is where to place our faith. There is no "safety first" in ethics or politics. Every activity carries with it its own peculiar sureties. Empty will can no longer masquerade as spiritual force. We can rely neither on facts nor, like the hero of the old-fashioned novel, on our own "strong will," but only on a full acceptance of all the responsibility involved in our part in that unfolding life which is making both "facts" and ourselves.

To put this still another way: integration, the resolution of conflict, the harmonizing of difference, must take place on the motor level, not on the intellectual level. We cannot get genuine agreement by mere discussion in conference. As our responses are governed by past habits, by what has been incorporated in the organism, the only way of getting other responses is by getting other things incorporated in the organism. We have not understood this: a man goes home from an international conference and wonders why he cannot carry his people with him in regard to what has there been agreed on. We assign a number of reasons for this; the real reason is that agreement has to come from and through what is going on every day in that nation. To persuade his people into verbal acceptance means only a pseudo agreement, and the underlying dissent (the dissent which is synonymous with unchanged motor sets) will only crop up again in some other form. The unadjusted *activities* in the situation will continue their conflict. Genuine integration occurs in the sphere of activities, and not of ideas or wills. Hence the present aim of our international conferences is wrong; the aim should be not intellectual agreement alone, but to provide opportunities for actual agreement through the activities of the nations involved. The task therefore of political scientists is not that of making a conceptual picture of the world, but to test the validity of a certain process. This, by the way, is the profounder reason why the coercive power of the majority will not work in the long run.

To sum up this point: the psychology we are considering teaches us that the ideas of people are not formed in their "minds" by conceptual pictures, but depend on their activities. Europe is trying to get Germany *to agree to pictures* instead of opening the way for her to *respond to conditions*. Diplomats may talk, statesmen may make plans, the journals may write on indefinitely, but we shall make little headway as long as we suffer from the illusion of pictures as independent of behavior. The only thing which will help toward any genuine solution of our world problems today are methods which will open the way for those responses which will help to create a different situation. Concepts can never be presented to me merely, they must be knitted into the structure of my being, and this can be done only through my own activity.

Thus we are taught the freshness of each moment, we cannot bind our activity to a preconceived purpose. When we see people who dislike to plan ahead, our tendency is to think either that they do not want to burn their ships behind them, or else that they dislike to assume obligations. It may not be either, but a clear seeing that the plan must always be a function of the activity.

We can never catch up with life by any other philosophy; we shall always be eating the soft part of our melting ice and meanwhile the nice hard part is rapidly melting too. This is why the English unwritten constitution is better than our rigid American constitution, why some union of nations is better than treaties, why we are seeking changes in our marriage laws. Because we want to find the law *of* the situation *in* the situation and yet still be guided by law and not by personal or national whims or a narrow self-interest —that is the problem set for sociology and jurisprudence by our formula. We are today in our private, national or international affairs, seeking a larger freedom, but a freedom based on law, yet a law evolved from the situation, yet not the "objective situation" but the "total situation."

The path is short and easy between conceptual pictures and the stereotypes Mr. Lippmann warns us against; nothing can save us from stereotypes but an understanding of the behavior process.

Another important thing to remember about conceptual pictures is that they tend to become typical, and it is already the weakness of too many writers that they classify too quickly under types. Every conceptual picture becomes progressively less typical as it is broken up into its several activities; to dwell in a photograph parlor of conceptual pictures is prison or illusion, it is not life.

Mr. Lippmann uses this phrase, but does not fall into the dangers involved. I wholly agree with his thought on this subject, and I think it one of his most valuable contributions to political science, that concepts should rest on facts. The "objective situation" cannot be overemphasized if we understand it as part of a total process; I am objecting here merely to those who speak of it as if there were an inherent nature in a "fact" to be revealed to the devout. This is opposed not only to psychology but to science as well, for was it not several centuries ago that scientists began to look at objects as processes? Moreover, "conceptual pictures" is with many the cumulative idea which was part of the nineteenth-century notion of evolution, but our idea of evolution has now become different with the profounder thought of experience self-evolving. of the *continuous* process of self-renewal.

I gave in Chapter V an illustration which I said a Freudian might call a rationalization of the social worker. He would do so if he did not note that the self there being considered is a self whose future experience will unroll itself, and does not depend on any conceptual pictures held by social worker of present or future consequences. Also it is not a self stripped of the integrations of its own past experience. I spoke there of the total situation, but the total *present* situation has a specious adequacy; we want to know how far the submerged experience of the past enters into the present. Here the Freudian too, as well as the rest of us, has perhaps something to learn. Properly on his guard against the rationalization of purpose in terms of overt consequence, he has not always thought sufficiently in terms of the *situation* of the past, but has often been more concerned with the *self* of the past. The importance which the *Gestalt* theory has given to the total situation raises the question whether there should not be some fresh scrutiny of Freudian conceptions about the way in which situations of the past enter as submerged experience into the situations of the present. The Freudian's interest always centres less in the overt activities of the self in the present, always carries him back to the past, but his view of the past sometimes envisages a too subjective aspect of that self. The past experience that the psychiatrist is dealing with, buried in the mind of the patient, is a functional total, an interweaving of self and circumstance, so that not only the self of the past is coming into the present, but also the situation of the past. The psychiatrist oversimplifies, therefore, when he is unduly occupied with the subjective aspects of the past. This shows in his technique. He should not expect to exorcise the morbidness of his patient merely by letting the cat out of the bag. The experience which occasioned the present morbidness was a past total situation; there has been an unsalutary interaction of self and circumstance. The psychiatrist should work out a technique, as some indeed are doing, which will allow for salutary interactivities now; these *activities,* not conceptual pictures, will exorcise the complex. The psychiatrist can not rely on conceptual description of the past; he certainly cannot occupy himself merely with probing for primal urges. In the illustration given, the social worker was thinking of the total situation which is functional for her client, but that serves only when you are contemplating the *present* situation. And does not alone serve then, for all the emphasis of total situations requires the social worker, the psychiatrist, to bear in mind that there have been past total situations. Above all let us remember that conceptual description is fraught with equal danger for social worker, psychiatrist or political scientist, for every one of us. The only legitimate use for concepts is as the medium by which the organized aspects of past situations may enter functionally into present situations.

IX

EXPERIENCE AS CREATING

INTEGRATION, the most suggestive word of contemporary psychology, is, I believe, the active principle of human intercourse scientifically lived. When differing interests meet, they need not *oppose* but only *confront* each other. The confronting of interests may result in either one of four things: (1) voluntary submission of one side; (2) struggle and the victory of one side over the other; (3) compromise; or (4) integration. Enough has been said of domination whether obtained by show of power or use of power; unless we can learn some other process than that we shall always be controlled by those who can summon to themselves the greatest force of the moment, militarist, economic, or whatever it may be. As one nation gains power, others, to that extent, come under its dominion. As trade unions gain power, they use it against the rest of the community; and the effect of this is merely that other groups wait to gather force for their moment.

But compromise too is temporary and futile. It usually means merely a postponement of the issue. The truth does not lie "between" the two sides. We must be ever on our guard against sham reconciliation. Many, unfortunately, still glorify compromise. I have just read that the spirit of compromise shows the humble heart. What nonsense. In the first place it doesn't, as you will find if you watch compromise; in the second place, that kind of humility, if it existed, would not be worth much. Humility needs to be defined: it is merely never claiming any more than belongs to me in any way whatever; it rests on the ability to see clearly what does belong to me. Thus do we maintain our integrity.

What do we mean by integration, the fourth method of dealing with confronting interests? Someone gave me what I thought at the time a good illustration: "If you are trying to decide whether you will go to New York by boat or by train, and are weighing the advantages—fresh air, etc., on the one hand, speed, etc., on the other—and a friend comes along and offers to take you in his aeroplane, where you will have the advantages of both train and boat, that is an integration." It happened that a week later a friend of mine who is president of a large industrial plant said to me, "Just what do you mean by integration?" I gave him this as an illustration and he replied, "No, it's not exactly that. I have been watching the committees in our factory for some time to see if I could discover when and why a joint decision is most satisfactory, in your language when and why we get integration. If you or your friend had *invented* the aeroplane to take you to New York, it would have come nearer the process as I see it taking place. That is, when we cannot decide in one of our committees what to do, because part of the members wish to take one course and the rest another, I find that the best way out is always when someone invents something new." I think, however, that bringing the aeroplane into the discussion *was* invention, but my friend went on to give me an illustration which was interesting. He said: "At a meeting of our manufacturing committee recently the following question came up. Our paper had been six cents, and the competing firm reduced their price to five and three-quarters. We then cut to five and a half and they replied with a price of five and a quarter. The question before us then was whether or not we should make a further reduction. Part were in favor; part, against. The solution came when something quite different was suggested: that we should stand for a higher quality of paper and make an appropriate price for it."

The following is an illustration of a decision which seems to me an integration and not a compromise. A coöperative association had a large number of members who had signed five-year contracts which legally bound them to market their crop with the association. When the executive committee met, it was reported that only about one-third of the members were actually adhering to their contracts. The question then arose as to what should be done about the members who were not selling their crop to the association? Should they be prosecuted under the law, or should they be allowed to violate their contracts with impunity? Sides were sharply defined and the debate became heated. The chief arguments for strict enforcement by prosecution were: if contract-violaters were allowed to break their contracts, the authority of the association would soon be undermined and the whole coöperative marketing movement doomed to failure, since it is based on the legal contract, on the belief in the possibility of contract enforcement; moreover, slightly more than one-third of the membership could not maintain the organization, as the cost of overhead machinery was based on total membership; and also it was pointed out that the speculators would use contract-violation as the means of undermining the cooperative movement by offering slightly higher prices in order to encourage violation.

The chief argument against prosecuting all contract-violaters was the following. There are in many cases extenuating circumstances which make it difficult if not impossible for individual growers to live up to their contracts, such as previous loans on the crop, loans higher than crop and price now warrant, etc. It would be difficult for the headquarters legal department to know all of the circumstances in each case of violation, and it would be fatal to the association to proceed on the principle that every violator was a wilful violator; many enemies would thus be made for the coöperative movement.

The controversy finally ended with a resolution which instructed the officials in regard to future policy. This resolution stated that the headquarters office was not to proceed with prosecution unless the specific cases were handled through a committee of the association located within the local community or the county in which the violators lived. That is, the initiation for prosecution was to come from the local community after it had thoroughly investigated each case.

Thus both sides were satisfied: one because the policy of prosecution was to be continued; the other because the responsibility for prosecutions was placed in the hands of the local group. The secretary and one or two of the more advanced members of the committee were more than satisfied, because they saw in this step a move in the direction of using the coöperative movement as the basis for a wide-spread education programme; that is, they felt that the door had now been opened for an educational process through which the coöperative movement might hope for permanency.

A conviction that both sides of a controversy could find a place in the final decision was part of the wisdom of John E. Williams, the well-known labor mediator of Streator, Illinois, and arbitrator for some years for Hart, Schaffner & Marx. In his testimony before the Civil Service Commission on Industrial Relations in 1914, he said: "The action of the Commission is that of discovery, of contrivance, or *invention* to find a practice that will serve the interests of both sides."[1]

Here is the way of progress. Compromising between the old ways, or even combining the old ways, keeps us always with—the old. But we must not make the error of thinking that our search for the new means the abandonment of the old; that is a shallow thought to be wholly repudiated. Has Russia been able to abandon the old? I wish to call special attention to the fact that creative activity does not disregard the past; the past is of course the material with which it always works. Hence we must use the word invention carefully. There are many objections to this word. I said in an earlier chapter that it suggests too much causeless spontaneity and too little specific response. Moreover, a Freudian might think that invention meant an evasive displacement rather than a true discrimination. For a number of reasons, therefore, I like better the term progressive integration, for most integrations by the

[1] *Survey*, January 18, 1919.

time we know them as such have been arrived at through many successive integrations. Take a recent decision at Harvard, that the first seven of the graduating class of any school whose course is approved by the university may be admitted to the university without examination. It is expected that the result of this for Harvard will be more students from the large agricultural states, since the entrance examinations have hitherto kept many students in those states from coming to Cambridge, as their state universities admit without examination. The result of this rule, it is thought by many, will change the proportion of Jews at Harvard. How far this rule was deliberately intended to affect the Jewish question I do not know, but as far as it does affect it an integration and not a compromise has been made, because both sides have got what they really wanted: the Jews are not discriminated against; at the same time there will be fewer relatively if the expectation of largely increased numbers from west of the Mississippi is fulfilled. My manufacturer friend would claim that this was a good illustration of what he means by saying that integration is always invention. From one point of view it certainly was an invention, yet what one would like to do would be to follow that whole controversy, including both the formal and the informal discussion, and see if there were not several on-the-way integrations before that suggestion was made.

But we need not go to such striking or publicly-discussed issues for examples of decisions which unite the desires of both sides. It is surprising how often we can succeed in finding the unifying solution in our everyday affairs when once we begin to search for it:

either with members of our family, with our servants, or our friends or fellow-workers. For instance, some friends of mine could not agree on a school for their boy: the man preferred one for its standard of scholarship, his wife preferred another for the companions the boy would have. As a way out of the dilemma they decided not to send the boy away (the question had been of a boarding-school), but to keep him at home where his mother could have a good deal to say about his companions and where there was a school his father liked. This was not a compromise because neither gave up anything: the father had a school with standards he respected and the mother was more pleased than with the arrangement first considered. This settlement of the question involved the further decision that the boy should be sent to a summer camp and thus he did get some of the benefits of the boarding-school.

And one could imagine still another integration in a case of this kind. They might in their predicament have decided to start a school themselves. If it turned out to be a good school their original dispute would then have had community value.[2] All diversity wisely handled may lead to the "something new" of Chapter VI, but if one submits to the other, or a compromise is made, we have no progress. Each must persist until a way is found by which neither is absorbed but by which both can contribute to the solution. This means a great spur to man's inventiveness. Difference is always a challenge. We should never avoid it. The only things we should condemn are muddle and hypocrisy.

[2] This is not too far-fetched an idea, as I have had two friends who established schools which turned out to be of great value to the community, but which were started in the first place for their own children.

Not all differences, however, can be integrated. That we must face fully, but it is certain that there are fewer irreconciliable activities than we at present think, although it often takes ingenuity, a "creative intelligence," to find the integration.

Integration might be considered a qualitative adjustment, compromise a quantitative one. In the former there is a change in the ideas and their action tendencies; in the latter there is mere barter of opposed "rights of way." The mal-adjusted activities (action tendencies involved) in the situation continue their conflict. For example, if the Genoa conference had agreed on a loan for Russia, the new coöperative attitude would have released harmonizing activities. As it was, the situation continued to be disruptive.

In compromise, I say, there is no qualitative change in our thinking. Partisanship starves our nature: I am so intent on my own values that other values have got starved out of me; this represents a loss in my nature, in the whole quality of my personality. Through an interpenetrating of understanding, the quality of one's own thinking is changed; we are sensitized to an appreciation of other values. By not interpenetrating, by simply lining up values and conceding some for the sake of getting the agreement necessary for action, our thinking stays just where it was. In integration all the overtones of value are utilized.

Whoever advocates compromise abandons the individual: the individual is to give up part of himself in order that some action may take place. The integrity of the individual is preserved only through integration—and the similarity in these words is not insignificant. Moreover, if you believe in compromise it means that you still see the individual as static. If the self with its purpose and its will is even for a moment a finished product, then of course the only way to get a common will is through compromise. But the truth is that the self is always in flux, weaving itself and again weaving itself.

Again, those who advocate compromise have failed to gather the fruits of recent psychological research, for compromise is suppression, and as we have been shown that a suppressed impulse in the individual will be his undoing later, so we see again and again that what has been suppressed in the compromises of politics or labor disputes crops up anew to bring more disastrous results. If according to the Freudians the sane man is one in whom there are no thwarted wishes, the sane industrial group would be one in which neither employer nor workman had compromised, the sane nation would be one not based on log-rolling, the sane league of nations one in which no nation had made "sacrifices," but where each sought enrichment. Suppression, the *bête noire* of modern psychology, is, in the form of compromise, the evil of our present constitution of society, politically, industrially and internationally.

It is interesting to notice that the adjustment of difference becomes increasingly important as coöperation increases, for coöperation instead of automatically absorbing difference, as is sometimes thought by theorists, does nothing of the sort actually. When men come together to do something, the first thing that is obvious is their differences; the question then is what to do about it. Take the movement today towards industrial corporations made up of a number of plants: an engineer who spoke to me of this said, "We must solve the problem of uniting men without crushing them."

Those who accept integration rather than compromise or domination as the law of social relations will seek the method. The first step in integration is to break up wholes: to analyze, differentiate and discriminate. I can best explain this by an illustration. An interesting example of the necessity of breaking up wholes has been given by Mrs. Sheffield in the case of an unmarried mother.[3] Most of the people who knew Jessica's case dismissed it with: "She's a prostitute, what more need be said?" But Mrs. Sheffield broke up this whole. She said: "You say she's a prostitute because she lived with two or three men, but that does not necessarily make her a prostitute. A prostitute is one who takes any man; Jessica took every time the man she wanted: in each case there was a selective process. If we want to compare Jessica's sex-conduct with the sex-conduct of someone else, we shall never understand it by comparing it as a whole, but only by breaking it up into its several aspects or conduct patterns. Her wish for success in her work, for a good time, for what she considered a higher social position, her maternal attitude: these are what have to be considered."

In other words, Mrs. Sheffield's point was that comparison cannot be made between total processes but must be made between factors of the same kind within these processes. It is equally true, to be sure, that Jessica's case could not have been understood by any atomistic method of study, for her "whole" activity was constantly influencing each separate activity. I

[3] Unpublished Paper by Mrs. Ada E. Sheffield.

am of course using activity here for implicit as well as overt action.

The calling of Jessica a prostitute was an example of two things: first of using a mere epithet to explain a situation; the people who called Jessica a prostitute without further consideration simply had the block notion of goodness and the evangelical idea of the soul. The second error involved was that of dealing in this manner with a whole. But we see the same fundamental error in many scientific people. For while it is true that the method of psychoanalysis is to make the patient break up his whole and deal with the separate parts,[4] yet we often see psychiatrists take one part of a multiple cause and treat it as *the* cause. The same error occurs constantly in labor disputes, the error of taking one factor from a multiple cause and connecting it alone with the effect. This comes from not trying to see clearly and to estimate separately the constituents of the multiple cause.[5]

Akin to this is the mistake we often see in discussion of not breaking the question up into its various parts; either the disputants are discussing a vague and non-existent whole, or else they are discussing different parts of the question without knowing that they are doing so. This is a frequent and fatal error. The disputants must first agree to differentiate the question into its parts and then to take them up one by one.

One way of breaking up wholes in conference is to split the question up as minutely as possible and take the vote as you go along. I have seen this done with

[4] At the same time the psychoanalyst tries to get his patient to consider the situation in its complete bearings. Both these methods are always necessary; they are integral parts of a "whole" method.

[5] See pp. 108–9.

marked success. Professor Ripley in a recent article says, "As always happens, each side voted for itself." But in the case I am referring to this did not happen, and I think the reason was entirely due to the differentiation of the question into several parts. Instead of voting on the amount of wages, in which case the line-up would of course have been according to sides, we voted on the amount needed for board, lodging, clothes, recreation, self-improvement, savings, etc. On many of these questions the vote showed employers and employees on both sides.

Everywhere I see what we called in Chapter III differentiation, as the first step. The men who succeed in business are not those who look at their competitors as wholes. They look at all their many activities and compete with these one by one. When it is decided that coöperation will pay better than competition, it is always because certain differentiations have first been made. If I have a shop in a country village and spend my life in the illusion that the shop-keeper across the road is my enemy, and that I shall prosper in proportion as he fails, it may be that neither I nor my village will prosper. But if I see that by uniting forces at different points (provided there is enough trade for two), we can make our joint capital more productive, I shall have made this discovery by breaking up the idea of "keeping store" into its separate activities; in the case of many of these activities I find that I shall do better by joining with my enemy than by fighting him.

Again, labor and capital can never be reconciled as long as labor persists in thinking that there is a capitalist point of view and capitalists that there is a labor point of view. There is not. These are imaginary wholes which must be broken up before capital and labor can coöperate. Or when you label a man a farmer or an artisan and then treat him as if his action tendencies were all farmer or artisan you make a grave mistake. You have to break him up into a number of things, I mean of course a number of activities. Parts, aspects, factors, elements—all these words are too static; we must differentiate into *activities.* The man sitting next me on a certain board represented the public. Have you a preconceived idea that the man who represents the public represents "social interests"? This man was part owner of a leather business, he was president of a bank and it was a year (1919) when the scarcity of money and the difficulty of getting credit affected more than usual the relation between banker and employer; he was a Mason, he was a member of the Presbyterian church, etc. All these things influenced him.

This breaking up of wholes, involving always the examining of symbols, seems to me very important. Comparison, we all know, is an integral part of scientific procedure, but we now see more clearly *what* to compare. The behavioristic question, "What is the individual really doing?" I have changed to, What does the individual really want?—the same question in another form. Take the workman's demand for an eight-hour day. Compare this with the attitude of the school-boy toward his hours. Twenty years ago he would have told you that he wanted a four-hour day, you could not have convinced him to the contrary; but now, with the country-day schools, he loves his eight or nine-hour day. So it was not, after all, a four-hour day that he wanted. Is it an eight-hour day that the workman really wants? This is a whole which has to be split up to find what he really wants, and we have to split it not into ideas but into activities. In all wage controversies this is important. We can say, at the very least, that the workman does not "really want" wages above the point that will keep the factory open; that the employer does not "really want" wages low enough seriously to impair the productive power of the workman.

The first question is then always: What is the demand a symbol of? Someone on a certain occasion, a philosophical conference, said that he would like to ask me a question. He asked it in triumph as if it would certainly floor me. He said he lived with his mother, and quite amicably except on one question. His mother wished the dining-room table in the middle of the dining-room and he wished it in the bay window, and "I don't believe," he ended by saying, "even you could integrate anything as solid as our dining-room table." As unfortunately the conference ended at that moment, and I have never seen him since, I have not been able to pursue this further, but what I should have liked to say to him was, "What is dining-table-in-middle-of-room a symbol of to you and what to your mother?" Or the question might be put: "What did you and your mother *really* want? Perhaps not table-in-window or table-in-middle-of-room at all. Perhaps what she really wanted was to have it where it would be near the butler's pantry, where it would be easy to walk around, or where it would be near the radiator. Perhaps what you *really* wanted was more light, or the view of the river. The integration might have been to take down the curtains." That would not have been a compromise because neither would have lopped off a part of his desire; both would have got what they really wanted. I like his using the word solidity; it is the solidity of symbols which make them a danger to us.

One of the most important results of recognizing and refusing to have anything to do with imaginary or verbal wholes, blanket expressions or mere subjective epithets, one of the most important results of analysis and discrimination as the first step in the resolution of conflict, is that we find that our decisions must be based upon intelligence as well as upon morals. And I know no lesson more necessary to learn. On one occasion during a conference on wages one of the members of the committee talked to us much of self-sacrifice and altruism, but these were empty words, for not only not one of us had any intention of sacrificing ourselves, this man included, but in any case such self-sacrifice has no social value. No sound solution of the wage question depends on sacrifice. As our discussions went on, it became increasingly evident that there was a figure between the $12 which the employers were willing to give and the $15 which the girls wished, which would be of equal advantage to both sides, not so high as to mean unemployment for the girls, high enough to secure the greatest efficiency from them; it was a matter of intelligence to find that figure. We approached it only as far as we were willing to give up those never-on-land-or-sea wholes.

I believe any talk of the sacrifice of interests on the employer's part because of altruistic feelings is pure sentimentality; we do not want either side to sacrifice its interests for we want nothing lost, we want all the interests to be united. A good example of this kind of sentimentality is the talk of the sacrifice of sovereignty in a League of Nations. Audience after audience has been asked by lecturers on the League of Nations if, for the sake of the peace of the world, they would not sacrifice part of their sovereignty. But as a matter of cold fact nations want the League when they see that they are going to get more out of joining the League than by not doing so. Yet while I think that all talk of the sacrifice of interests is ruinously sentimental, there is something else which is an essential part of any unifying process, and that is a revaluation of interests. For individuals and nations alike this is the course of progress. We wish to join the League of Nations when a revaluation of our interests shows us that it is to our advantage to do so.

The confronting of diverse interests each claiming right of way leads us to evaluate our interests, and valuation often is evolved into revaluation; not in the sense that sour grapes hang high, or that a *pis aller* must be accepted, but a genuine revaluation. It also draws into the field of attention other values which otherwise might not be taken into account, for our choice is a choice of activities in which all the values have a stake. The revaluation of interests comes about in various ways. Consider what influences a change of opinion in regard to the League of Nations: (1) changes in the situation which make me see my interests differently, (2) changes in myself caused by the situation, (3) other things which may give me a deeper understanding of this situation, (4) values when put together look different from the same values considered separately, for in the act of comparison there is a simultaneous view of all values in the field which register themselves in their relative claims, they acquire perspective. Values depend largely on relation. Certain values emerge as values when we are thinking of joining the League of Nations which we should not have considered if that question had not arisen. Or take the case in the co-operative associations of prosecuting defaulters, those who break their contract to sell to the association. The conflict is between individual members and the coöperative association, but the values at stake take on efficacy as values because of the conflict between the coöperative and the middlemen.

Thus value does not appear on the mere viewing of interests: it is more than a process of inspection, introspection or retrospection. The realizing of a second value involves activities which change my attitude towards the first value. The evaluation of my interests changes as I *do* things. The evaluation of interests comes from the interbehavior of men. Values are "eventual things." Experience is the creator of all criteria. Thus the distinction between subjective and objective values takes on new meaning. While we think we are coolly comparing and judicially weighing, we are at the same time doing something; that doing is helping to build values for us. To be sure, in the present organization of society official criteria are supplied by those who come to the top; sometime we hope the way will be open for an integrating and evolving experience which will give us integrating and evolving values.

I have said that ethics cannot be divorced from intelligence, that these two are one. Now many people do not like the effort of using their intelligence; they fight because it is easier. The thinking out of a solution by which the interests of both sides shall be satisfied means sometimes long and arduous labor. That is often the reason of conflict, that it is the line of least resistance to fight. It is far easier for labor to fight for higher wages, shorter hours, continuous employment, than to solve the problems involved in these. We see this often too in our everyday decisions: we can more easily choose one way to the exclusion of the other; it takes more effort and far greater intelligence to give both a place. We have here the question of allegiance, so important in both politics and ethics. Writers on ethics often talk of narrower and wider loyalties, of smaller and larger duties. I do not think that we have any smaller duties, any narrower loyalties. All that we feel of loyalty to our children should be gathered up into our loyalty to our country. All our interests, ties, obligations, should be brought together in order that each shall enrich the other. There should be no conflict in the sense of one conquering the other, or of a compromise, a "middle-road"; but conflict there will always be in the sense of a confronting, a facing, to be followed by an integrating. Reciprocal reinforcement is the task of existence and that can never come by abandonments. But to control coöperating allegiance requires a higher order of intelligence than to choose one of two allegiances.

While we are speaking of the ethics of conflict, one point should be mentioned which is rather subtly insidious: to keep to our original opinion is sometimes considered a kind of moral self-preservation. But the question is: Do we want to preserve that self or grow a bigger self? The progress of individual or race is by integration. The biological law is growth by the continuous integration of simple, specific responses; in the same way do we build up our characters by uniting diverse tendencies into new action patterns; social progress follows exactly the same law. To understand this we need not go to the larger conflicts of industry or nations. Take a disagreement with someone: if we find that it was caused by a mere misunderstanding, there is little development there, but if we find that there was real difference and that we can unite what was of value in each point of view, it is a step in our growth. To keep to our own "side" either in the hope of downing the other side or in order to delimit the boundaries of the compromise is against all growth. We must guard against Mill's "deep slumber of a decided opinion." Our "opponents" are our co-creators, for they have something to give which we have not. The basis of all coöperative activity is integrated diversity.

We get a kind of pseudo-integration when we accept a speciously verbal solution, when we "save face" by cloaking with verbal ambiguity, as in the resort in religious controversy to understanding the creed symbolically. This is sometimes, however, a very good thing. Professor Ripley gives an interesting example.[6] In the Cambridge Rubber case, when the agreement was finally reached, the employer demanded that the men sign as a committee of his own workmen. "To this the union representative demurred, refusing assent unless his name too went on the peace treaty in his official capacity. On this point of 'recognition' the employer would not budge, although in fact all of the essentials of recognition had already been granted.

[6] *Survey*, pp. 170–171, February, 1922, *Bones of Contention.*

And so the fracas lasted literally for hours, long after the battle was really over. . . . We finally got round it by subterfuge. H. Grorolitzki (stitcher) and W. Wenens (cementer) finally put their names to the document as men who 'as employees of the Cambridge Rubber Company have witnessed the ratification of an agreement between the said company and its employees, now belonging to the union, and their representatives, by a unanimous vote of said employees.' . . . But even then, in order to save the face of the union, a separate document had to be signed by the employer and by David Kaplar, actually the union agent, but he was not allowed to add his official title. The second document was signed as if by a couple of American citizens who happened to be passing that way at the time."

Thus they "saved face" and at the same time reached a harmonious settlement.

When the arbitrator of industrial disputes tells you that the first thing to be done is to find out what both sides represented at the conference will accept, it is wise to see just what that means. It means that integration occurs in the sphere of activities rather than of ideas. Business men try to make agreements court-proof, but a finesse in wording your agreement is not what nails it down as an agreement. Unless it is heartily ratified by both sides it seldom lasts. This has been shown in the number of violation of contracts in the southern coöperatives during the last two years, both in the tobacco and the cotton associations. It is also shown in the series of articles in the *Survey* by Professor Ripley, official arbitrator during the war period in many industrial disputes. Any agreement that is to work must enlist the action tendencies of both parties. Verbal agreements are—verbal agreements. Here we see the difference between mere arbitration and mutual strike-settlement. The most successful arbitrator is one who does not "arbitrate," but who gets the parties in the controversy face to face and helps them to work out the decision for themselves.

Integration of activities usually outruns integration of ideas. We have all of us noticed this in conference where we see ourselves and fellows influenced both by the situation as it was when we entered the conference, and also as it has developed during the conference. This means that the life processes integrate faster than our minds can integrate them. When Lloyd George said, as he so often did, "We were able to find the formula," he meant that the solution had already been found in the field of action. The agreement had come off but could not be released because they had not found the intellectual terms for an agreement which had already established itself subliminally. Professor Sheffield has shown how in controversy the real consensus takes place subterraneously in the motor activity of the controversy, while the intellectual form of the controversy must proceed in terms of language and does not keep pace with the real integration.

Mr. Sheffield has thrown light on another aspect of this consideration by pointing out that all controversies have certain postulates and that postulates taken behavioristically are habits, modes of action. Take Gompers' postulate, for instance, freedom to strike. The moment we look at that behavioristically we have a different attitude toward it; we see that it is true only within the postulates of the present situation.

Gompers assumes the *laissez-faire* conduct of industry. Therefore the workman can take or leave his job, for by that postulate he is a free agent.

I have said that our main consideration is always with the integration of activities. It is thus impossible to speak of the integration of persons. An individual as an abstraction does not meet another individual as an abstraction; it is always activity meeting activity. There is no use chasing through the universe for a "real" you or a "real" me; it is more useful to study our interactions, these are certainly real. What happens when I meet another person for the first time? He comes to me always pushing in front of him his picture of himself; as I get to know him, do I see that picture gradually disappear, leaving his real self? Not at all, I put my own interpretative picture in its place. Where, then, is the real person—for me? It is in his behaving (and his account of his behaving is part of his behavior) plus my interpretation of his behavior *as shown by my behaving.*

It goes without saying that integration is a far more complex matter than I can indicate in the space of this chapter. I have different wants to integrate; you have different wants to integrate. Then there are your wants and my wants to be joined. But the process is not that I integrate my desires, you yours, and then we together unite the results; I often make my own integration through and by means of my integration with you. In international disputes this is obvious.

We need now careful studies of the method of integration. We must observe and analyze industrial controversy, international controversy, personal controversy, to see when and why and how we get compromise, when and why and how we get genuine integration. We need more than this; far more than observation, we need experiment. We want participant-observers who will try experiment after experiment and tell us which succeed and which fail. For integrating is the fundamental process of life, either as between organism and environment or between man and man.

In my emphasis on integration, it must not be supposed, however, that I ignore the part of disintegration in the creative process. The medieval church broke up and this was a wholly liberating phenomenon. We should always see the relation between disruptive and creative forces; disruption may be a real moment in integration. The breaking up of the German Empire might be a signal sign of advancing liberalism. When the American colonies broke away from England it is generally agreed that there was a wholesome disruption; here we see clearly disruption itself as a constructive process. This point ought to be much further developed, for it would prevent us from too superficial an optimism; by dwelling so exclusively on integration, I have rather tended to oversimplify the process of life. Yet however often it is disruption which leads to fresh and more fruitful unitings, however often it is the salutary means by which formal wholes give place to functional unities, yet disruption is only a part of that total life process to which, in its more comprehensive aspect, we may give the name integration.

X

POWER: THE CONDITION OF ITS VALIDITY

THE psychology of integration gives us hints of a new conception of power. Yet much empirical study must be made before we can draw any valid conclusions. I know of no definition of power which has come from the actual observation of the behavior of men. Political scientists transfer power, divide power, confer power, but do not analyze power. Biologists give us power as the mainspring of activity but do not tell us what it is. Some of the psychologists give us "the urge to power" and leave us there. To many it is a good word, "God is all powerful"; to others it is a bad word, the desire of evil men. Some writers tell us that there is a satisfaction merely in the possession of power: Kohler, the eminent jurist, says, "The love of power is inherent in most human beings"; another writes, "Man's will for power is his most distinguishing characteristic." On the other hand, many writers deny this point of view and say that power is desired merely as means to end. An economist however speaks of "the struggle for bread *and* the struggle for power," as if they were different "urges." But whether "good" or "bad," whether or not there is an "instinctive" urge to power or only an urge for the means to satisfy desire, the attempt to gain power is the predominant feature of our life. A few years ago I thought of making some group-studies. I talked about it to both my academic and my business friends. I expected the former to be interested, but thought the latter might think such studies unnecessary. To my surprise I found that my academic friends listened chiefly out of politeness, whereas the business men were keenly interested. This was explained, however, one day, when one of the latter said to me: "Go ahead, you can have all the opportunity you want for study in my plant; you write a book telling me how to manipulate groups and I'm in your debt." My contemplated book against "manipulation" was to be a contribution to it! Much of the "applied psychology" of which we hear so much nowadays has exactly this for its aim: to teach power over others. The salesmanship classes teach this; the men taught how to conduct business interviews are being taught this; "the psychology of advertising" is not the psychology of giving information but of gaining power. Many of the trade unionists in the labor education movement wish training for power, that is, increased power in the fight with capital. But the object of all education has been largely power—power over others. The paradox of American democracy has been that its slogan of equal opportunity has meant, often, equal opportunity to get power over your fellows.

This chapter only hints at the questions we shall have to try to answer in studying power. Just what is the alleged urge to power? Is power force, influence, leadership, manipulation, managing, is it self-control, self-discipline, is it capacity, is it self-expression? Are these different species under the same genus or are there generic differences among them. What is the relation of the idea of power to the biological notion of survival? What is the relation of the idea of power to the political and legal notion of sovereignty? Shall we perhaps have to reconsider "the power of all over each"? Is success power? Is "will to power" the hasty snatching of end results without paying the price of real influence? Is power a sign of intellectual bankruptcy, is it a short-view solution? Is power one unintegrated difference usurping the claim of all the differences? You have an urge to power; so have other people; their urges can be used against you unless you combine them with yours.

Is there a distinction possible between power and influence? I have a friend who thinks power a short-cut to influence, that there is no "urge to power" but a desire to be influential. A legitimate desire, in my friend's opinion, for while power does not presuppose relationship, that is interacting relationship, influence does: it means the enrichment of interacting personalities; it is the vibration between two terms each of which is active. I do not agree with this, but I think it interesting.

If it were possible to analyze power before we have decided whether it is a "good" word or a "bad" word, our conclusions would be far more valuable. All control means a sense of power. The athlete has control over his muscles, and this brings him a satisfying sense of power. Control of circumstances, all achievement, gives the same gratification. One might go further and say that all activity brings a sense of power, certainly successfully coördinated activity does.

Another thing to be studied is the "balance of

power." It has obviously failed in international affairs and yet many plans for a pluralistic state rest on this theory. If you divest the balance of power theory of the pomp of diplomacy and the sanctity of academic controversy, the doctrine is no more dignified than the behavior of the two men (each having taken a course in "applied psychology" and learned that he must not face the light in a business interview) who dodged each other round the room until they found themselves side by side on the window seat. In every contact we should watch ourselves to see how far we are trying, if not to gain power, at least to produce an equilibrium. For instance, is self-justification an example of this? Again, jurists tell us that "compensatory equalization" (the layman's *quid pro quo*) is the urge to keep or to restore the balance of power. Jhering says: "There is no idea which man feels to be so compelling as that of 'compensatory equalization.'" Let us watch ourselves and see. If you do something for me and I am "grateful" and want to do something for you "in return," is my calling that gratitude a "rationalization"? In other words, is there such a thing as gratitude or is it always "compensatory equalization"?

One trouble with the balance of power theory is that we have no progress here. For instance, gratitude should do more than "restore an equilibrium"; it should lead to further action.

We must consider also the relation of self-assertion to the "balance of power." For instance, how far does the farmers' present self-assertion represent an "inferiority complex" due to the "hayseed" stigma? The present demand of domestic servants for high wages is partly due to the stigma that has been attached to domestic service; there is an inferiority complex here which demands money as the only way to its overcoming, the only way to reach a "balance of power."

People often like to keep or acquire power even when they have no immediate use for it, as we like to have a reserve in the bank for emergencies. A farmer with unused water power on his farm would not sell to the summer colony the right to use it for an electrical plant. He did not anticipate any need of this fall of water for himself. Moreover, water experts were brought to show him that such use would not interfere with the flow from another spring, which he ignorantly feared; lawyers were brought to tell him that the granting of this use would not affect the title to his farm. All his objections were met, but he would not sell. It became pretty evident that he wished to keep his fall of water as a sort of balance of power with the rich summer people.

We must also consider how far groups are power-organizations. For example, the trade unions' demand for higher wages is the demand (desire) of individuals, not of a group; they join in order to put power back of the demand. There is no group "instinct." My loyalty to my group is stimulated when I need the power of the group to satisfy needs; my loyalty to my trade union is stimulated when my children have no shoes. This must all be watched. We must observe in all our groups whether group cohesion increases or not with need of power. (Of course it is a commonplace that group loyalty increases with opposition or attack.) To be sure many associations exist to perform some particular service. And there are others, like a Women's Municipal League, which exist to educate their members, to release energy and to render service, and only secondarily to get the power which comes from combination. Some trade unionists are beginning to see the finer function of combination, combination in order to develop power in themselves rather than power over others. How is it in the coöperative movement? In coöperative marketing, or collective selling, we have another form of collective bargaining. How far then are the coöperative associations power-groups? The commercial power developed by the Citrus Growers of California is no by-product of their organization. In all the farmer organizations it is interesting to balance motives: higher and more uniform prices as against the wish to get power equal to other groups. What we have to do is to discover how to integrate the power trend in an organization and the freeing trend.

The subject of power needs, I have said, much empirical study, but at present the greatest light on the subject is, I think, that given by the psychological principle of integration. The integrating of wants precludes the necessity of gaining power to satisfy desire. In the library today, in one of the smaller rooms, someone wanted the window open, I wanted it shut. We opened the window in the next room where no one was sitting. This was not a compromise because there was no lopping off of desire; we both got what we really wanted. For I did not want a closed room, I simply did not want the north wind to blow directly on me; likewise the other occupant did not want that particular window open, he simply wanted more air in the room. Therefore, by the process I gave in the last chapter—breaking up wholes, finding out what we really wanted—an integration was possible without resorting to power. By reducing the area of irreconcilable controversy, you reduce the area of arbitrary power.

Let us look further at the psychology of Chapter III in its relation to the conception of power. We saw there that experience is a self-generating, self-sufficing, all-including activity. Here must be the origin of power. When the political scientists ask where we shall place power, when they talk of transferring it from one group to another, it almost sounds as if power were a definite, preëxisting quantity which could be handed round; they tell us nothing of how it can be produced. Psychology by showing us the origin of power at the same time shows us its limit. We see that the integration of responses means concerted and controlled action. We get control in any instance just to the extent of the organization, or rather they are the same thing. Also we can get no continued action without this concerted and controlled activity. These three are bound together: the unifying, controlling, the sustaining are one. Whenever we are talking of actual power, then, we are talking of something which is generated by circular response; no, of what is being generated by circular response. It often has tragic consequences when our control attempts to run ahead of our integration. As far as our control and our integration correspond, we have a legitimate situation, a valid process: we can always thus test the validity of our situation.

Napoleon ran ahead of his integrations. The people

of Boston did the same by not knowing how to integrate with the rapidly increasing Irish element. Again, the wealthy residents of Milton doing business in Boston rush out to Milton on town meeting day to swamp the farmers instead of integrating with them; if the farmers could, they would try to swamp the "capitalists"; but in neither case is this genuine control. All pure majority control is getting power *over.* Genuine control is activity between, not influence over. Le Dantec talks much of power [1] and it is all the time power over another of which he is speaking. And Le Dantec is right for primitive man, who has not advanced far enough to analyze power. And neither have we; therefore Le Dantec has been right for us too. But we are now about to take a new step: to find out what power is and to create it consciously. What the formula I am using shows us is that the only genuine power is that over the self—whatever that self may be. When you and I decide on a course of action together and do that thing, you have no power over me nor I over you, but we have power over ourselves together. We have, however, no authority over John Smith. We could try to get "power" over him in a number of ways, and that is what Le Dantec would call power, but the only legitimate power we could have in connection with John Smith is what you and John Smith and I could develop together over our three selves.

We might try this in our households by saying to our servants: "I wish no authority in my household but genuine authority; I do not wish any over you, I

[1] *L'Egoisme, seule base de toute société.*

do not wish you to have any over me; together we will control *ourselves.* If you wish to do your work in a certain way or at certain times, we will find the way and the times which will suit us both." Many mistresses say, "I pay, therefore I have the right to decide." Many servants say or think, "I do the work, therefore I have the right to decide." But neither pay nor work bestows the right to power—over another. We can have power only over ourselves. But we cannot join as wholes and become "ourselves"—another whole; the process is analysis, discrimination and integration. Again we see, as I so often try to show, that the making of wholes and the breaking of wholes are equally necessary.

This kind of power, power-with, is what democracy should mean in politics or industry, but as we have not taken the means to get a genuine power, pseudo power has leapt into the saddle. In the present situation between coal operators and miners, the miners carefully measure their "power" and pit it against the "power" of the operators; the operators do the same. But miners and operators are bound together; until this is fully recognized and acted upon, they will not be able to control their lives. Their interests are not the same, but indissolubly united. It is one situation, not two. Only when it is treated as one situation will the authority of that situation appear. To make the situation single is, I know, an impossibility as the industry is at present organized. It should be so organized that the will of the total situation—miners and operators—could appear; then the relation of that industry to the state should be such that their will uniting with the will of the consumers should be the authentic will of the coal industry.

I have been asked if this is a conservative or a radical point of view. It is both: it is conservative because it is concerned with only *actual* power, and it takes time and education and training to develop that; it cannot be got by revolution, it involves a process and a slow process; it is concerned with neither granting power nor grabbing power but with evolving power. At the same time it is a radical view because opportunity must be given for this process.

What exactly do we mean by the single situation? Do we not find here too, as in every question where we go below the surface, that we wish to do away with atomism? Surely we must abolish any conception of power that has an atomistic taint. The only possible way of getting rid of the greed and scramble of our present world is for all of us to realize that the power we are snatching at is not really power, not that which we are really seeking, that the way to gain genuine power, even that which we ourselves *really* want, is by an integrative process.

To sum up this point: there is no power-over in the single situation, therefore the aim should always be to create the single situation, that is, to make a working-unit or functional whole: as between employer and employee, landlord and tenant, or whatever the case may be. But we shall never succeed if we conceive the single situation as produced by coincidence of interests; this only twists and distorts the facts and that way lies failure—in the long run. The single situation is produced by the union of interests. For the moment, then, awaiting further study, I am inclined to make this distinction: genuine power is power-with, pseudo power, power-over. This is not a fanciful or personal distinction, for these two prepositions are used to mark a distinction in law: juridical relations imply rights "with," that is the expression used. Juridical relations are possible only between persons who enjoy legal rights; we cannot have juridical relations with aliens, with slaves, etc. That is, you can have, jurists say, a right over a slave but not with him; but in engaging a servant the law gives you rights with him but not over him. Juridical relations then imply always rights with, not over.

I do not believe that there will ever come a time when one class has not more power than another, one nation than another, one individual than another. But the more power any one has the better, if we mean by power integrated control. The more the better if it is used to join with the integrated control evolved by other units; we certainly do not want to abolish power, that would be abolishing life itself, but we need a new orientation toward it. The power of the strong is not to be used to conquer the weaker: this means for the conquerors activity which is not legitimately based, which will therefore have disastrous consequences later; and for the conquered, repression. As an example of the former one might instance the "urge to power" of the trade unions which got too much support during the Wilson administration, and from which they are suffering now; and as for repression, that means in society as in individual a pathological condition.

The more power I have over myself the more capable I am of joining fruitfully with you and with you developing power in the new unit thus formed—our two selves. The more power America has over herself the more capable she is of joining fruitfully with other nations and thus developing power in a new unit, a union of nations.

Influence then in the wrong sense is when you choose to appeal to those tendencies which will help your purpose, not mine. Influence in a good sense is when you do not try to bind (me to you) but to free.

The influence we wield is valid only *within* a certain process; what we must understand is the conditions of the validity of influence. We have, as a matter of fact, to make some decision in regard to this every day; we see in a given instance that we can easily make our influence potent if we would do certain things, but are we willing to do these things? It depends on whether we care most for my way or your way, or for the whole psychic significance of that which is connected by myriad threads with every other situation in life. From this point of view power-over disappears. Try it any day in your humblest activities from hour to hour, in your contact with friend or stenographer or grocer, and you will see it. Any attempt at arbitrary control sets up antagonisms in the other person or group that will defeat you in the end.

Power-over is resorted to time without number because people will not wait for the slower process of education. We can see this every day in the countless meetings held to persuade people of this or that. A man said to me, "You are never going to get people to accept government ownership or free trade by your discussion meetings," but I do not want people to accept government ownership or free trade—that is power-over. Yet it seems impossible to convince the "reformers" of this. Many people, confident that their object is for the good of society, are willing to take measures to attain it which are essentially coercive. For example, when the southern coöperatives began to organize, they found that they must control the commodity, its flow to market. Five hundred tobacco growers could not have obtained the facilities for curing, drying and storing, could not have secured the necessary credits. In order to get these it was necessary to control 75% of the crop, which meant that more farmers had to be persuaded to sign contracts to sell to the association than were fully permeated with the coöperative idea. This was practically coercion instead of education. In some cases the Workers' Education movement has suffered from the brass-band style of inauguration; it is better that little groups shall slowly create their own clientèle. Certain movements begun through national associations instead of through the development and education of local units have shown the same weakness.

There is an idea prevalent, which I think very harmful, that we give up individual power in order to get joint activity. But first, by pooling power we are not giving it up; and secondly, the power produced by relationship is a qualitative, not a quantitative thing. If we follow our rule throughout of translating everything into activity, if we look at power as the power to *do* something, we shall understand this. When a grower signs a coöperative contract, he does not give up his "power"; he expects that his marketing capacity will be increased by joining with others. The same question is discussed often in regard to freedom, but, to name one instance out of a thousand, what more pitiful delusion have we had than the freedom of the "independent" farmer?

We sometimes see in political writing the expression "the justification for power." If the time has come to write apologies for power, then the time has certainly come to analyze further the conception of power. We read in the book of a thoughtful writer, "Power which promotes the ends of society is justified . . . ," but ideas seem rather hopelessly confused in this sentence, for who is to decide what are the ends of society? An interweaving experience produces social ends *and* power. The origin of power in experience is what we do not sufficiently consider. Interweaving experience creates legitimate power. Power by fiat can never persist. Arbitrary will cannot, in the long run, take the place of a psychological will.

In Part II of this book, in the consideration of democracy, we shall have to seek the connection between what political scientists have called "the ultimate source of power" with power psychologically developed. What is this "repository of power" we hear of? I fear some day we shall go to it and find it empty. Is that perhaps exactly what we are doing today in nation after nation? At any rate we want to know the laws which govern its flow from reservoir to specific place of use. "The moral right to self-determination" must be analyzed. We have as much "moral right to self-determination" as we are capable of genuine self-determination. Psychological and moral power are synonymous. The moral right to power which has not been psychologically developed is an empty ethics; it is an ethics, alas, which we have to combat daily in politics and industry.[2]

To sum up this chapter: Power begins, as far as our study goes, with the organization of reflex arcs. Then these are organized into a system—more power. Then the organization of these systems comprise the organism—more power. On the level of personality I gain more and more control over myself as I unite various tendencies. In social relations power is a centripetal self-developing. Power is the legitimate, the inevitable, outcome of the essential life-process. We can always test the validity of power by asking whether it is integral to the process or outside the process.

And is not power, thus defined, freedom—freedom and law too? In the life process freedom and law must appear together. We can see that when we unite opposing tendencies in ourselves, the result is freedom, is power, is law. To express the personality I am creating, to live the authority I am creating, is to be free. From biology, social psychology, all along the line, we learn one lesson: that man is rising into consciousness of self as freedom in the forms of law. Government and industry must express this truth.

I have intended in this chapter only to ask questions, not to answer them; I have wished merely to point out the importance of this subject. For throughout history nothing is more apparent than: (1) that the urge to power goes on *pari passu* with unsatisfied desire; (2)

[2] I have tried to show in *The New State* that the state cannot create power but only recognize it.

that every shift in power brings a change in our ideas and ideals. The connection between shift of power and revaluation of interests must be carefully studied. Society should be so organized that standards and power evolve together; social tragedy comes when they are in different hands.

PART II

AN EXPERIMENTAL ATTITUDE TOWARD EXPERIENCE

XI

"CONSENT" NOT THE TECHNIQUE OF DEMOCRACY

THE problem of democracy is how to develop power from experience, from the interplay of our daily concrete activities. The expert cannot dictate and the people consent. This is the voice of the wax-doll; it has no reality. "Less bread, more taxes," the people cried under the palace windows in Lewis Carroll's political farce; but what else are we doing today when we "consent" to the tariff? We might be told here that we need from the expert the facts by which to understand the tariff. Certainly, but we need just as much a method for connecting those facts with our own lives. The relation of facts to my "will" is the thesis of this chapter.

As "consent of the governed" is perhaps the most important conception of political science—it is the crux of the problem of dependent nations, it is the fundamental matter involved in all the talk of a unitary or pluralistic state, it lies below every discussion of local self-government—we ought to give it careful consideration.

Many write as if the problem of government would be solved when we had devised methods to obtain the consent of the people to the garnered wisdom of the expert. But assertion and assent, no matter how the latter is obtained, should not be the political process. You can often get a specious consensus on the intellectual level which in virtue of the prestige of verbal agreement arrests the activity of your mind, but the only real consensus is that which arises on the motor level. The theory of consent rests on the wholly intellectualistic fallacy that thought and action can be separated. The theory of consent rests on the assumption that we think with our "minds" and we don't. Political leaders are supposed to put something before our minds to which we respond with our minds. Yet how often we see cases where we have not been able to persuade people, by our most careful reasoning, to think differently, but later, by giving them an opportunity to enter on a certain course of action, their "minds" are thereby changed. The colleges which have adopted some form of student government could give us illustrations of this. Mill long ago told us of "torpid assent"—it is not a vital process.

Thus the fullest freedom in passing on policies is not self-government, because the participation has to take place further back, in the activity from which the policies emerge. Unfortunately a great deal of out-of-place ethics has been mixed up with the arguments against consent; it has been thought not "right" for the few to decide and the many to assent, but the fact is that it is an impossibility. We cannot really carry out the will of another, for we can use only our own behavior patterns. If we consent to the will of the expert or administrative official, it is still the will of expert or official; the people's will can be found only in their motor mechanisms or habit systems. If Wilson had had creative genius he would have known the futility of the formal acceptance of principles.

One of the best examples in history of a practical understanding of this was given by the founders of our American government. The Constitution united the colonies largely on the intellectual level. Our early statesmen saw this and were wise enough to forge the bonds of a real America. The unifying of America was brought about by the building of the Cumberland Road, by the relation of the national courts to the state courts which not only unified federal law but tended also to unify state law, and by our whole financial system by which the bank became not only a steadier of finances but an adjunct of government—the national currency, the system of paying off the debt, the state branches, all tended to hasten and strengthen the unifying of the states. Again, the history of the welding of East and West as "West" became first west of the Alleghanies, then west of the Mississippi, and finally west of the Rockies, has not yet been adequately written, but it was made possible by the "progressive integrations" which took place day by day as the pioneers integrated with the frontier that which they had never left behind them.

The "will of the people" then is found exactly where our own will is found, in our concrete existence. Men study "the art of persuasion," the method of obtaining consent, but it is usually merely a method of obtaining "power-over," the pernicious aim of much of our activity. The case of expert and people should be wholly a case of "power-with." The validity of the "will of the people" depends on the distinction between power-over and power-with.[1] In many of the methods used to "persuade," consent becomes hardly distinguishable from coercion, as in some of the features of picketing during strikes. The remedy for coercion is not consent but co-action. When our political scientists talk of gaining assent, they are usually thinking of overcoming wills. But our legal science has outgrown the error of talking of wills;[2] as it no longer thinks of the conflict of wills, so political science must give up its idea of the overcoming of wills. It is not a sound political process.

The difficulty of all revolutions is this: the leaders think they can substitute new ideas for old before they have changed the action tendencies, habit systems, of the people. As this cannot be done, revolution after revolution fails. The first thing a normal class for revolutionists should be taught is that behavior must be changed through experience, that it cannot be changed by the impact of ideas. The Bolsheviki are intellectualists. When we say that "evolution is better than revolution," it is not because we are afraid of blood and battle, but because it is only by the slower process that you can get the habit systems changed. The question all leaders, all organizers, should ask is not, how can we bring about the acceptance of this idea, but how can we get that into the experience of the people which will mean the construction of new habits? This means a keen and inventive intelligence; good intentions, noble ideas are not enough. Leaders often act on the assumption that if you destroy existing institutions you have a *tabula rasa* on which to begin

[1] See Chap. X.
[2] See p. 264.

anew. But there is no such thing as a *tabula rasa.* Again and again in our own lives we act on this assumption, always to find it a vain illusion. The Englishman dressing for dinner in the wilds is not making an empty gesture, it is a defence movement.

Thus a popular revolution is often followed by some one man seizing the power. You will always in the end be ruled by force unless you are governed in accordance with tradition—a developing tradition. President Lowell says, "The result is that a popular vote against a despotism is often followed by an autocracy not less despotic, and indeed more so, because, not having behind it the traditions which incline the bulk of the population to obey the government to which they are accustomed, it is under a greater necessity of using force." The psychology, in this aspect, of the four revolutions in France in the hundred years between 1770 and 1870, and also of the Russian Revolution, is given in President Lowell's last book on *Public Opinion.*

We are willing to blame the revolutionists because they are revolutionists, but the expert faces exactly the same difficulty. His facts do not impress themselves on people's minds as words upon the blotter. The process is far different. We are now ready to take our understanding of that process a step further. I said in Chapter I that we could not put the objective situation at one extreme and the will of the people at the other with the expert in between, that the will of the people is already in the situation. This is forgotten by those who tell us that Yes or No is all that the people can contribute to government. According to these writers the process would be: first, an objective situation, so objective that there is no will (!) in it; then the administrative official constructs his policy based thereon; then the people say Yes. Of course they never say No because the expert sees to that as part of his job. (I hear in this Utopia the continuous murmur of assent rising from the earth like the murmur of insects on a summer afternoon.) But I do not think this the political process. Facts, objective situations, are activities, the activities of interacting men. The will of the people is already there; I do not see any *way* of eliminating it if one wished to. I believe that the political process consists in connecting the will of the people which is in a situation with the will of the people which passes on a situation. How to do this is the problem of democracy. This is the step forward which we have now to take. I have spoken of the necessity of making connection between expert and people, but more fundamental even than that is the necessity of providing for such activity of the people concerned that the true will will be the political will. This is the subtler meaning of democracy. We cannot be satisfied with a political will which is not a psychological will. We can have no sound politics until psychological and political will are one. We must plan all our reorganization of industry, our coöperative enterprises, all new political units or reformed representation, all international experiments, on this principle. Our test of all political structure should be whether it allows for coincidence of psychological and formal will. Will after the event is as bad as will before the event; there is only will in the event.

Moreover, if the experts are to go round with cameras, and the administrative officials to sit at their desks and construct policies, and the people to assent, who is to do the living, who is to make the "objective situation" to be reported on? Its "objectivity" seems rather shadowy. But the people do live, do carry on their activities from day to day, and all that the advocates of democracy want is that this shall be recognized in its full significance. Democracy is a denial of dualism in every sense; it is an assertion that the people who do the doing are also thereby doing the thinking, that a divorce of these two is impossible. Our real problem is to connect the will of the people as it lives daily in the multitudinous activities of men with the political will.

We have been told recently that our problem is how to give up the belief in the omnicompetence of the individual and still have faith in human nature. But I do not find this dilemma in actual existence anywhere. Among my own acquaintance those who have least tendency to entertain a belief in the omnicompetence of the individual are those who see most clearly the vast possibilities of human nature in our mutual supplementing, reciprocal reinforcing, each of the other.

Again, those who advocate "consent" as the rôle of the people are apt to tell us that there is no instinct for self-government. This is both true and untrue. In the sense of an urge or drive like hunger or sex, it is of course true. What seems like the urge to self-government is often, if you examine it carefully, the urge to power; the demand for *self*-government often merely masks a desire to govern *others*. But I do not see anyone who really wants the trouble of self-government. In our own individual lives a serious problem arises and we often think, "Oh, if someone would only tell me what to do"; we are by no means always yearning to decide for ourselves. But we do not get the advice we crave; it would be against every law of the universe if we should. There is no "instinct" for self-government, but it is the law of our being; we escape it only to our harm, but as a matter of fact we cannot escape it. Suicide is the only alternative. A cynical Englishman came to America during the war and said, "Why *don't* you let the Germans come over and govern you? They would probably do it much better than you've done it for yourselves." Even if that had been true, we could not have let the Germans govern us. The canker in that idea rots any society in the long run, not because in some mysterious way self-government is better than "good" government, or because it is what "ought" to be, but because it is the only thing possible.

The relation of his own activity to the satisfaction of his desires should be a part of the education of every citizen. And we must learn not to juggle with words in regard to our desires. There is a tendency to translate specific desire into abstract words and then to think that we are longing for the abstraction; this seems in some mysterious way to dignify our desire. It is more noble to ask for liberty than a latchkey. A number of years ago in England I knew some Norwegians whose conversation became a wearisome bore because they talked all the time of the freedom of the soul, and their "freedom of the soul" seemed a black hole, a contentless abyss. But when one came to know them better one found that it was the desire to do certain specific things that they had translated in this way. How our poor "souls" are unnecessarily overburdened. The abstraction never comes first. You cannot tell people they "ought" to want to govern themselves, and then look around and try to invent something for them to do. You can only feed open mouths. When we see the relation between desire and attainment of desire through self-activity, we shall understand self-government better than we do at present. The development of the farmers' coöperative movement is rather interesting here. From California to Virginia it was presented to the farmers as a marketing proposition purely. They heard nothing of their "right" to control their produce on its passage from field to factory; they were told simply how they could get more money for the product. Now they are demanding a larger share in the overhead control and more power for the local groups. This has come directly from certain dissatisfactions, that is, the desire for increased control has come with the need.

To sum up these pages: psychology now shows us how experience generates its own thought, will, purpose. This means that between expert and people is a chasm which ideas cannot cross. It means too that there is no magic by which consent can be converted into will: if the expert or administrative official wills, it will be forever the will of the expert or administrative official; there is no will of the people except through the activity of the people. Will and activity do not dwell in separate spheres. Consent is not the technique of democracy. We want the information of expert or official, not to turn us into rubber stamps, but as the foundation for the social process. The "consent of the governed" is intellectualistic doctrine; the will of the people is not to be found on this plane at all, but in the concrete activities of everyday life. The fallacy of consent is the fallacy of dualism—a fallacy exposed by biology, psychology and philosophy. To talk of consent is only to cling to that dualism for which the eighteenth century so preëminently stood but from which we have ever since been slowly emerging. Dualism must go in law and government. For those who have been deaf to our most profound philosphy, psychology is now pointing the way.

We see now that within every process is its own momentum; therefore the guiding power is always within—and this is the vindication of democracy. Every living process is subject to its own authority, that is, the authority evolved by, or involved in, the process itself. We see this clearly in international relations: we shall never be able to make an international settlement and erect some power to enforce it; the settlement must be such as to provide its own momentum. We have been trying ever since the war to make international will run ahead of international activity. It is an impossibility. Consider reparations, indemnity, allied debts, etc. We can pile up "accurate" information on accurate information and sit around the council table looking at it, but no international will can be born at the council table. That the collective will produces collective activity is one of the most harmful of our political fallacies. We see this every day, but nowhere is it so strikingly shown as in the history of Europe during the last five years. When Rathenau went to Rapallo and wished the revived business relations between Germany and Russia recognized in the treaty, Lloyd George preferred to assume that no such relations existed until the treaty was made.

But Germany and Russia *were* dealing with each other. International unifying (the "progressive integrations" of Part I) is a process which is worked out not in conference alone, but in the day-by-day activities of the nations, in international behavior. Statesmanship of the first order will recognize and act on this; it will of course wish frequent conference, but for the purpose of making possible a certain process and giving validity to it.

Thus we see that there is no static collective will nor "group mind": we have continuing activity; at any one moment the function which that activity is of the situation is the collective will. Thus its nature is wholly dynamic. We must think no more in terms of social institutions but of social activities. It is the same on the social level as we have already seen on the personal level. As we no longer think of personality as a static entity, but as "so far integrated behavior," so the collective will also is "so far" integrated behavior. Here, as so often, the parallel development of social research and psychological investigation is interesting. In our studies of social activities we gave up the idea of a collective will as a union of "wills" when we began to observe that the joining of men's wills always took place *in reference to* a situation, when we saw that we were always studying, not men's "minds," but their activities in reference to a situation. And then we learned that that was the phrase most essential to behavioristic and realistic thought, "in reference to." But our older psychology has much to answer for in the attitude of certain political writers on this subject. We were told, and I have seen it repeated recently, that "psychology deals with mental phenomena and not with objective conditions"; hence we have tended to think that the unifying of wills was an accepted psychological process. But what preëminently distinguishes our present from the older psychology is the inclusion of the object of behavior in "the total situation." The idea of a collective will as a unifying of wills must go; there is only a collective will as a unifying of activities—a different matter. The group will as an intellectualistic conception has no place in our most progressive psychology and should have none in political science.

What then is "the will of the people"? The deeper truth underlying all that I have said on this point is that truth emerges from difference, not from the difference of opinion chiefly, but from all the countless differings of our daily lives. If assertion and assent were the political process, then the political process would be different from the life process as described now by biology and physiology and psychology, which hardly seems probable. Political seeing should grow exactly as physical seeing. In the organism's effort to respond to total environment we have the multitudinous responses which constitute the growth of the organism. Respondings never ceasing, in their progress refine respondings still further, until afferent and efferent neural chains, muscles, etc., appear. Physical seeing creates itself by ceaseless integrating of response and situation, by refining itself into greater and greater sensitiveness which means for the individual wider objective environment and wider awareness. Thus we see the genesis of all new percipience.

Public opinion should be created by the same law by which all else is created. Thus we come to the conclusion again that the "will of the people" arises on the motor level. It is part of the whole social process: stimulus from total environment and response to total environment;[3] interactions between people, and interactions between people and their environment. Here, as in all stimulus and response, we have the releasing of energy which produces new energy. The will of the people scientifically evolved must bring out all the constitutive processes, must implicate all the necessary processes of all the citizens. We have the will of the people ideally when all desires are satisfied. In a power-society, however, it is the desire of the dominant classes which by the sorcery of consent becomes "the will of the people." The aim of democracy should be integrating-desires. I have said that truth emerges from difference. In the ballot-box there is no confronting of difference, hence no possibility of integrating, hence no creating; self-government is a creative process and nothing else. Thus the suggestion box of the modern factory is not a democratic device although often so-called. Nor is a factory democratically organized when questions are put formally to a committee of workmen and a Yes or No vote taken. Democracy does not register various opinions; it is an attempt to create unity.

An interesting example of a very genuine misunderstanding of this occurred on a Minimum Wage Board in Massachusetts. Of the six representatives of the employees, five were girls working in the industry concerned, one a labor leader from a strong union. This man, after one or two meetings, long before the questions involved had been threshed out, suddenly proposed

[3] Of course not total "total environment"; see p. 109.

that the vote be taken on the minimum wage for that industry. Before the chairman could say anything however, the Secretary of the Board of Labor and Industry, who sits with all Minimum Wage Boards, announced that the Board of Labor and Industry did not convene Minimum Wage Boards in order that they should take a vote, in order, that is, that they should register the preëxisting opinions of employers and employees; they were called together to see if by discussion based on a review of all the facts involved they could come to some agreement. If they could, or to substantial agreement, and should send in a report to that effect to the Board of Labor and Industries, the latter would probably accept the report. It was thus expressly pointed out by an official of the state that this group of employees, employers, and public had been called together and given the job of trying to create unity. Our Minimum Wage Law in Massachusetts is far from perfect, but it has recognized the principle that a conference should not merely record existing differences of opinion, nor should it be a fight, with the vote registering the outcome of the struggle, but a sincere attempt to find agreement.

And through that attempt we learn the process of creative thinking, the process which gives the unceasing increment of the increment. The final blow to the consent theory of government is that the plus-values are found always in the interweaving.

XII

A PARTICIPANT ELECTORATE

THINKERS about democracy then have passed the stage of merely perfecting mechanisms of voting and representation; their aim is to train minds to act together constructively. The democratic problem is now recognized as the problem of how to get collective action that is socially valid, that is satisfying by the criteria of enlightened living; the problem of how to maintain vigor and creativeness in the thinking of everybody, not merely of chosen spirits.

But the creative attitude has to be created. The people by virtue of being the people are not going to think creatively unless they have a rationale that sets them about it. Our first question might be: how is legitimate connection to be made between experts and people? Many are telling us of the importance of gathering accurate information; the way of conveying that information is still an unsolved problem. The large meeting is the method most in use in cities at present, and there is an honest endeavor, by having both sides presented, to bring all the facts before the people. But the approved method is to find a man who believes passionately in socialism, for instance, who is also a crowd orator who can play on every emotion, and ask him to give a talk on socialism. Then the next week you find a man who is passionately against socialism and is a good crowd orator. The idea seems to be that truth will emerge from this process; that out of all this bias and high feeling will, because there is equal prepossession and high feeling on both sides, be produced calm and reason and unbiased men. It is like the sculptor who tried to make a sexless head by using both a man and a woman as models.[1]

But can we find a better way? For "accurate information" seems to bore people. How to give the people facts without an amount of dulness which leaves us with empty halls is our problem. A good many experiments should be tried in order to see if we could hit on one that might be successful. Democracy in every country in the world today needs not propaganda but ingenuity, inventiveness, in method. I should like, for instance, to try experience meetings. The first step in these would be to present the subject under consideration in such a way as to show clearly its relation to all our daily lives. This is very important and usually neglected; I have never heard anyone tell people the actual difference in their own lives a League of Nations might make. The second step would be for each one of us to try to find in our own experience anything that would throw light on the question. I am hoping that this might prove sufficiently interesting to induce us to put up with the "accurate information." Also that after such meetings have become a part of

[1] I do not mean that the ardent advocates of certain causes are always unduly biased or are always willing to use crowd methods to win an audience, only that there seems often a tendency to secure such speakers for public meetings.

our community life, we should begin to observe and analyze our experience much more carefully than we do at present; it is almost wholly insignificant to us now as having social value. And I am hoping much more than this: that we shall take an experimental attitude toward our experience, and have many experiments to report with reasons for their success or failure, and suggestions as to what direction new experiments should take. The third step would be to see if we could unite our various experiences, one with the other and with the material provided by the expert. The material of the expert would always thus be thrown into the situation, not put up for acceptance or rejection. In the case of the farmer, get his experience and add to that of the agricultural expert. The scientific manager in the factory needs the experience of the workman. The Red Cross agent in the village needs the experience of the mother. We want to be governed neither by experts nor by the "innate" ideas of an all-born-equal people; what we want is coöperating experience, which means coöperating activity, which means a progressively more efficient activity.

I have said that such meetings should have definitely two objects: (1) to give the information of the expert, and (2) to elicit from each individual how far that corresponds with his own experience. Take our referendum in Massachusetts year before last as to whether trade unions should "sue and be sued": in order to make up my mind how to vote on that question, I had to get certain information from a lawyer; but my own experience also gave me some light on this question, not technical experience, not even experience with the bodies in question, trade unions, but experience in regard to the effect of responsibility and so forth. It is the uniting of these two kinds of experience on which public opinion is to be built up.

Moreover, in regard to the passing of a certain law, there have usually been laws simliar to it, or ones in the carrying out of which the same difficulties have been experienced as this one will probably have to face, or this same law may already exist in a partial form. The people therefore have had a chance to know how that law or a part of it or a similar one has already worked. In the effort to get the referundum upholding the Volstead Act passed, I think it would have been worth while to try to learn something from the audiences addressed. I do not know whether that was anywhere done.

One of the most valuable things about the Cincinnati Unit was that it was trying to work out the relation of the expert to democracy. In that plan the expert had a recognized place and a recognized relation to the rest of the community, a place which instead of separating him from the community in order to operate upon it, gave him an integral part therein by means of which he could both influence and be influenced by the community. Through such experiments, humble as they may seem to the political scientist, must we work out democracy.

A non-comprehension of the relation of expert to people is the weakness, I think, in the southern coöperative movement. This movement emphasizes the expert. The coöperative tobacco associations frankly tell the farmer that he is not an expert. These organizations are subdivided according to experts: the warehouse department, with men who know how to handle warehouses;

the grading department, with men who know how to grade tobacco; the sales department, with men who know how to sell tobacco. In other words, a high value is put on technical experience, but there is no effort made to add to that the farmers' experience. The field-service department gets information *to* the farmer; there is no recognized method of getting information *from* the farmer. Even if you should think the farmers' experience of little value (with which opinion I do not however agree), it could be made more valuable if the farmers were told that one of the principles of the coöperative movement was to make use of their experience, that they were expected when they became coöperators, to watch their experience; more than that, to take an experimental attitude toward their experience, to try experiments and contribute the results to the association for the benefit of all. Thus would the southern farmer be answering the problem which we must all solve: how to live life scientifically, by experiment and observation. A by-product for tobacco and cotton growers of such an attitude on the part of the coöperative associations would be increased self-respect which would improve their work and condition generally. Many persons' idea of increased democracy within the coöperative movement is to democratize the organization: to have it less hierarchical than at present, to have more democratic elections, etc. This is not enough, to elect the officials and then to listen to their policy and consent. The farmers must also contribute. There is no democracy without contribution. And an interesting commentary on this is the difficulty, mentioned above, which the southern coöperatives are now meeting within their associations, the dissatisfaction with the overhead. This will continue until the coöperative movement becomes in fact what it is in theory, a democratic movement. It is honestly *for* the farmer; it is not honestly *by* the farmer.

I am not hereby glorifying "the people." We no longer declare a mystic faith in a native rightness of public opinion; we want nothing from the people but their experience, but emphatically we want that. Reason, wisdom, emerge from our daily activities. It is not the *will* of the people we are interested in but the *life* of the people. Public opinion must be built up from concrete existence, from the perceptual level.

We should notice here an important fact: in regard to the so-called interpretation of our experience we should remember that interpretation, like everything else, originates on the motor level. I have already in my behavior given my interpretation to that experience; that is, actual interpretation exists in advance of formal interpretation. Yes, it is the *life* of the people with which we must concern ourselves.

Experience meetings as an experiment in democracy I am urgently advocating. We are not now master of our experience; we do not know what it is and we could not express it if we did. We need an articulate experience. And I should like to add, for it seems to me important, that from such experiments a new type of leadership might appear. When at the end of the war the western farmers became dissatisfied with the agents of the Department of Agriculture and organized the Farm Bureau, the leadership of the new movement fell to Howard, a plain Iowa farmer, because of his ability in interpreting the farmers' experience. This means the emergence of a new type of leadership, and to me a significant type for a genuine not a fictitious democracy.

Of course there are innumerable problems to be worked out when once we decide that we want a participant electorate. We have inherited many forms which canalize activities. We need geniuses to work out the problems of organization. We need inventive novelties in the way of functional organization, experiments in other than hierarchical organizations with ramifying authority. Moreover, would it be possible for the executive policy to be presented in such a way that we do not have to take a for or against attitude? It is this attitude which makes conflict. Also there must be found ways of our revaluing our interests while they are in solution. This is very important. Above all, is there any way of preventing an executive overhead, which is at first a functional agency of the whole body, from acquiring a solidarity of its own and drifting apart from the rank and file which created it? Many trade unionists feel that Gompers and his followers are acting in ways mainly intended to keep themselves in power. In such cases the organization keeps on after its function has ceased. The central body acquires a self-interest of its own apart from the functional relating. This is the danger of the group-mind; some of the pluralists have proved more than they meant to in what they have claimed for their groups. The problem is how to keep organization and function together, how to keep up the activity between central body and rank and file. There is sometimes a confusion of mind here; people blame "collective activity" for what is only the fault of an executive divorced from what it originally represented. There is no danger in a genuine collective activity.

I should like to carry the argument of these two chapters concerning a participant versus a consenting electorate a little further by connecting them more explicitly with the psychology given in Part I. I said above that we need the coöperating experience of expert and people. That might be understood as a matter of addition merely if we do not recall what was emphasized in Part I in regard to relation: that in social situations my response is to an activity which my response is changing while that activity is changing my response; further, that my response is not merely to the other activity but to the relating between the self-activity and the other activity. When the process of coöperation between expert and people is given its legitimate chance, the experience of the people may change the conclusions of the expert while the conclusions of the expert are changing the experience of the people; further than that, the people's activity is a response to the relating of their own activity to that of the expert. Here we have the compound interest of all genuine coöperation. Industrial and political organization will take different forms when we understand coöperation not as addition, but as *progressive* interweaving.

An understanding of this is very important in regard to the relation of state and individual. Let us briefly summarize, even although doing so means repetition, the central idea of the psychology given in earlier chapters, for much light is thereby thrown on the relation of individual to group, of group to state or larger unit. The circular reflex is a law which we see operating not only on the infra-personal level, in the functioning of the neuro-muscular apparatus, but also on personal and social levels. Bok in his account of the reflex circle shows us: (1) stimulus and response as a unitary experience; (2) that the important thing for us to notice is the functioning of the individual. He tells us that the character of the functioning of the effector depends largely on the effector and not only on the stimulation which incited it to function. Bok is speaking for the infra-personal level, but on the personal level we can all see for ourselves that our own activity is influencing that activity as much as the stimulus which incited it; we see "the occurrence of stimulations in consequence of" our activity, exactly as Bok expresses it for the neuro-muscular system. Again on the political level we see the same law in operation: the activities of the people "cause, actualize, alter the stimulations" which cause the activities. On no level of life do we find that "consent" which has been foisted upon us in the name of democracy. In the political process as well as in the physiological and psychological, we see that "the activity of the individual" is the central feature. The state is being made daily and hourly by the activities of its citizens; and as the activity of the citizens changes the state, the state exerts a different stimulus on the citizens so that their activity is different. Thus their activity is "causing" their own activity exactly as in Bok's law; the doctrine of circular behavior is as important for politics as for psychology or physiology.

The people of Massachusetts at the time of the policemen's strike took sides either with Governor

Coolidge or with the policemen. Both sides talked as if the policemen's will was set up against that of the state: some thought this legitimate; others thought it wrong. But what seemed to be forgotten was that the policemen had already, with others, made the state. The policemen whom I happen to know personally belong to the Tammany Club. These men by their adherence to Tammany are helping to make the autocratic state; then when they become the victims of their own tyrant, they cry out against him. But there was never a question, really, of the will of the policemen *against* the will of the state, against the will of a state which existed apart from themselves. That kind of a state is a myth of the pluralists.

Many people, moreover, talked of the policemen's oath to the state as the important point in the controversy, but I should deny that I owe less loyalty to my state than a policeman on the ground that he has taken an oral oath. Society could not exist for a moment unless it were based on more oaths than the spoken ones, or rather on an allegiance which is not external enough to require an oath but which is inextricably bound up in the nature of the relation. The policemen's allegiance to the state rests on exactly the same basis as my own: we have made the state, we must recognize the authority of the state. There is something inexorable about life that in the end sweeps away all but the most fundamental things. These naked things need neither oaths nor contracts, for they themselves provide their own laws; they proceed inevitably by the laws of their own being whatever external laws one may solemnly set up or futilely talk about.

This is very closely connected with what I have said of purpose as constituent, not as object, of creating activity. When the political pluralists would allow individuals or groups to decide whether the state is fulfilling its purpose, they tend to make the state purpose static. And the moment they make the state purpose static, they are back in the block universe they have repudiated. Governor Coolidge made the same mistake when he did not see that state will and state purpose must integrate at every moment with the facts of every separate situation, thereby creating a new will and a new purpose. When we have a participant electorate instead of a consenting electorate, we cannot stand outside and judge the purpose of the state; we ourselves become part of that purpose. A flood of light is thrown on the conception of purpose in politics by the psychology we have been considering. The political pluralists say that the state wins our loyalty by its achievements. But it doesn't. Our loyalty is bound up in the interweaving relation between ourselves and the state. That interweaving is the dynamo which produces both power and loyalty.

With the recent development of psychological thought then, we should have a different attitude toward the conception of "obedience" from that taken by the pluralists, who repudiate obedience as a loss of individuality, as an abandonment of moral integrity. What they forget is the dynamic nature of their "moral individual." Our main duty toward the state is not the contribution of a static self, but of a developing self. Hence obedience takes on new meaning.

Thus the "consent" which the pluralists give the various groups composing their state has but little connection with the soil and roots of our existence. The only valid consent is a growth, a long and slow process of education. The assent-obsessed historians would write history merely in its dramatic moments. Spears clashed assent in the valley of the Rhine many years ago, and not far from there today one can see on any Friday the picturesque Dutchmen, beside the thousand cheeses piled on the quays, striking hands as the sign of assent to the bargain. But one of the objects of this book is to urge the examination of symbols. Our ballot-box is certainly a symbol that needs examination. We must find in every case what is *mere* consent, for it is not consent which we really wish, even those who apotheosize it wish far more than that; it is power which we are seeking, that is, integrated control, "so far" integrated behavior. What vitiated the social contract theory was that assent, mere assent, was in that theory the foundation of power. When we are able to see ourselves as integral part of that process which at one moment and from one aspect we call state or industry or coöperative association or whatever it may be, we shall see that consent is hardly the proper word. The consent error is seen in all that the pluralists write against that theory of sovereignty postulated by legal science. They do not see that there is another theory of sovereignty possible, a sovereignty psychologically developed.[2]

Yet there is a strong argument for political pluralism. It is not that the various groups of a pluralistic state are voluntary associations (sometimes a great deal is made of that), not that they are functional

[2] See M. P. Follett, *op. cit.*, Chap. XXIX, Political Pluralism and Sovereignty.

associations (usually everything is made of that), but that they are close to the actual life of the people; men meet on the basis of their everyday interests and in small enough numbers to make an attempt at agreement possible. Everywhere we see that the kind of experience which develops us most is that which increases our motor reactions. For instance, ordinary travelling does not as a rule develop people because it does not produce vigorous motor reactions. But where we have stake, personal responsibility and vital interests, we make vigorous response. Here where our action tendencies are formed, democracy must begin. Thus alone can psychological and political power coincide.

But our industrial and political structure must be such as to allow legitimate outlet for our motor reactions. When labor leader and ward boss get control of these, harm often ensues, for when dormant motor reactions are roused to activity by other stimuli than those which produced them, they are divorced from necessary safeguards and correctives, since every activity contains its own protective, a protective bound up with its genesis. When the labor agitator speaks to working men, like every crowd orator he aims, to use the expressive phrase which psychology has given us, to arouse certain motor impulses, but these motor impulses, separated from the conditions which have given rise to them, are put into activity by a stimulus which allows no check from those originating conditions. The motor impulses produced by the life of the factory have often become dormant because there is no opportunity for outlet. They can be aroused by ways that are not legitimate, that are outside the normal process. The problem of democracy is to find an outlet for our motor impulses within the conditions which produce them. Any other way is fraught with the gravest danger. We want to give to the local neighborhood unit political, economic and social activity; we want to make possible vigorous motor reactions and at the same time provide for their outlet. As progress is through the release and integration of the action tendencies of each and every individual in society, way should be provided for such activity to take place normally. This is perhaps the sentence in this book which I want most to emphasize.

"Oh, you Americans," said Sir Horace Plunkett, speaking to the coöperatives on his recent visit, "you always begin at the top." Whenever we begin with an overhead organization rather than with the local units, the underlying fallacy is in thinking that consent will take the place of participation. I think it will be found that the only kind of coöperation which will succeed against the capitalistic or joint-stock organizations is that which begins from the very bottom and gathers into its activity every member. Moreover, when we begin with the local units we shall more easily succeed in welding the various interests into a working relation. When we begin at the top we are more likely to get a number of opposing interests to agree to fight under one flag because of the common enemy; not being really united they tend easily to fall apart. Current international experience shows this.

The most essential thing to remember about government is that control must be generated by the activity which is to be controlled. Therefore in industry, in coöperative undertakings, in government, control must begin as far back in the process as possible, else, to use the language of an earlier chapter, we shall have power-over instead of power-with. Joint action must know its source. We have seen the advantage of a coöperative gathering of facts before discussion begins rather than the presentation of different "facts" by the two sides of a controversy. We shall see in a later chapter the advantage of trying to combine interests before they get crystallized, of valuing interests while they are still capable of *re*valuation. We shall see that the workman's request is more easily dealt with than his demand, his suggestion than his complaint. We shall see that the whole secret of a sound system of representation, in politics or industry, is to make the necessary movements for agreement far enough back in the process. In short, the secret of sound government is to know what your *unit* is. It is as necessary as in the sciences.

Moreover, in considering that which educates or "influences," we must remember that influence is not all from the newspapers or the platform or what gets displayed in the limelight; people are influencing one another all the time. Instead of that influence being casual, we should be able to make more of it; there is much divergence going to waste. What I hope is that we shall be able so to vitalize small meetings of people that something shall be created in them which will be fundamental for our political life. Psychology gives us "progressive integratings" as the process of all organic life; the "progressive integratings" of men are the substance of democracy. We must free the way, create the conditions, for the productive relating of human beings.

In the small group then is where we shall find the

inner meaning of democracy, its very heart and core. We can begin with shop committees or neighborhood groups or where you will, but we must begin with small local units. The difficulty is that we have not yet found the way of vitalizing the local unit, of making it the means by which all men shall function, shall participate. The Republic of Germany saw this difficulty and the "*Interfaktionnelle Arbeit*" was appointed—somewhat like a Royal Commission, representing all parties, and composed of deputies to the Reichstag—to study the best ways and means of solving local problems, of meeting local needs. Every attempt at democracy will find that its first problem. Meanwhile let us try to know what democracy is. Now, when we want to photograph democracy we take a picture of a mass meeting. I have such pictures from various parts of the United States. They are sent me with letters which say: "We are getting right down to the real thing in our town; I enclose a picture of democracy in ward two." But numbers and flags and music are certainly not the symbols of democracy. Democracy means a genuine interplay and a coöperative constructing.

Yet we have not exhausted the significance of democracy by brandishing aloft "the local unit." Consider where such doctrine may lead. In Boston many of us oppose such federal bills as the Shepard-Towner because it will take something from the sacred rights of Massachusetts. But we all know the suspicion city-hall has of "the hill," where our state legislature sits. And again the ward politician is often more interested in his ward than in the city. Finally, in one of our wards you must be "loyal" to your precinct to be a good American. Is this democracy? Well, it is the apotheosis of the local unit carried to its furthest extreme.

Involved in this error is that common but most deplorable misunderstanding of federalism which conceives the individual as genuine member of his local unit but not of the larger group of state or federal government. I heard a discussion recently on the pros and cons of extended federal legislation. What was durprisingly omitted in that discussion was the fact that *we* are Washington just as much as we are the local unit. Either Washington is we ourselves or it is a myth. But it was assumed that when we allowed our federal government to do things, we were thereby giving up doing them ourselves—a strange illusion. The question is not *who* does it, because there is no one but ourselves to do it in any case, but *how* it is to be done: whether it is possible to have centralization of the right kind with at the same time a greatly increased decentralization. Far from thinking these opposed I think that one is involved in the other. Philosophical controversy throughout the ages has been concerned with the relation of the whole to the parts; any solution of this question in the realm of politics which does not consider the contribution which our most profound thinkers have made to it runs the risk of being superficial. If federalism means necessarily a struggle between whole and parts, there is menace for our future development in America.

We must understand federalism as a vital process, not merely as a governmental institution, a process as important for ethics and philosophy as for political science. Power not "granted," not "derived," but self-evolved, implies always federal relation; that is, a unifying from below, a continuous unifying which involves the progressive increase of power.

To sum up this section. Most of the weaknesses of pluralistic thought in politics could be included under one heading: it has not accepted the profound truth that response is always to a relating. The individual or group does not respond to the state, but to the relating between self and state. To use the language of Chapter III, the pluralist is not studying the activity-between, is not studying the effect of the activity-between on variations of individual or variations of state, does not see that the activity of the state is influenced not only by the behavior of individuals but by the interweaving between state and individual, individual man or individual group. In other words, the pluralist ignores the increment of the increment; he gives us a new theory of politics leaving out the law of geometrical increase. Is it probable that the law of political growth is different from the law of all organic growth? Political science must accept this law if it is to be equal to the problems it now has on its hands. For we must seek ever the plus-values of experience if we wish for progress. We advocate democracy for no sentimental reason but because we believe it will, rightly understood, give us the plus-values. The pluralists have much to contribute to political thinking, but their whole argument must take a different form if we are not to remain deaf to the recent contributions of psychology and the physical sciences. The pluralist idea of the relation of groups, of the relation of groups and state, belongs with the old idea of adjustment. Adjustment harmonizes the existing; it does not create. Only integration creates.

If you should say that to harmonize is a sufficient ideal in this world of clash and chaos, then we should have to carry the argument a little further into the region of philosophy and try to show that harmonizing itself, except of the most superficial kind, involves creating. That this should be so is one of the glories of existence, but this is not the place for philosophical doctrine; I hint at it because I hope it will be seen by some to underlie everything I have written.

Finally, the pluralistic state is often thought of as new *structure*. This is unfortunate. I believe so wholly in decentralization that I dread to think we may lose its fruits unless we are basing that decentralization not on mere changes in structure but on vital modes of association. Moreover, as Kappers and Bok have shown that functional correlation precedes anatomical correlation, that activity becomes structure, the same holds good in political development: the activity must precede the form. You cannot go against the law of all nature. The form cannot be imposed and the activity follow.[3] Many political scientists are basing their hopes, as so many have done throughout the ages, in adding one more institution to our government, in increasing the machinery. The political pluralists want a third chamber in Congress based on the principle of vocational representation; those who are putting their faith in the gathering of information want intelligence departments at Washington. I am not opposed to either of these institutions, but I believe that our hope for the future lies not in increasing institutions but in improving process.

[3] Of course in both social and physiological structure they influence each other simultaneously.

The fundamental thing is not functional delimitation in politics or labor representation in industry, but vital modes of association. The pluralists are simply proposing another basis of representation, the functional basis. But we have been for many years improving our scheme of representation, and yet it is a fact patent to every honest student that the essential thing has hitherto eluded us, that whatever the plan of representation the individual has been lost, that one usurpation has followed another. The political pluralists now run the danger of merely substituting group tyranny for state tyranny. The fatal methods of the past which have wrecked us again and again are the fatal methods of today, in trade union or city council or Paris conference. It should now be recognized that no scheme of representation, functional or otherwise, can save us, but only a different method of association—in shop-committee, industrial council, legislative commission or international league. The problem of democracy is how to make our daily life creative. People talk of the apathy of the average citizen, but there is really no such thing. Every man has *his* interests; at those points his attention can be enlisted. At those points he can be got to take an experimental attitude toward experience. The result will not be a mere satisfaction of wants—that alone would be a somewhat crude aim—but the emerging of ever finer and finer wants. The lamp of experience is both to illumine our way and to guide us further into new paths.

Have we anywhere in these two chapters seemed to overemphasize the part of "the people"? Certainly at no time has there ever been greater need of the expert than today. The plea for accurate information is as timely as it is important, but after we get the accurate information we must know what to do with it. For political "science" is a misnomer; politics is science and philosophy and art, the highest art we know. Concepts appear from the interweaving of response and situation. The political scientist may record the level of the moment which the interweaving of response and situation is attaining. The political philosopher may presage the tendencies of the strivings and their possible fulfilment. But the political architect, the statesman who takes these living concepts into the arena of factual happenings and makes them part of the interplay of concrete reciprocal servings, shows us the full creative process of his world. It is he who welds the generating centres of the community into coöperating creatings of new factual happenings and new awareness—the ceaseless progress of existence.

XIII

THE DYNAMICS OF REPRESENTATION: A NON-INTELLECTUALISTIC VIEW

THE acceptance of recent psychology means a greatly enriched thinking to bring to the study of representation. I can here, as in the chapter on Power, merely give hints of the direction that study should take, indicate the problems, not try to solve them. Indicate the problems while bearing in mind that as we are basing our thought on a dynamic psychology, we wish to see where a dynamic rather than an intellectualistic attitude toward representation would lead us.

The first question perhaps that we should ask is: can men with one set of action tendencies represent men with another set? For instance, the labor leaders who represent labor at joint conferences of labor and capital are not, like the people they represent, working daily in the industry in question. Thus they are not directly affected by the decisions reached in the same way as the people for whom they are acting. They are paid by trade unions to work for the amelioration of industrial conditions and higher wages. One of the chief forms such work takes is strikes, or threatened strikes, and preparation for strikes. Here, therefore, we have very different behavior patterns. Their work is largely fighting, they are paid to fight, they gain their leadership largely because of their ability in fighting; their organism is set to fight.

In Massachusetts the law requires that Minimum Wage Boards shall be composed of six representatives of the employers of the industry, six representatives of the employees and three representatives of the public. But the representatives of the employees are of two kinds: as the law makes no restriction, any one or several of them may not only be labor leaders and so outside the industry under consideration, but even when from inside the industry, they may not be taken from those about whom the whole discussion is to turn, that is, from those receiving a minimum wage. And on the Boards on which I have served not only not one of the representatives of the employees has been a minimum wage girl, but most of them have been the most highly paid in the industry. The reason is of course obvious: the initiative, energy and ability which have put them among the most highly paid wage earners in their particular industry, are the qualities which secured their appointment on the public board. The reason is obvious but the fact is there, and the importance of this fact has been much overlooked. Not only their stake is different but their whole lives are different and this greatly affects their attitude in conference.

Now compare the attitudes of these two different kinds of representatives of employees on Minimum Wage Boards. The more highly paid girls in the industry are often willing to concede too much, are less urgent than the girls actually suffering from the lowest wages. On the other hand the labor leader is far more urgent than any minimum wage girl would be. Neither represents those she is supposed to represent. The girl who is getting $18 a week naturally feels lenient toward employers who are paying her that amount; moreover, she does not fully understand the hardships of the girl trying to live on $8 a week. In the case of the labor organizer the difference in attitude is even more marked. It is not merely the fact that she spends her day in her own office instead of a factory, it is not merely that her stake is different, it is not only that her whole life is spent in controversy; there is also, very important, her relation to her trade union, her relation to the whole body of organized labor. Whereas the girl from the shop represents the girls individually, the labor leader represents a group. There are all the traditions of the group; there is perhaps more loyalty to an organized group than to individuals; there is certainly the question of one's standing in one's group. Yet there seems something artificial about mere trade-union representation: roughly speaking, very roughly speaking, the trade union representatives on the Minimum Wage Boards tend to represent trade union "stereotypes," the girls from the shop to represent "facts."

Yet I am not speaking against either type of representation; much more study is needed before anyone is competent to do that. But we see, I think, that the present discussion of craft-union representation versus shop representation must take a new form: has the shop representative, because of the common shop experience, because he has more in common with those he stands for, a wider basis for representation than the craft representative? Is there something more significant passing between people in the shop than in the trade union? Or vice versa? There is something to be said on both sides. Or if you should put the question in this form—how far is the total personality of representative and represented in question in representation?—one might answer that the man who represents the shop lives a life which in its totality is more consonant with the lives of the men he is representing; that the man from the trade union is by virtue of his craft representation a more specialized personality. Just as much could be said on the other side. I am not trying to answer questions in this chapter, but to point out what some of the questions should be.

I say that we should ask whether common experience in the shop gives to the shop representative a wider basis for representation than the craft representative, but we have also to note the behavior patterns peculiar to the type of representative when employees in a shop are also members of a craft union. This is a new type of representative. A representative from a shop, but from a unionized shop, as compared with a representative from a non-unionized shop, has the quality of his representativeness much affected by this fact. Men in a unionized shop have a certain social discipline, minds disciplined by common action; they proceed more or less by a certain process the steps of which are familiar to them.

Again, the question of labor representation might be put thus: do you want paid professional leadership with its incentives and tendencies, or unprofessional leadership with a different kind? Many questions spring to mind here. Why did Henderson lose the leadership of the labor movement in England? When Frank Hodges left the ranks of the miners how far and in what way did he separate himself from them? The question of leadership in connection with representation involves many interesting points, such as that of outside leadership versus indigenous leadership. Compare the intellectual leaders of the English labor party with the workingmen leaders. In our Congress, Senator Capper was referred to as the leader of the farmer bloc; in what did his "representation" of the farmers consist? There could be no more interesting case of leadership in its representative aspect than that of Sidney Hillman, President of the Amalgamated Clothing Workers of America. And the relation to the marketing coöperatives of Sapiro, the brilliant lawyer who is not only their legal adviser but promoter and representative before the public, would repay study. The question of the relation of the real leaders to the official leaders should also be given attention. In what sense, for instance, did Townley represent the Non-Partisan League? It would be fruitful to watch shifts in leadership and discover the reasons therefor.

The psychological members of a group are those who share in its activities. Let us from this point of view consider "labor leaders," who have only indirectly a personal stake in the solution, "personnel managers" who may be oblivious of the underlying motor forces, "impartial chairmen," whose detachment may cut them off from a developing situation, "agricultural experts" sent from Washington to the Farm Bureaus. Can a mind that irresponsibly contemplates the situation be sufficiently caught up into it to move with it?

We often hear the expression that labor officials have "lost touch" with the workers.

The chief trouble with democracy is that it has been put on a supposedly ethical basis: it was not "right" to legislate for people. The question psychology asks in regard to democracy is: *can* you do things for people? Can people with one set of action tendencies act for people with another set? Any theory of representation must take this very carefully into consideration.

Another current discussion in regard to representation very much affected by our present thinking is that of consistency of behavior in your two groups, the one from which you go and the one to which you go. Whether you think it proper or not, it is inevitable that our ideas should undergo some change from contact with the new group; in what way is this to be reckoned with in planning methods of representation, in developing standards of conduct for representatives? If the trade unionist in the conference with capital votes differently from the way he has voted in his trade union, is he to be denounced as a traitor? On a recent occasion I voted differently on the same question in different groups, a question which required the joint action of these groups. It would be interesting to find the reason for this. It was not merely that I was affected by additional facts or by additional arguments, for if so then I should have gone back to the first group and reversed my decision. But I did not do that; with the first group I still voted as I had before, for I saw that both groups were right. Yet these two rights blocked the road to action. In order to get action these two committees had to find a new way.

which would include the advantages both were seeking. I think they did it. The question of honesty or consistency when a representative acts on a new orientation to the issue needs much study, is in fact one of the most important questions of representation. Before we hastily use such words as traitor, we must inquire whether new facts have been discovered, whether the situation has changed (perhaps changed by the very act of holding this conference or by its deliberations), whether, of great importance, the man has grown by his new contacts. The question might be framed thus: how far does the integrating of the representative's own personality count in his representative rôle? Yet this is putting it too narrowly. The most important thing to consider is whether each group may not have developed a perfectly legitimate will or purpose, and whether a way cannot be found wide enough to include the purposes of both groups.

To those writers, therefore, who consider it wholly wrong when you develop loyalty to the new group, I should reply that that means an intellectualistic not a dynamic conception of representation. You are not necessarily disloyal to your primary group by being loyal to your secondary group because, and this is the whole point, they are both *your* groups. If you are a part of the second group, you *are* a part of it; if you are not, then by being there you are merely pretending to be a part of it, and business cannot be done on that basis. You lose your moral and spiritual integrity; you lose your opportunity for the most fruitful way of conducting the matter in hand. Loyalty is the very essence of all existence, and has its corresponding meaning on physiological, psychological and sociological levels. There *is* no group, there is no genuine conference, unless there is loyalty; it is imbedded in the innermost meaning of all human relations. This must be recognized in any sound theory of representation. I have heard the question of allegiance discussed in regard to the conflict in England between craft unions and shop stewards; again in this country, several years ago, in regard to the shop committees and the trade unions of the General Electric Company at Lynn. Much of such discussion seems useless to us, however, when we see allegiance as an automatic part of the behavior process, when we see that it is bound up with the whole matter, that it is never an arbitrary decision. Whether you show a greater loyalty to your legislative committee in Congress or to your party at home or to a particular faction of that party, depends on whether you have made the most vigorous response to committee or party or faction.

To be sure, if you are a trade unionist and suddenly embrace the capitalist point of view, you might be accused of treachery; some suspicion might attach to such a change of front. But when you go to a joint conference (even if you are the only one there on your side), the very fact of your consenting to confer means that you agree for the time to be a member of a new group, not a capitalist group, but a group of capitalists plus you. The capitalists make the same undertaking. If you come to some agreement in that conference it should never be assumed, without strong proof, that you have been won over to "the other side" either by the arguments or the prestige of that side.

A writer on philosophy said to me after a discussion we had had: "I think the chief point of disagreement between you and me is whether one thinks the nearer or the larger loyalty the more imperative." But I utterly disavow narrower and wider loyalties. I am going to be loyal both to my family and to my country; both to my trade union and to any other group to which I may be sent as trade-union representative, loyal not to the people on "the other side" but to the new group we all of us together make.

Another friend said to me: "What, then, exactly, do you think happens, or may happen, when a man goes to a conference and comes in contact with a new group?" I think the question impossible in this form; "conferring" and "coming in contact with a new group" are two mutually exclusive expressions. If the conference *is* a conference, we do not "come in contact with a new group," we altogether make a new group. The two processes are wholly different. When I "appear" before a legislative committee at the State House, I come in contact with a group; when I am asked to confer with people, they and I together make a group. If I go to push through something already decided on, it is not a "conference." This gives some hint as to the method of conference; one or two representatives should not "appear" before a body to state their case and then those before whom they appear talk it over by themselves and render decision. Genuine *conference* must be the rational technique. To be sure commissions, boards, legislative committees, etc., call people before them for facts or opinions, and this is, of course, a very useful proceeding, but it is not a conference, and on these occasions it is indeed not called a conference, but when you do call it a conference it should be a conference.[1]

But we must take the whole matter of representation a step beyond this. There are two integrations a representative has to make: first, the integration of the point of view he brings from his constituents with that brought by the other representatives from their constituents; secondly, the representative should go back and persuade his constituents not that a better way than theirs has been found, but that they must try to unite their old point of view, or their present point of view as developed since his election or appointment, with that formed in the representative group. Let us note what the process will be when we have worked out a method of continuous intercourse between constituents and representatives in city council, legislative assembly, international conference or labor conference. We are often told that the representative must keep in constant touch with the group from which he was sent; this usually means that he must bear in mind the wishes of his constituents, and also that he must keep them informed of the actions and deliberations of the representative body. But there is something beyond this: he should go back to his constituents not merely to bring information to them, not only to receive fresh instruction from them, but to take back to them whatever integrations of ideas and interests have been made in the representative body in order to unite these again with the ideas and wishes of his constituents. For in the representative

[1] The matter of the change in views consequent upon a new group formation has the widest application. The presenting of reports of sub-committees to the primary committee and the consequent discussion, realignments, etc., must be carefully studied.

body his ideas have been enlarged by all that he has discovered of the objections to what he has presented to his fellow-representatives, with all that he has heard of the possible consequences of the legislation he is proposing, with all that he has learned of the advantages of other plans, etc. Then, turning back to his constituents, he should unite all this with their developing ideas and wishes, and again go to meet his confrères in assembly or conference reinforced now by the larger point of view thus gained. Our relation to the people we are representing is interweaving at every moment with our relation to the new group. We need much further observation in regard to this, for people often talk as if the two things existed side by side and a kind of invisible scales were weighing them against each other and registering the result. It is the interweaving that people have not sufficiently studied.

Perhaps nowhere do we see a more superb indifference to recent psychology than in many theories of representation. If we had no neuro-muscular systems, we might perhaps be one man in one group and another in another, but alas, we are burdened with ineraseable inner activities. Every response we make to life is registered in, is built into the structure of, our internal mechanisms, becomes part of the integrating of our habit systems. We cannot leave these at home when we go to represent our fellows. The new experience will conflict or unite with these, and we must go back to our constituents with the mechanisms we then have. We have no choice. Someone I know told me that she was aware of the complexity of her personality and always chose which side she would show as she walked into a room. I wonder. She thought she could separate her action systems, but this is an impossibility; it is the whole organism, the integrating action systems, which makes response.

The fact that every new contact inevitably means change is, however, not accepted by everyone as a good thing. G. D. H. Cole evidently thinks this unfortunate. He says that Rousseau explains in one of the most illuminating chapters of the *Social Contract* that all action through representatives involves to a certain extent the substitution of the wills of the representatives for those of the represented. Moreover, that all groups of men through experience of acting together tend to develop in some degree a "common will" of their own; chosen to express the common will of those whom they represent, they acquire a common will of their own different from that of the represented. "However faithfully the members of a committee may try to fulfil their whole duty to their members, an element of committee loyalty will almost inevitably enter into their actions. . . . It is for the body of the members to counteract the tendency to clannishness and even conspiracy on the part of the elected persons by being clannish and alert in pressing forward their own common wills."[2] But I do not think that this is a tendency to be counteracted; I think it is far too valuable. We should recognize it and decide just what to do with it, for our task is always to learn how to make human meeting productive. That should be our guide in all such questions: how to enrich our lives, not to counteract and eliminate but to add—no, more, to multiply.

Although I have said that by coming into contact

[2] G. D. H. Cole, *Social Theory*, pp. 120–122.

with the new group we may broaden our ideas, may see that our interests are, while not the same, yet interdependent, perhaps I have not emphasized sufficiently that the very fact of our doing something together creates a bond. We are doing something together if we merely sit round the table; if we walk down the street together afterward, that increases the bond; if we dine together, that still further increases the bond; if we have to mend the car together before we can get home—but the jump here is incalculable. The "little" things of life are much overlooked. The place of meeting is always important. Shop committees meet in the shop; trade unions meet in a hall outside. This very largely influences the discussions. In international conferences we must estimate the influence of the country in which the conference is held, as, for instance, the influence of France in the Peace Conference.

To sum up this section, our problem is as follows. Let us put it in the language of psychology since in this chapter we are considering the contribution of recent psychological thinking to the subject of representation. In a group we make responses to certain stimuli; our own actions contribute to those stimuli, and those stimuli produce more comprehensive activity on our part. We have certain motor mechanisms which are much like those of the others in the group. Then we go to another group. Here, too, we meet specific stimuli; here, too, we contribute to the stimuli to which we react. One of the gravest dangers in some of the current notions of representation is the stereotyping of behavior patterns, for here perhaps more than anywhere else in our political system we have been reluctant to allow opportunity for development. When therefore we see the question of representation put thus: do we expect our representative to vote according to the new light he receives in conference and as the whole situation develops, or according to the ideas of his constituents as they had crystallized at the particular moment he was sent?—we can only reply that our thinking on this subject has gone beyond this stage. The core of the problem of representation is how to make the people I represent have a part in my own specific-response activity in the second group, that is, how to make people share vicariously in their representative's activity. We have had a too intellectualistic treatment of representation. There has not been sufficiently taken into account the very basic fact that new stimulus must always mean new response, that we grow through more and more contact, that progress means "progressive integrations." Nowhere is this psychological expression more fitly applicable than to the conception of representation.

I think we can now see both the strength and the weakness of "functional representation," so much talked of in England. Cole says that purposes, not men, should be represented, that "representation is always specific and functional, never general and inclusive." But this theory of representation spends its strength in looking backward and does not see the possibilities ahead. While Cole says that the state is not a coördinator, yet his representative assembly, inasmuch as its members represent specific and to a certain extent static interests, is more of a coördinating than a creating body. Coördinating is the old idea of adjustment, but that view is against our more progressive thought and is inadequate to meet our life. We should now think of a representative assembly not as a coördinating but as a creating body. Cole says that in a functional democracy, because the electors remain in being and in activity, you have an opportunity for the representatives in their functional assemblies to receive constant counsel from their constituents. Good. That is the strength of "functional representation." Its weakness is that it leaves the representative assembly as a mere registering and coördinating body.

One might ask, "Every representative must then be a great creative genius?" That would indeed simplify the matter.

Moreover, in Cole's functional theory of representation we come up against a very practical difficulty. Cole says: "We must assign to any association its function as the purposes which its members have set before themselves in creating and maintaining it."[3] But I have examined a number of associations and found that their function was not "the purpose which its members had set before themselves in creating and maintaining" them. Function is what an association is doing. Function is de facto purpose. Every step in activity is a step in purpose. The way in which recent psychology corroborates observation of social situations on this point is very interesting. "Functional representation" needs more searching analysis of the conceptions therein involved. For instance, you cannot, as we have seen, integrate purpose without developing purpose; it is part of the same process. This is not always recognized by those who wish society organized on a functional basis; they have a tendency to connect a certain function with a certain

[3] *Op. cit.*, Chap. III.

purpose, and do not see that functions cannot meet without purposes meeting, and that more happens in that meeting than they are taking account of. This is a very important consideration for those who are advocating a "functional state."

Another difficulty about the functional theory is that it obviously concerns the relation of "part to whole," and here we often go astray. When Cole says "in order that each may make its proper contribution to the whole," it seems to me that he goes rather near the danger line in thinking. When I "do my part in the whole," is the whole for me a "wish-phenomenon," that is, is it something which I posit in order to give greater dignity to my "part"? It *might* be just that. The functional theory of representation needs, I think, the doctrine of circular behavior which explains the relation of parts to the only possible "whole" there can be.[4]

The question of leadership in connection with representation was spoken of above in regard to the effect on any situation of outside leaders rather than those developed from inside. We have now to ask the further question: how far is the official representative accepted gladly as a leader, perhaps a leader who forms the thought of his community? How far is he given a mandate to think out things, how far is that exactly his job—to do their thinking for his constituents? The consciousness of their own inadequacy may have been the uppermost motive with his constituents in their selection of leader or representative. Lord Haldane has pointed out that ministers may be held deeply responsible for carrying out the fiery words

4 See Chaps. III and V.

of a general election instead of following their sober judgment as the situation develops. He says that there may even devolve on the representative "the duty of taking the initiative and acting for his clients freely, as a man of courage and high intelligence should act, and he may have been chosen more on the ground of faith in his possession of these qualities than in order that he might take some specific action which the nation feels that it has not adequately thought out." We see this often in committee work. We go to represent our committee at city hall or state legislature and are told to use our own discretion and judgment; this is not always merely because of what may develop there, but for the reason just given, that our committee has not been able yet to think out the question adequately.

There is always the question of how far the representative shall deal with questions which have come up since the election. This has been a particularly interesting question in England. The questions of leadership and of representation merge. A separate chapter should be written on leadership, but much more study is needed before that can be done. Its connection with behaviorism, however, is so obvious that to all students of political psychology it must appear as one of the most interesting studies before us.

The most significant contribution, however, which contemporary psychology can make to the subject of representation is connected with that conception of progressive integrating which I have already referred to in this chapter but which must now be further considered. We must note that there is a time and place for integrating, and that there is no way in which these can be artificially changed. The integratings that must be made between workmen and foremen cannot be left to the moment when the foreman goes to meet a committee of foremen and superintendents. The integratings that must be made between foremen and superintendents cannot be left until the superintendent goes to meet the board of directors. The integratings that must be made in shop committees cannot be left for a later moment. The non-recognition of this is a weakness I think in Cole's theory of representation. He tells us that shop committees should be composed entirely of employees, not of employees and management, in order that the fight shall be clear-cut, the issues not blurred. But if one sees the world not as a scene of continuous fighting, not as composed always of conquerors and defeated, if one believes that we should try to find the way of uniting our interests, then we have to consider at just what point the uniting most easily and naturally, most fruitfully, takes place.

The question of whether foremen rank with the management or the workmen is significant here. In most plants they are considered as part of the management, but occasionally they belong to unions; this makes an interesting situation. A case of a foreman discharged for belonging to a union came before the Railroad Labor Board in 1921. The question had to be decided whether a foreman of a section gang might properly become a member of the Brotherhood of Maintenance and Way Employees. The Butler County Railway officials declared that the foremen, men who acted on their behalf to see that work was expeditiously, economically and properly performed, owed an undivided allegiance to the company. The foreman who had been discharged was acknowledged to be competent and industrious, but he refused to renounce his membership in the union. The Railroad Labor Board ordered his reinstatement.[5] One would like to know upon what principle this was done. The Board probably realized, whether fully or only partially, first, that it is coöperating allegiance rather than choice of allegiance which is going to further the development of industry; secondly, that such allegiance cannot be theoretical, that the foreman must act with both workmen and management; and third, that the unifying of the diverse interests of employer and employed can take place more successfully through this early linking of the two than after crystallized grievances have been sent up formally to the management.

The most important consideration for any theory of representation is *where* the uniting of interests should take place. Guild socialists, like most advocates of group government, push it too far forward; by the time the diverse interests confront each other they are so crystallized that it is difficult or impossible to unite them. The pluralists pit groups against each other, against the state; it is the fundamental weakness of their theory. Democracy must find those methods by which the uniting of interests shall take place before they have become crystallized. The most acute thinkers in regard to the problems of industrial organization see this clearly. The labor manager already quoted, Mr. Earl Howard, has given me the following as his key to industrial controversy: interests can be revalued only as long as they are kept in solution. What this

[5] *The Survey*, Sept., 1922, p. 647.

means to Mr. Howard practically is that he tries to prevent a controversy from reaching the stage of alternatives; that is, he finds reconciliation difficult when two bare alternatives confront each other.

Recent events in Canada have thrown some light on this question. For four years, 1919–1923, Ontario had a farmer-government. The farmer party had not a majority in parliament, but it had the largest number of representatives of any one of the parties, and was therefore asked to form the government. A difference arose in the party's councils as to whom this farmer-government represented. The prime minister, Drury, insisted that it represented the whole province. Morrison, Secretary of the United Farmers of Ontario, the organization which placed Drury in power, did not agree. He insisted just as firmly that farmer-government is farmer-government, and that there can be no union with other parties. He preferred to have the farmers sit in parliament as an opposition rather than coöperate with any of the other parties.

The problem is: when a representative of farmers is elected by a constituency does he represent merely farmers or the whole of the constituency? If he represents only the farmers, do the urban populations of the constituency go unrepresented? If, on the other hand, the farmer-elected representative represents all the people of his constituency, how are the interests of the farmers to be kept distinct? That is, if the edges become blurred will the interests be practically lost? The question seems to me to be one of where you can get the most fruitful uniting. If experience shows us that the cleavage of class interests becomes too sharply marked by the time the representatives reach parliament, then we ought to begin back in the constituencies. I might add, by the way, that the question of a Labor Party in America has not yet been sufficiently discussed from this point of view.

Incidentally another interesting point might be noted in the Canadian situation: do we get better leadership from groups? We might consider Drury from this point of view. And if "better," in what way and why?

In this chapter I am trying merely to hint at a way of approaching the subject of representation. There are many important points which I cannot consider here. It must always be noticed, for instance, whether our representative is dealing with the representatives that he meets or with the group back of them. We saw Lloyd George sometimes dealing with France, sometimes with Poincaré. Another interesting question, partially touched on above, is how far the representative represents his officially recognized constituents or a party or faction among them. I have sometimes found it necessary to watch just what effect a rapprochement of the two sides of a representative group has on the alignment of factions in the primary group; to observe how far success in the representative group means a new alignment of factions in the primary group. We need a deeper study of representation than we have yet had, with more extended observation and with more experiments. Such a study would be a valuable contribution to the problem of labor: the relation of labor to capital, of industry to the state. While we have theories of representation which are called "the representation of interests not men," others which tell of "the representation of values," the chief function of the state being the official recognition of values, it should be noticed that both these theories are involved in that given in this chapter, the representation of activities. Both the theory of the representation of interests and that of the representation of values often fail to take account of two things: first, the *evolving* of interests or values; secondly, the part representation itself plays in the evolving of interests or values.

Let us pick out the principal points in this discussion of representation.

1. We should send our representatives not to win a victory but to come to some agreement on the basis of an enlarged understanding on both sides. We should send men to a "conference" to confer, not to fight for something already decided on before meeting; if the latter, they will use the balance of power of the moment, will rely on diplomacy and the handling of groups.

2. We should expect our representatives to maintain an integrating relation with the representative group as the situation changes.

3. The representative must keep in touch with his constituents not only on the intellectual but on the motor level. It was no crystallized public opinion that Wilson had to meet in the sense of America's mere intellectual assent or dissent to the Versailles proceedings, for war and post-war happenings were producing fresh public opinion every moment. The great leader or the true representative—I consider them the same—must look ahead and see what public opinion is going to be, and that means no prophetic insight, it means only that from the daily occurrences in the life of his

constituents he reads public opinion before it gets formulated as such. In other words, the "prophet" is the good behaviorist; he reads from the Book of Behavior.

4. Finally, we find here in considering the subject of representation the same principle at work which we noted in the last chapter in regard to people and expert, in regard to individual (man or group) and state: that response is always to a relating. We see this when we apply our rule of Part I, namely, that we must always study things as they vary in relation to the varyings of other things. We watch the representative in his relation to his constituents, then to the people in the representative group, then again to his constituents, again to the representative group—it is like getting X to the *n*th power in compound interest. Here we have the dynamics of representation. The intellectualistic view of representation did not allow for the increment of the interweaving.

At the risk of some repetition I wish to sum up the connection between these three chapters and the thought of Part I. The empirical emphasis of recent philosophy and psychology has not yet been sufficiently applied to politics. The doctrine of consent is the "rationalization" by which arbitrary authority is to-day possible. All autocrats must advocate this doctrine; in a modern world it is their only weapon. Genuine authority is not a matter of "will," even of the "will of the people"; it is an interweaving *activity*. This means that it is found buried deep in the actual life of men as lived from day to day, from hour to hour. For instance, the truth about what we euphemistically call the "rights" of the minority is that the habit tendencies of a minority have to be taken into account else a mere majority vote would not last. You may crush or ignore "wills," but the motor mechanisms of men are not so easily blotted out. Again, the greatest difficulty in finding a just system of representation is how to get activities rather than ideas represented. The whole question of government responsibility is that of discovering a method by which experts, officials, judges, etc., shall be responsible, not to our "minds" but to our lives. This is the difficulty in the international question: how to connect any kind of an international authority we may set up, with the activities of the people concerned. An international mind—a dangerous expression—is otherwise an abstraction.

But if the connection of authority with the actual life of those concerned is the first point to be considered in the political process, the second is not less important, that that actual life must be considered as gathering its force from the interrelatings involved. Power is the intermingling of many psychic forces. Many people seem to think that the "rights" of a minority are founded on our tenderness for the under-dog. Not at all. Besides the reason just given, that it is impossible in the long run to ignore the minority, we wish to add to the social structure what minority has as well as majority. President Lowell has shown us this in writing of the formulation and expression of the views of minorities.

The phrase which sums up the two emphases of this book is integrating activities. *Social* activities does not give us the process described here, because social, as I have tried to show in Chapter II, does not mean necessarily the actual, concrete uniting of men; as ordinarily used that word means what some person or persons think good for society. To most people the word social does not connote that *functional unity* which I think the most valuable conception of contemporary thinking. For the abstract word social we must substitute the wholly concrete word integrating. But integrating *wills* does not give us the democratic process because genuine union can take place only on the motor level. Control—in government, national or international, in industry—must rest (1) on the concrete activities involved, (2) on the interdependence of these activities.

XIV

LAW AS SELF-CREATING FROM THE DAILY ACTIVITIES OF MEN

I HAVE spoken of the contribution which the modern school of legal realism is making not only to jurisprudence but to all our thinking. One discussion of present-day jurists throws some light on the question we are considering in this book: the part of the daily experience of all men in creating a life within which that experience shall flow on to fuller development and greater enrichment. I refer to the discussion of the place in jurisprudence of economic determinism. This theory would have many more adherents, I believe, if it were not often misunderstood as synonymous with class conflict; those, therefore, who do not see the whole of life in the terms of class struggle often deny this doctrine altogether. But this is to conceive economic determinism far too narrowly. No one denies that the different development of common law in England and America was for a century due largely to the pioneer conditions and agricultural interests of America. Yet this is economic determinism. While I do not carry this interpretation of legal history as far as some writers, while I think its exponents are apt to give too little value to other factors in legal development—such as the conscious determination on the part of many of the legal order not to be influenced by class struggle, to "uphold justice,"—yet I think it is evident that law has, on the whole, registered at any one moment the stage of the conflict at that moment between interests. Law has followed power.

This is written clearly enough on the pages of English history: in the long struggle between Crown and Court, and in that industrial and business expansion to which English law ever responded. In America, too, both legislation and judicial decision have, on the whole, reflected the moneyed interests as their chief influence. Jhering gives us many examples in the past of law following the dominant interests. The history of law as regards the property of the peasant, the credit of the merchant, the honor of the officer shows this most interestingly. Again he tells us:

> "A theocracy brands blasphemy and idolatry as crimes deserving of death, while it looks upon a boundary violation as a simple misdemeanor. (Mosaic law.) The agricultural state, on the other hand, visits the latter with the severest punishment, while it lets the blasphemer go with the lightest punishment. (Old Roman law.) The commercial state punishes most severely the uttering of false coin, the military state insubordination and breach of official duty, the absolute state high treason, the republic the striving after regal power; and they all manifest a severity in these points which contrasts greatly with the manner in which they punish other crimes. In short, the reaction of the feeling of legal right, both of states and individuals, is most violent when they feel themselves threatened in the conditions of existence peculiar to them."[1]

When, therefore, we are told, as an innovation in the conception of law, that law must respond to social facts, we are a little bewildered, for that is what we have seen it do in the past, what we see it doing every

[1] Rudolph von Jhering, *The Struggle for Law*, pp. 48–49.

day in the present—responding to manufacturers' associations, trade unions, railroads, bankers, etc., exactly in proportion to their power. Cardozo gives as an example of the courts' recognition of social values, the development in the attitude of the courts towards the activities of labor unions. "The suspicion and even hostility of an earlier generation found reflection in ludicial decisions which a changing conception of social values has made it necessary to recant." But this change has not been produced chiefly by a changing conception of social values, but because the trade unions have been steadily gaining power. When and where they lose ground is usually reflected in legal decision. Or as far as we have "a changing conception of social values" that too has come from the shift in power. Again Cardozo tells us that "Rules derived from pre-established conceptions of contract and obligation have broken down before the steady action of justice." This is certainly too vague; there have been many very concrete things at work to change our ideas of contract.

But most of us are realists enough nowadays, I think, to accept the fact that law follows interests. It is after that is acknowledged that the whole crux of legal procedure, of philosophical thinking, arises: are the interests to be those of the most powerful class in society at the moment? If not, in what way are the interests of less powerful classes to be taken into account?

First of all it must be noted that legal thinking has now reached a further stage even than that of "interests." Although the notion of interest is far better than the nineteenth-century "will," it is still too subjective, still has a hint of abstract values or prejudged purposes. There is a biological interpretation of law which says that it is the reconciling of *instincts* which must take place if the race is to endure, a philosophical interpretation which says that it is a reconciling of *wills* (this has occupied by far the largest place in the theory of jurisprudence), and an economic interpretation which says that it is the reconciling of *interests* —although to be sure this school has spoken so far not of the reconciliation but of the domination of interests. Pound cuts under all these interpretations when he substitutes for instincts, wills, interests, the word desire: "the problem of the legal order is one of reconciling or harmonizing or compromising, conflicting or overlapping human claims or desires or demands." But the question remains: what is the *process* of reconciliation? How is the "value" of these various conflicting desires to be estimated? There is only one test for the value of wants: their confronting or conflict, but conflict constructively conceived, not as resulting necessarily in adjustment, mere adjustment, but as opening the way for integration. Our psychology has shown us integration as the "something new" which specific response always involves. This means that landlord rights and tenant rights, or rather landlord and tenant desires, can be satisfactorily reconciled only through the something new which our study of that particular landlord-tenant situation must uncover.[2] Every honest confronting of interests helps men to conceive their interests more largely. Our success depends not on the firmness with which we adhere to purpose

[2] It has been explained that "something new" does not mean spontaneous invention but progressive integration.

but on the penetration with which we discern purpose.

There is a theory of law now emerging which recognizes this, as I have said in an earlier chapter. It is based not on the battle of interests with the crown to the victor, but on the uniting of interests. It must be noticed, however, that both these theories, that of law as battle of interests and law as uniting of interests, recognize conflict; but while in the former theory conflict must always result in victory for one side, in the latter doctrine, while the conception of conflict is still valuable, it is valuable for a different reason—because it reveals desires. This revealing is of the utmost importance, for only when thus revealed is there any chance of there being found some method by which they can be united, some method by which to avoid conquest as the result of war. As long as we do not understand this, as long as we do not seek that method, law will continue to follow power. Holmes says "Whenever a doubtful case arises ... what is really before us is a conflict between two social desires, each of which seeks to extend its dominion over the case and which can't both have their way. The social question is, 'Which desire is stronger at the point of conflict?'" But that may not be the social question. The social question may be: is it possible so to conceive conflict that *both* desires may receive satisfaction?

The relation of law to conflict has engaged many writers. Many agree with Richard (*L'Origine de l'Idée de Droit*) that the function of law is to reduce conflict; others with Adams that "Law is the result of forces in conflict—and crowns the victor." We need not necessarily see conflict ending with crowned victor and prostrate foe, but on the other hand we should not seek to reduce conflict, for to reduce conflict is to reduce life. Law emerges from conflict. Yes, and from conflict constructively conceived a progressive law proceeds. Let us look further at this matter of law in relation to conflict. One writer tells us that the coincident purposes of individuals create social purpose which generates law. But the discovery of coincidence is not the social process. Again we are told that law comes always from struggle; the right conquers. All the errors of this way of thinking come from one: the ignoring of the creative possibilities of conflict. We do not wish to put up with strife for the sake of the peace that follows. Existence should not be an alternation of peace and strife. We should see life as manifold differings inevitably confronting each other, and we should understand that there is no peace for us except *within* this process. There is no moment when life, the facing of differings, stops for us to enjoy peace in the sense of a cessation of difference. We can learn the nature of peace only through an understanding of the true nature of conflict. It seems to me unfortunate that we are seeking something which does not exist. Only when we are willing to accept life as it is can we learn how to deal with it. To battle for a preconceived right involves the same error as to work for a preëxisting end, for it leaves out of question the never-ceasing movement of life which is always revealing to us new "rights" and new "ends." Rights and purposes emerge from the ceaseless differings of concrete existence. Rights develop as needs develop. There is no reason why we should not hold to a theory of rights now that we understand their origin and meaning. The slogan of "equal rights" has no value for us until it is translated into the right to do specific things: the things we want to do represent our desires; what we have to find out in the so-called "struggle-groups" of society is simply what people want to *do*—thus do we escape from "the philosophy of the will."

What contribution does the psychology I have tried to indicate briefly in earlier chapters yield for jurisprudence in regard to the doctrine of the will? In its analysis of the behavior process it shows us the identification of will, desire, purpose, thought, with some concrete activity. Since Aristotle we have had the dualism of the law of reason and the law of the will, and in the last century the struggle between the two was tinged by the doctrine of the "sovereign" will; but now that we see the relation of reason and will, and now that the nineteenth-century "sovereign will" has been, or is being, abolished, such dualism must go. One jurist makes a distinction between will and purpose. The "cause" of the activity of the will, he tells us, is purpose. Purpose always relates to the future. "Purpose is the idea of a future event, which the will essays to realize. . . . This begins in man with the faculty of ideation." But we cannot find in "the conception of purpose" "the generative forces of morals and laws." Both genetically and progressively purpose must be studied in relation to an activity of which it is an aspect.

There are students of both political and legal science who have tried to make purpose take the place of will, but with a deeper understanding of will and purpose we find that there is no antagonism between the two. The controversy between will and purpose has many forms. One it frequently takes is the discussion whether law rests on will or needs, or as Tanon, President of the French Court of Cassation, puts it, "the dominance in law of 'internal spontaneity' or 'external causality.'" Here obviously the difficulty is a misunderstanding of the will. If Duguit seems confusing when he considers whether law is based on the will of the people or on social conditions, it is for the same reason, that he is thinking of will in its older, not more modern, meaning. When a recent writer on government tells us that, "The State is based on will, but the wills from which its will is eventually formed struggle against each other for survival," this is, in so far, or rather as expressed, old-fashioned doctrine based on an outgrown psychology. The "conflict of wills" must disappear both from our theory of government and from our theory of law, as it has with some writers. When Pound denies that law has to do with the assertion of "wills," the reconciliation of "wills," he thus gives up the old legal theory of "the conflict of wills." He is dealing with human desires as manifested in concrete activities.

The school of realism in politics or jurisprudence cannot be realistic enough for us if it does not see the essential process of life. We have been told that there are two parts to law, exchange and association, that the first rests on the difference of needs, the second on identity of needs. But identity of needs is not the basis of association (if it were we should have very little successful association), but the reciprocal fitting of needs one to the other. Meredith's definition of love is I think the best definition for every human relation: "His need and her need rushed together somewhere down the skies." To have need each of the other—nation and nation, capital and labor—is very different from the identity of need. It is when law discovers that my need and your need may both be satisfied that it renders us its greatest service. No, when it goes a step beyond this and sees the reciprocal relation of these needs, sees that my need and your need may both be integral to the situation. No, when it takes a step even beyond this and sees that the reciprocal supplementing of your desires and mine leads inevitably to something further—to a greater need and therefore a larger "right."

What then is the aim of law?—the question asked in all juristical writing. Jhering steps out of the philosophical and practical difficulties involved in the nineteenth-century doctrine of law as protector of will and maintainer of rights, and gives us law as the guardian of interests; with Kohler the aim of law is "to meet the requirements of advancing culture"; with Duguit law protects man in his functions, secures social interdependence. But Pound, in giving us the end of law as the satisfaction of human desire, brings the school of legal realism in line with our most advanced psychology. The statutes of our legislatures, the decisions of our courts, and the rules of our administrative officials, are based on desire. The sovereignty of will or purpose will always remain intellectualistic doctrine until we translate will and purpose into terms of activity. If, as we are told, men have ceased to think in terms of a hierarchy of authoritative wills, they must also cease to think in terms of a hierarchy of authoritative purposes. The key-word for jurisprudence and politics as for psychology is desire. But this desire can be the desire of a dominant class or the unifying desires of all classes, of all men. It is for us to choose. We must remember, however, that law both satisfies desire and opens the way to new desires. Law neither reflects nor dictates progress, although it is interesting to watch how often it is supposed to do either one or the other. The aim of law is, I believe, to free, to "release energy." I like to use here the physiological expression, I am glad to find the same process in legal adjustment as in "functional adjustment," for then we cannot be accused of a shallow "idealism." The high mission of law should be forever the release of energy, thereby leading us to new levels of experience. For every harmonizing should emerge on a higher social level.

We can now revalue our nineteenth-century individualism, for we do not want to abandon it. The doctrine of the equal claims of individual units, that is the doctrine of "equal rights," finds a place again in our thinking, but now within the doctrine of integrating desires. For more than two centuries individualism held sway in one form or another. The theory of the maximum of individual self-assertion for each as the end for which the legal order exists found both support and direction in Kant's doctrine of the freedom of the will, which provided for the "freedom of each and freedom of all" by the establishment of boundaries, and the acceptance of "universal" laws. Thus the idea of right and freedom followed closely on that of the will. The will of each was to have as much scope as left equal scope to the will of others. It was the function of the legal order to secure this. Legal right at this point mingles with philosophical right as so often in the history of law, that is, right and law become synonymous. At just what moment law becomes officially connected with freedom it is hard to tell, but at this moment the liaison between law and ethics gives way to that liaison between law and politics which was so powerful a factor in social development throughout the nineteenth century; the idea of liberty was the end of law as it was the political aspiration par excellence. When the difficulties of this doctrine became so apparent that they had to be admitted, we swung away from the word individual to the word social, but the danger in the doctrine of the individual will is not in the word individual but in the word will. With our present understanding of will, with the doctrine of integrating wills or integrating activities, with the idea that conflict itself may be made creative, with a deeper comprehension of freedom, the individual may with safety be reinstated. Much of what was written in the last century of the individual will as securing individual needs is true today if we understand by will the pressure of desire, and if we confine desires to actual desires, operating desires.

Pound has thrown much light on this subject by what he has written of relation. The significance of this part of his thought is so great that I should like to quote his own words:

"The central idea in the developed Roman system is to secure and effectuate the will. . . . In our law, by contrast, the central idea is rather relation. . . . The Romanist develops all his doctrines [of partnership] from the will of the parties who engaged in the legal transaction of forming the partnership. . . . We speak instead of the partnership relation and of the powers and rights and duties which the law attaches to that relation. . . . The Romanist speaks . . . of a letting of services and of the effects which the parties have willed thereby. We speak of the relation of master and servant and of the duty to furnish safe appliances and the assumption of risk. . . . We do not think of what is willed by the parties but what is involved in the relation. In the case of mortgage and mortgagor, as in the sale of land, we do not ask what was agreed, but what is involved in the relation. . . . We have established that the duties of public service corporations are not contractual, as the nineteenth century tried to make them, but are instead relational; they do not flow from agreements which the public servant may make as he chooses, they flow from the calling in which he has engaged and his consequent relation to the public. . . . Even more significant is the legislative development whereby duties and liabilities are imposed on the employer in the relation of employer and employee, not because he has so willed but because the nature of the relation is deemed to call for it. . . . Anglo-American law is pervaded on every hand by the idea of legal rights as incident to relation." [3]

Here we have a new idea of will in line with that given us by contemporary psychology, for here there is only verbally a distinction between will and relation; it is actually a distinction between the will involved in an activity and a preëxistent or contentless will. It is de facto will as against what was once the legal will. When Pound speaks of the difference between will and relation as fundamental notions, he is speaking of the difference betwen de facto will, that which is involved in the situation, and a theoretical will. That the legal profession is now recognizing the unreality of ante-facto will is significant. I do not think it is chiefly because of the influence of psychology; the parallel development in psychology, politics, economics, and jurisprudence has been to me the most outstanding and interesting event in the development of recent thinking. Correspondence between legal and psychological think-

[3] *The Spirit of Common Law*, pp. 20–31.

ing, besides the one just given, we see in all of Pound's writing. To sum up the most important: his definition of law in terms of human desire, his "de facto wish" explicitly so given, and all that he has written of relation which takes away from "social interest" the possible stigma of an empty abstraction. This part of his teaching shows us too that among the many mitigations of the rule that law follows power, among the many reasons why the war between the classes has not been fought out crudely to extreme positions, the chief among legal conceptions, and apart from the service of our great lawyers, is the idea of relation inherited from feudal law. He shows us that the influence of feudal law gave to our legal system a fundamental mode of thought, a mode of dealing with legal institutions and with legal problems, which has always tempered the individualism of our law. Thus the idea of relation has ameliorated the fullest effect of the tendency of law to follow power. And yet I think Pound does not give enough emphasis to one point: the legal order, and all the rest of us, are influenced in our *interpretation* of the demands of the relation by the relative power of the parties concerned. When world conditions are such that the balance of power is in the hands of the workmen, the employers interpret the situation very differently from the way they would had they the balance of power; the duty involved in the relation then makes it necessary to put safety devices on machinery, to give higher wages, etc. Yet, with this understood, the influence of this legal conception on all our life can hardly be overestimated. It is necessary to notice too that every relation is affected by its own relations. For instance, the relation of landlord and tenant is connected with all the rest of our life—with conditions in the building trade, with real estate values, with heating facilities, etc.; as the circumstances of our industrial and commercial life change, the relation of landlord and tenant changes, their "rights" change.

To sum up this chapter. The interweaving of desire, not the domination of the desires of the strongest, should be the social process; the service of law is to help find those methods by which desires shall more and more fruitfully interweave. This does away with the notion that the function of the legal order is to delimit demands or claims. The psychological suppression, the political compromise, by which part of one's claim is waived, and the legal delimitation, are notions which belong together. When the social sciences are based, as they should be, on the concept of desire, we shall understand many correlations which escape us now. If contemporary psychology gives us integration in the place of suppression, if the effort of our sanest political writing is to secure a place for minorities as well as majorities in our government, to make majorities coactive instead of coercive, so also the legal order must understand that its problem too is not that of delimitation but of integration. With the nineteenth-century notion of freedom based on right went the idea that the function of the legal order was so to delimit individual self-assertion that all could be "as free as possible." With the idea of social interests which supplanted the false individualism of the nineteenth century went also, with some writers, the same idea, that the function of the legal order was to delimit, but this time it was to be done not in the interest of other individuals but of society. Both these notions should be replaced by the conception of the uniting interests of individuals. Law is to find the way of uniting interests. It is to seek to limit the area of mutually exclusive interests, but it is to do this not by arbitrary declaration, but by suggesting and encouraging those activities which will produce interests that are capable of uniting. Law should seek far more than mere reconciliation; it should be one of the great creative forces of our social life.

XV

THE LIMITS OF A PRAGMATIC JURISPRUDENCE

IF experience can be looked at as the confronting of diversity, if we can see that the problem of experience is how to make use of such confronting to preserve the individual and enrich the social life, we shall have taken a long step forward in our thinking. Here is the source of every gain in civilization. Our judges are not endowed with the sense of right and justice as they are invested with their robes. We hear much of the "reason" of the judge, but what is this reason to which we are to pin our faith? Grotius and his followers emancipated law from theology, but the reason they put in its place was not that which dwells in experience. Those jurists who ask whether law should conform to the demands of our present civilization or to reason, forever the crucial question in the philosophy of law, do not see that reason develops on the perceptual plane. Human reason is what human desire, working indirectly of course, makes it. We cannot bring percepts to the bar of reason because reason is the outgrowth of percepts. As often as we are told of the reason or the intuition of the judge, we must remember that our reason, our intuition, are themselves the fruits of experience; they too have emerged from the conflict of interests or, the expression I prefer, the confronting of desires.

Moreover, what are called the standards of the legal order, as the standard of "due" care, the standard of the "fair" conduct of a fiduciary, the standard of "reasonable" facilities to be furnished by a public utility, these are standards of the community: the interpretation we give to "due," to "fair," to "reasonable," is the gradual outgrowth of the confronting of diverse interests. I do not wish to minimize the juristic effort, in the administration of justice, to make law conform to ideas of right and justice, but only to recognize where these have their origin. Ideas unfold *within* human experience, not by their own momentum apart from experience. Law does not develop by its "inner force"; it is part of the stuff of human experience. Every ideal comes from desire, from the interknitting desires of men as evolving in their everyday activities. Experience is the unchallengeable foundation of all our thoughts and ideals. This does not mean that we need take a cynical attitude toward right and justice. On the contrary it shows that right and justice have a solid objective basis, and that upon every one of us rests the responsibility for their appearance. In juristical writing we read much of "logical reasons," "ethical motives." We can deny the existence of these, or we can erect them into things whose value rests on something outside experience, or we can recognize that logical reasons and ethical motives have come from the conflict of interests in the past. The "conviction of right" is the sureness felt in regard to the satisfaction of desires. Right is the satisfaction of *all* our desires. Absolute right appears—in infinity.

When therefore we are told, as we have been recently, that "law is authoritative because of its ethical character as embodying a rule of right," we reply that law is authoritative because it is the outcome of all those activities involved in the confronting desires of men which give us at the same time our ethical ideas, our political institutions, our legal organs. The custom of the community, the ethics of law, the conscience of the judge, are being made by the same process.

We are warned, however, that formulated experience may give us natural law again in another form. That will not frighten us. Indeed the feat which modern psychology and jurisprudence have accomplished in salvaging natural law is a contribution to all our thought. But this has nothing to do with deductions from the abstract nature of man pronounced by logician or judge; this is a developing law, a formulating experience to which all men contribute. Law is not a body of formulated experience; it is an activity of formulating experience. We shall never have the right idea of law as long as we think of it as a "body" of anything.

But so far we have looked at only half the story. If from our daily activities come all our conceptions, it is equally true that these conceptions are embodying themselves continuously in concrete forms. Much juristical writing assumes that it is the part of the judge to decide how far the legal concept shall be allowed to influence the situation, taking no notice of the fact, equally true, that it has already influenced the situation before the case comes to the judge. Facts do not happen irrespective of concepts and then change the concepts. One flaw in the theory of the economic interpretation of legal history is that it is often set up *against* the ethical theory of the judge administering justice, but our conceptions of right and justice are already working in that conflict of interests on which economic determinism concentrates its attention. I have said that right is the outcome of desire, yet it is equally true that our conception of right influences our desires, but not from a separate sphere; what I have wished to emphasize is the evolving of these together.

A pragmatic jurisprudence goes a little too far. We wish indeed to discard "the method of deduction from predetermined conceptions," but we can do that without discarding these conceptions themselves, which is in fact an impossibility. You do not throw over juristical conceptions when you base your law on the concrete case, because the concepts are already in the concrete case before us, to a certain extent. The business practice of America has given us certain juristical conceptions which we did not have at the beginning of our history, but the conceptions of the beginning of our history have undoubtedly influenced our business practice which in turn gives the new conceptions. But "in turn" is an inaccurate expression. Legal conception does not follow experience, and experience follow legal conception; they are bound up together. Here again we have an example of that circular response described in Part I. If you take a legal idea, such as gift or obligation, and trace its stages through Roman law, you find each "discarded" principle contributing something to the "next" stage of thought but always through concrete activity. If our judges rule differently in regard to liberty of contract from those of the last century, if state regulation of individual self-assertion in the interest of health is now given larger areas, this is not because our legal order, comparing the conceptions and the concrete situation, get different results from those of the legal order of the last century, but because the conceptions which gave liberty of contract and restricted state regulation have, by their operation in the concrete world, worked out to other conceptions. Conceptions do not develop by themselves; by mingling with concrete situations they do. The nineteenth century tended to look on legal conceptions as final, and yet those very conceptions eluded their grasp. While the legal order thought they had them under lock and key, lo, they were out the window, taking the road and bringing back all that they could gather there.

Thus when law "discards" a principle it does not annihilate it. Because it cannot; the roots of the principle have branched in too many subterranean directions for that. "Off with his head" was what Alice's Queen decided the simple life to be, and it would indeed be far simpler for us too, and for our judges—if it were possible. We are told that law should be based not on abstract principles but on social facts, but we do not want to set up a jurisprudence of facts *against* a jurisprudence of principles; we must unite them. Tanon says that we must not connect law with metaphysical principles "because we thereby leave the highway of observation and science." This is not a necessary consequence of the recognition of metaphysical principles. We do not want to give up principles except in so far as they are divorced from experience; the empirical road leads always to principles and these are principles in which we can put our faith. I read the other day in a chapter on legal philosophy, "Should facts rule or Ideas hold sway?" (Capitalization not mine.) This shows, I think, a lack of understanding of the relation of the two. Holmes has given us a good definition of a principle as "a felt reconciliation of concrete instances." Concepts should be based on facts, not governed by fixed logical construction. Psychological, not logical, concepts are the concepts of dynamic thinking.

But our chief thought in reading the denunciations of a conceptual jurisprudence and the advocacy of a practical or pragmatic law, is: when has jurisprudence not been practical, what is the whole history of our common law but a pragmatic development? Our difficulty is that in much juristical writing we have to separate legal history and legal theory; one is as pragmatic as the other is not. Or perhaps our legal theory has been peculiarly pragmatic if it has made it possible for us to live comfortably in the same house with our legal history. And in many cases where it is thought that jurists are sacrificing needs to legal conceptions, they are by no means doing this, but are using certain legal conceptions to further what *they* consider the needs. Moreover, new juristic generalization has seldom been on the side of theory. The new situation has needed a new generalization—and got it, as is the way with needs.

I think the writing on "pragmatic jurisprudence" shows several confusions of thought. Cardozo tells us in somewhat loose language: "The rule that functions well produces a title deed to recognition." This is where a pragmatic jurisprudence breaks down, not because of its pragmatism but because it is not pragmatic enough, or rather it is not empirical enough, for exactly what we mean when we say a rule functions well is the difficult point in the whole matter. Whether a rule functions well or ill usually means whether it functions in the interests of the dominant class, dominant at the moment everything considered.

When a "conceptual jurisprudence" has been justly criticized, the validity of the criticism has depended not on the conceptualism of the jurisprudence, but on the mechanical manner in which it has been administered. We have noted in an earlier chapter the inadequacy of the doctrine of verifying. Thus we see that our judges cannot go to pigeon-holes to find correspondences. A mere mechanical intelligence could do that, but no judge has been great who has not had a creating intelligence. The development of law in England and America would not have had the broad and dignified history it has had if our judges had had the passion for classification shown by some writers. The fact that we have had great jurists in England and America is because we have had men who have not used old classifications when they would not serve, who have not tried to ram life into pigeon-holes, but who have created law through the welding of principle, precedent and present experience. Precedent is principle as at that time embodied plus experience as at that time interpreted. It is sometimes thought that the ability of the judge is shown by the clearness with which he sees under what head any particular case belongs. On the contrary, his ability is shown much more by his keenness for difference than for similars, by the acuteness with which he sees exactly where this case is different from all others. Here is where a constructive intelligence gets its opportunity. For in every circumstance there is always something unique. This is the part that escapes classification but cannot be ignored. "No two cases of negligence are alike. It is not the general features of such cases, for which mechanically applied rules would be appropriate, but the special circumstances . . . that are significant. There is nothing unique in a bill of exchange. Every case of human conduct is a unique event."[1] Here is where the legal order has gone beyond the sociologists. Many of the latter stick in the old idea of adjustment, a manipulation of that which already exists; the legal order by combining principles with individual application, that is, the application made necessary by the uniqueness of the particular case, does more than manipulate, it creates. For every concrete solution becomes part of legal doctrine. Whenever judges try the feat of reconciling justice and utility, they are apt to find themselves in difficulties. Their task is ever those larger utilities which extend the idea of justice. It is true that there is always an effort to keep "the body of law" consistent, but this is often an effort after the event, after the demands of the concrete case have been met. Our history teems with examples of law meeting a need and afterwards finding the legal justification. The Juvenile Court was an innovation accepted because its value was obvious; after it had been accepted and established a precedent was found for it in the jurisdiction of chancery over infants.

Thus if we see some hint of the "philosophy of hypothesis" in a certain tendency in modern jurisprudence which, while it is reacting against "natural

[1] Pound, *Interpetations of Legal History*, p. 155.

law," against a theory of law as *a priori* truth, yet keeps law apart to compare with a developing society, at the same time we find in the increasing sense of judicial responsibility, a large understanding of the share of law in the coöperative creating of a developing society.

And yet no amount of judicial effort can carry law beyond this "share." The standards of the past and those of the present can be united not by law makers or judges but only in the meetings and differings, the confronting and integrating, of the daily activities of men. The fruitful uniting of fundamental principles and social facts takes place in no man's *mind*. We rise from the perceptual to the conceptual plane through our concrete activities. Thus is our conception of "right" evolved. Thus does law develop. To paraphrase a sentence of Holmes: To find law in experience is not a duty, it is only a necessity.

The exigencies of logic and the exigencies of the situation both press upon the legal order. When we dislike economic determinism, we talk of "reason" and "the sense of right and justice"; when we wish to denounce a "barren" conceptualism, we talk of facts. And the same person may do these in different moods. I know of no better way to stimulate that juristic activity which Pound gives as the task for twentieth-century jurisprudence than for jurists to show the connection between these. Juristic fatalism will disappear, I think, as fast as we perceive (1) that legal experience and the experience of all men must be united; (2) that concept and percept, reason and fact, are alike rooted in our concrete existence.

To sum up this chapter. As far as pragmatism has

influenced jurisprudence unduly, that influence must be overcome by recognizing that there need be no controversy between conceptual and pragmatic jurisprudence. A jurisprudence of results cannot supersede a jurisprudence of concepts. (I want to apply the teaching of this book to my own thinking, and integrate, not discard, either pragmatism or conceptualism.) Much of the attack on conceptual jurisprudence shows a lack of understanding that concepts may be psychologically evolved rather than built up on fixed logical constructions. One jurist repudiates a jurisprudence of concepts because he is "determined to keep in touch with the facts of life." But life itself is uniting at every instant concept and fact, and the jurist must keep in touch with this process. Again some jurists discuss "the boundaries of the justifiable operation of the conceptual process," but it is not a question of limiting a process which is good if restrained, but of finding a legitimate process. Concepts pregnant with concrete daily living we need have no fear of. We must understand how concepts arise and how they are to be used. Holmes says that we must take a rule of law, trace it back, and find out the need in which it arose, and then reshape it with conscious, articulate reference to the end in view now. The contribution which Holmes has made to the development of American thought and life by himself following this teaching constitutes the debt which America owes him, but we must also bear in mind that other part of the process which Holmes probably takes so much for granted that he does not state. The idea of law serving ends is only half the story; by that serving it creates new ends. This is its most important function; as long as it merely served ends, if such a thing were possible, there would be no progress. It does not merely enunciate a way of meeting a situation, that enunciation then remaining as a precedent to test the next situation by, it helps to make the next situation. The creative activity of the legal order is not confined, as one might think from the writings of some jurists, to the *law* it creates; it helps to further all those concrete activities which, expanding and developing, soon demand new juristic activity which again extends and enlarges the scope of our life. We see this double function of the legal order particularly in the development of commercial law: we see it at the same time satisfying desire and creating new desire.

XVI

THE CREATIVE AREA OF LAW

DEAN POUND believes in conscious law-making, and he uses often that happiest phrase of twentieth-century thought, the "efficacy of effort," but that phrase instantly raises the question, "Whose is to be the effort?" One might tend to think because this comes from a jurist that it is a motto for the Bench alone, but a little reflection will show the part of all of us in making law. If we are in industry we must realize that we are not only producing goods and adjusting human relations, but in and through these processes we are helping to make law. We are always thinking of the influence of law on industrial relations but less apt to think of the influence of industrial relations on law. We are told over and over again today that law should not rest on any legal conception but on social facts; yet if this is so, then heads of industry and our new "industrial counsellors" should take it into consideration. As the production manager of the paper mill understands the process from tree to finished product, so the industrial counsellor should understand the process by which the social facts on which the eight-hour demand is based pass over into law. If that is understood, then he is not only helping industry, but helping to create a juster system of law.

Law should be the declaration of the interacting forms of life. But I need not emphasize industry. In almost every relation we are helping to make law. If you make a request of your landlord, that may eventually contribute to landlord-tenant law; the "Emergency Legislation" of Massachusetts came about, as rents rose higher and higher, from the repeated requests of tenants, "May we stay until we find another house?" If you make a rule that your maid disputes, that may influence the law of master and servant; if you have a quarrel with your neighbor, that may change property law; if you are rude to your wife, that may influence the divorce laws. Many of our acts contribute as directly to the making of law as the decisions of judge or enactments of legislatures. Law is concerned with human relations; my life from moment to moment is a matter of human relations; the way I conduct those relations contribute to the building of law.

The legal order may conceive its function as that of "striving to do justice and satisfy demands and secure social interests by principles of reason in order to eliminate wilfulness and personal caprice," but it cannot do all this alone. It cannot cope single-handed with "will."[1] We have a very complex social process in which the legal order is one factor. It does not watch over the world and provide it with new precepts and principles as the need arises. Percept passes into precept by a process of which the legal order is a part. It has many opportunities to play this part—as through the appeal to equity and natural law and by the use

[1] Further we have always to reckon with the personal bias and prejudice of any member of the legal order, his particular traditions and education and association.

of interpretation—but that this is always merely a part must be clearly understood. Take interpretation: some writers would tell us that when there exists no legal precept by which the judge can administer what seems to him justice in a given case, he invents one by interpretation; that is, that interpretation is the accepted technique by which new needs are met. Very true, but that case, and all the enormously complex circumstances ramifying in a hundred directions, perhaps, which have gone to produce that case, have often produced the interpretation—the fruit is ripe for the picking. It is, however, indeed true that it often takes greatness to make the interpretation; it takes the vision to see it and the courage to declare it, ever the two qualities which make greatness. As for the conceptions of equity and natural law, other agencies of which the judge may avail himself to make what are indeed creative generalizations, it is even more obvious that these have been largely evolved by the community. Moreover, in most controversies there is not one adjustment to be made, there are many; the legal order cannot attend to them all, if it points out the major we usually have to find the minor for ourselves. That is, in almost every decision of the court the legal adjustment merely leads the way to many other adjustments thereby made possible.

But by thus dwelling upon the part of all men in creating law, by insisting that the "effort" is not juristic effort alone, by recognizing that there are limitations to the juristic power to shape law, we take nothing away from the legal order. On the contrary we extend its function, increase its responsibility, enhance its dignity. For while we may deny that the reason and intuition of the legal order are the most important factors in social-legal development, yet it would be impossible to overvalue these as contributing to that development.

And yet law must never for a moment attempt to stand outside that activity to which it is contributing by legal enactment, judicial pronouncement, juristical doctrine. It is as important to recognize the limits of a "creative jurisprudence" as it is to emphasize its possibilities. Kohler thought that law not only maintains existing values of civilization, but that it creates new ones. It *helps* to do so. Law must always be conceived as part of the social process. Kohler made the mistake of looking at *law* as self-developing; human experience is self-developing and law is part of human experience. There is a vast difference here. Kohler's intellectualism occasionally gives his thought an unfortunate bias. It is perhaps Pound's uniting of idealism and empiricism which gives so great value to his thought. Moreover, the way in which he uses the expression "creative activity," a phrase which occurs frequently in his last book, gets us away from the juristic stagnation of the latter part of the nineteenth century without obliging us to adopt doctrines which would lead to a break with the past, for he is everywhere talking of legal development not of legal innovations.

Juristic thought of the eighteenth century preached individual rights. In the nineteenth century, when freedom was the watchword, the doctrine of freedom was added to that of rights and every individual was to be given a maximum amount of freedom as his "right." In the twentieth century we find much of juristical writing shot through with the word social. While this conception is enormously valuable as counteracting what was harmful in the doctrine of individual rights, yet the most interesting tendency in progressive juristic thought today is not the distinction between individual and social, but an abandoning of logical presuppositions in favor of a consideration of every aspect of the concrete situation, the aim being not merely the adjustment of relation, but the creating of those modes of association which shall provide the possibility of more and more self-adjusting as part of man's normal activity. This involves the recognition that conflict is not pathological, that the legal order does not exist only for the ills of society, but that diversity—of ideas, emotions and interests,—is normal, and that it rests largely with the legal order whether that diversity shall be made fruitful rather than wasteful.

The legal order is not to restore equilibrium merely, to find a "balance," it is so to take its part in resolving conflict that the conflict may lead to larger understandings, more comprehensive activities. The great judge does not "apply" rules and precedents to the situation; he creates from rules and precedents and situation. He creates what? New rules, new precedents? Perhaps, but more important, he makes possible in the future, situations enriched with further possibilities, more comprehensive understandings, broader and fairer relations. What the legal order may do preeminently, what we might consider its most important contribution to society, is to prevent the leakage of experience. Perhaps the most widespread fallacy in regard to law is that its chief aim is the preservation of peace and order. The administration of justice is not the orderly disposition of controversies; the administration of justice must be truly part of that social process which generates ever those further activities which are significant for the progress of men. Thus shall we get further and further away from the old expression (good in itself if it had not been abused) "the logical development of law," and come more and more to understand a psychological development of law. Thus the function of the legal order meets and mingles with other functions in a developing experience. Law is created on the motor level from the daily intercourse of men, from concrete "conflict." Not "law and order," but to make conflict creative, must be the part of law as of every other activity of our life. We have all of us to understand the process of creative conflict and trust to that process, not to the expert with his "facts," not to the judge with his "reason," not to the citizen with his "will"—not to any one of these alone, but to the whole process as each takes his share in the concrete activities in which all these are involved.

To put this a little differently, many think law a "necessary evil," that it exists because of the wickedness in all "poor human beings." This theory limits the constructive area of the legal order and is detrimental to the development of society. It is often expressed in terms of a restriction on freedom. We should, however, see law not as restricting or regulating freedom, but as increasing our freedom by making wider and wider the area in which that freedom may operate. I have theoretical freedom in the forest; I have actual freedom only with the freedom to *do,* to do and do, in wider relations, in more significant relations, by extending ever more and more the possibility of fruitful response. Men do not lose their freedom in relation but thereby gain it. We have found out by trial and error that liberty is not attained by marking off an area in which it is allowed to be operative. The trouble with the supporters of the idea of freedom which prevailed in the nineteenth century was that they misnamed their doctrine; they were not trying to preserve or extend freedom, but to reduce coercion, and the reducing of coercion is not the same as the extension of freedom. This, that era did not see and politics and law suffered in consequence. Moreover, the freedom of the nineteenth century, both of political and legal science, was an assumption, not a freedom gained and sustained through concrete activity. The freedom given us by our present-day psychology is not freedom in general, but a freedom to do certain things; it is not an inherent freedom, but a freedom achieved through doing certain things. No concept of jurisprudence is sound which rests on the claims of an abstract freedom. When one sees the place where mechanism and free will meet, as shown both by our present psychology and an older philosophy, one understands the place of freedom within the doctrines of jurisprudence. The notion of integrating desires synthesizes the conceptions of freedom and non-freedom; it is hopeless to think that liberty and conflicting desires can live in the same world together by any other process. Thus we see the place for the creative activity of the legal order. Its influence is always largely in anticipation. It may do far more than register what exists; it has a share in what may be called into existence.

Moreover, legal decisions do not "settle" controversies. The settlement must be worked out in life, and it is this working out to which law must contribute. The idea of the finality of legal decision is a notion we must abandon; legal decision is the beginning of something, not the end. It has been said that the law is to give the support of an "organized authority" to certain interests. It is to do somewhat less and far more than that; it is to help those interests to develop their own authoritative relation to the rest of society, not a dominating authority but an integrating authority. Law is something different from a command; the imperative nature of law is its most superficial aspect. It is neither a "fiat of will" nor a "rule of right." Perhaps we may conceive the function of law as follows. If we accept the doctrine that when two diverse interests confront each other, the task, before deciding that they are mutually exclusive, that a duel for right of way is inevitable, is to try to integrate them, then perhaps it is to the legal order that this task of integrating may more and more be given. And yet this does not mean agreement with that portion of legal literature which presents life to us as full of divergent interests, antagonistic wills, and law as stepping into all this maze of cross-purposes to make the necessary adjustments. For that same evolving activity which produces the confronting desires carries within itself the possibilitiy of harmonizing those desires. The legal order opens the way to that possibility.

In short the creative activity of law is possible because law follows life, not life, law—which is not a paradox.

It is interesting to notice that the juristic and economic stagnation of the nineteenth century are due in part to the same cause. Take the enunciation by the "classical" economists of the automatic supply of labor and capital out of which grew the wage-fund doctrine in all its unapproachable fixity: if wages were "too high" in any branch of industry, capital would automatically forsake it, and hence wages would fall; if wages were "too low" they would be raised automatically by the same beneficent play of natural economic laws, beneficent because "natural." What was overlooked, of course, as was soon discovered, was that if the workman did not consciously pursue his interest, he lost his interest; that "unduly low" wages did not automatically right themselves, for labor tended to adapt itself to the new conditions which "automatically" got worse and worse. Labor and capital would find a level indeed, but the level would be increasingly lower. In short, following "economic laws" pointed straight to the degradation of labor and hence to the retarding of economic progress and hence to the diminution of the fund available for both capital and labor. For that fund is not fixed but flexible, and really a product of psychological forces.

In economics and law, in politics and all our human relations, the field grows daily larger for the opportunity of creative activity as we recognize its possibility, as we recognize its fundamental truth: that we do not follow, but make law.

It is obvious that in this chapter I am emphasizing only one aspect of the subject. In a fuller consideration of the creative area of law one would, for instance, consider the power given more and more of recent years to administrative commissions. I wish here merely to refer to them as an illustration of one of the cardinal points of Part I: the relating of a varying activity to a varying activity, and the plus-values thereby created. When the Interstate Commerce, the Federal Trade or the Tariff Act came to be administered, it was found that those laws were made for such varying factors that wide discretion must be used in their administration; that is, as the law cannot vary we have administrative commissions which can. Here we see clearly what we have called the evolving situation: the interweaving of a varying activity and what is practically, through the possibility of different interpretations by the administrative commissions, a varying law. We have found that the basis of creative experience is circular response. Nowhere do we see this more steadily than in the history of law, and here in our administrative commissions is a very striking instance of circular response; between legislative enactment as administered by these commissions and the activity in question. On every level, in every field which I have looked at, I find circular response the fundamental activity of life.

To sum up these chapters on law: law cannot decide between purposes, set their various values, secure interests. Its task is to allow full opportunity for those modes of activity from which an integrating purpose may arise, and such purpose tends to secure itself. The function of law is not merely to safeguard interests; it is to help us to understand our interests, to broaden and deepen them. Law can never "protect" life, it can only find a legitimate place among life's many activities; whatever theory places it outside the general life process thereby condemns itself. Even if the task of law were adjustment, it could never successfully declare the adjustment arbitrarily; it could only open the way for the reconciliation to manifest itself. Law is not essentially a constraining power. Or rather law, properly conceived, like every process of life, contains within itself its own imperative. The authority, power, developed through those interactivities of man by which law is created, is the imperative of those activities. Law, I say, should not be conceived as a constraining power chiefly. As it should not help the vested interests to victimize the other members of society, so it should not, merely, protect those others against such aggressions. Law, one of the strongest forces of our life, should consent to no negative rôle. It is true that law is to remove obstructions, to give free play, and yet it has a far more positive function; not *laisser-faire* but "*faire-marcher*" must be its motto. When we thought that man could do as he pleased except when he interfered with others, and that the chief function of law was to mark off the boundary of that interference, there was not much chance of a creative jurisprudence, but that time is past. The creative generalizations of the legal order, founded on the exigencies of concrete cases, contribute to the evolution of law. But the legal order is not, alone, the custodian of social values nor the interpreter of social facts; it is an integral part of the social order, cocreator of a richer life for all men. As I have hoped to show that the "will of the people" should not be conceived as a crowd-induced phenomenon, that it should not be a mere "consent" to the "expert," so law should not be conceived as product either of legislature or judge. To life itself we must go, before ever expert or judge appears, and there in the ceaseless interweavings of our concrete existence shall we find the foundations of the "majesty of law."

XVII

PARALLEL DEVELOPMENTS IN PSYCHOLOGY AND LAW

I HAVE said that I think the most interesting thing in our thinking today is the parallel development in psychology, ethics, law and politics. For instance, when we hear from certain quarters that behaviorism must be applied to jurisprudence, we could reply that we do not have to urge the lawyers to "apply" behaviorism to law, because they can show as much behavioristic trend as any other department of our thinking. Take, for instance, the analysis of evidence. When it is a question of finding the intention of an act, the judge and jury do not try to look into a man's mind to find his intention; they compare the act in question with previous and subsequent acts and try to see what they can infer in regard to his intention. Of course, what he says about his act and the way he says it and the way he looks as he says it, etc., is part of his behavior; if the behaviorists have sometimes forgotten this point, the courts never have. Again, the fact that we now look at the workings of law, that we ask, What does law do?—is a behavioristic tendency. For instance, the legal conception of contract formerly rested on the will of the contracting parties; now we ask, what does the contract *do?* The whole doctrine of legal liability we relate now to the *activity* in question. Again, we have the reluctance of the courts to enforce "abstract promises," promises which cannot show objective basis. There is a wish to test the genuineness of the intention by behavior, by the payment of money or by the fact that the promissor has begun to act under the agreement. Thus is shown a "real" intention to assume a binding relation. This can be compared with "the reluctance of courts to apply the ordinary principle of negligence to negligent speech, with the doctrine as to seller's talk, with the limitations upon liability for oral defamation." One could easily extend such illustrations. The whole trend of law today is toward an objective basis for legal transactions. The very fact that lawyers are more and more giving up the narrow legalistic view which is concerned with rights and precedents and technicalities, and facing each concrete situation as it appears, the fact that less and less is ingenious reasoning being put in the place of the examination of facts, is a trend toward a wholesome objectivity. In business there is constant attempt to make binding agreements, and yet it is a matter of common experience that the most ironclad agreement cannot be carried out if purely intellectualistic.

Some of the origins of law, moreover, seem to have been decidedly behavioristic. For instance, in early Roman law, dispute over breach of agreement as such was not actionable, but if it resulted in assault, tribunals might be called on to act. Controversy as to possession of property the law took cognizance of because of the consequent trespass, breaking of the fence, etc., rather than because of any more abstract consideration. Again, in Hindu law the debtor is not one who owes an "obligation," but one who by withholding property which belongs to the creditor is in this respect a thief.

There is, to be sure, always the danger of over-emphasis. The objective trend of today, valuable as it is on the whole, has its dangers in law as well as in psychology: in psychology it demands that we shall ignore all that our senses or our laboratory instruments do not immediately give us; in law it sometimes takes away from our responsibility when it should not do so, that is, moral obligation may tend to grow dim, while on the other hand it only changes the field of manipulation for the unscrupulous. With superficial thinkers there indeed lurk many dangers in the objective trend of law. Mr. Pound sees this and on the last page of his *Philosophy of Law,* where he makes a plea for enlarging the domain of legally enforceable promises, he tells us that that good faith which jurist and layman alike see as essential to the integrity of men should be recognized more fully in legal technique without reverting to the "will" doctrine, without again injecting the subjective into law. The book ends without telling us how this is to be done, but surely it is by an enlarged understanding on our part of what "good faith" means. We hark back to less intrepid thought when we think that good faith has more subjective than objective meaning. A man promises me something; circumstances change; is he to keep that promise? Many answer Yes unreservedly, but one should discriminate here. That might mean life lived purely mechanically. Loyalty is not adherence to one moment or one person or one set of circumstances alone; my loyalty is tested by whether I am keeping faith with all the circumstances, with all that the present conditions involve, with the complexity of all my obligations. The other is a formal good faith, perhaps a half-blind good faith, or even sometimes a cowardly good faith. To be sure the loyalty I am advocating allows opportunity for greater self-deception, for doing more harm to others, the older doctrine was safer, but if we are willing to embrace the greater risk for the greater gain—gain in our spiritual development, in our individual and social progress—we shall accept the latter. It requires not only more courage, but more intelligence on our part; it renders our own responsibility greater and law more difficult, yet it is, I believe, worth all the demands it makes upon us. Of course there are many circumstances which should never affect our promises. I do not mean that when conditions are difficult or less to our interest that that should make adherence to obligation undertaken less imperative; there is often simply unquestionable justice in keeping a promise when it is no longer to our interest to do so. But understanding all this, it still remains true that this is not always so, and good faith must in the end mean loyalty to what is, in all its fulness and actuality. The meeting here of psychology, law and ethics is significant.

If, however, we do not wish to "apply" psychology to jurisprudence, still the recent development of psychological thinking as corroborative of certain tendencies in juristical thinking is exceedingly interesting. It gives us, to sum up briefly, a conception of purpose which shows it involved in the activity, not as something somewhere on in front; a conception of "functional adjustment" or integration, which supports the present-day juristical notion of the reconciling of desires rather than the old legalistic idea of "adjustment of rights"; it contributes toward the reconciliation of the controversy over law as conflict of wills versus law as the securing of interests by giving us a clearer understanding of the relation of will to interest, by giving us the de facto will, and it contributes toward another reconciliation of almost equal importance, that of the theories of a conscious and an unconscious evolution of law. For while it shows us that we must believe in the deliberate effort of the legal order, it shows us that that effort must be directed towards providing those interactivities of men from which *droit* in the sense of both right and law shall emerge. If law is the declaration of the interacting forms of life, practical men and women must establish in concrete existence those forms from which the written law may be declared. The controversy in jurisprudence today should not be between a conscious and an unconscious evolution of law, but between a mechanical and a developing theory of law. A "dynamic psychology" and a "creative jurisprudence" rest on the same foundations.

XVIII

CONCLUSION: EXPERIENCE AS EVOCATION

THINKER after thinker is trying to find some way to get rid of conflict. Moralists hope that this will be done by changing human nature. The political scientists who have taken fact-finding for their slogan tell us that facts are the solvent for controversy. Economists are seeking a way by which the struggle between capital and labor may cease. Many writers on international relations would rid us of the conflict between nations. Some of the biologists tell us that we could abolish conflict and live together in peace and harmony like the well-known instances of the animal colonies; they seem to ignore the fact that most of us, even those peacefully inclined, do not wish to live like the ants and the beavers.

But on the other hand there are biologists who give us the tooth-and-claw theory. There are sociologists who say that conflict is built into the structure of the world, that the world is cemented with blood and sweat. It seems to me that there is occasionally a little confusion of thought on one point both among those who wish to abolish conflict and those who regard it as beneficent and wish to retain it. What people often mean by getting rid of conflict is getting rid of diversity, and it is of the utmost importance that these should not be considered the same. We may wish to abolish conflict but we cannot get rid of diversity. We must face life as it is and understand that diversity is its most essential feature. I know a man whose fear of difference is so great that he looks alarmed if the most friendly argument appears at his dinner table; he always changes the subject immediately. But fear of difference is dread of life itself. It is possible to conceive conflict as not necessarily a wasteful outbreak of incompatibilities, but a *normal* process by which socially valuable differences register themselves for the enrichment of all concerned. One of the greatest values of controversy is its revealing nature. The real issues at stake come into the open and have the possibility of being reconciled. A fresh conflict between employers and employees is often not so much an upsetting of equilibrium, really, as an opportunity for stabilizing. Our unfortunate ethical connotations are a handicap to clear thinking. The conflict of chemistry we do not think reprehensible. If we could look at social conflict as neither good nor bad, but simply a fact, we should make great strides in our thinking. On every level the movement of life is through the release of energy. Psychology has shown us release and what it calls integration as one process. Social conflict is constructive when it follows this normal process, when the release of energy is by one and the same movement carrying itself to a higher level.

What I have tried to show in this book is that the social process may be conceived either as the opposing and battle of desires with the victory of one over the other, or as the confronting and integrating of desires. The former means non-freedom for both sides, the defeated bound to the victor, the victor bound to the false situation thus created—both bound. The latter means a freeing for both sides and increased total power or increased capacity in the world. The core of the development, expansion, growth, progress of humanity is the confronting and gripping of opposites. Integration is both the keel and the rudder of life: it supports all life's structure and guides every activity. This thought must be ever before us in social research. For we believe in the inexhaustible resources of life, in the fresh powers constantly springing up. The test of the vitality of any experience is its power to unite into a living, generating activity its self-yielding differences. We seek a richly diversified experience where every difference strengthens and reinforces the other. Through the interpenetrating of spirit and spirit, differences are conserved, accentuated and reconciled in the greater life which is the issue. Each remains forever himself that thereby the larger activity may be enriched and in its refluence, reinforce him. The activity of co-creating is the core of democracy, the essence of citizenship, the condition of world-citizenship.

We seek reality in experience. Let us reject the realm of the compensatory; it is fair, but a prison. Experience may be hard but we claim its gifts because they are real, even though our feet bleed on its stones. We seek progressive advancement through the transformation of daily experience. Into what, conceptual pictures? No, daily experience must be translated not into conceptual pictures but into spiritual conviction. Experience can both guide and guard us. Foolish indeed are those who do not bring oil to its burning.

In conclusion, the essence of experience, the law of relation, is reciprocal freeing: here is "the rock and the substance of the human spirit." This is the truth of stimulus and response: evocation. We are all rooted in that great unknown in which are the infinite latents of humanity. And these latents are evoked, called forth into visibility, summoned, by the action and reaction of one on the other. All human intercourse should be the evocation by each from the other of new forms undreamed of before, and all intercourse that is not evocation should be eschewed. Release, evocation—evocation by release, release by evocation—this is the fundamental law of the universe. The test of the validity of any social process is whether this is taking place—between one and another, between capital and labor, between nation and nation. It must be the test for industrial arbitrators, jurists and statesmen alike. To free the energies of the human spirit is the high potentiality of all human association.

No reform will be successful which tries to circumvent life instead of facing it. I believe in no happy (or unhappy) land where expert or leader can overcome diversity. I believe in no shadow country where vicarious experience can take the place of our own experience. I see no golden age in the past or in the future, but I believe in the possibilities of human effort, of disciplined effort, in truth in its Anglo-Saxon meaning (tryw) of faithfulness, and in the essence of relation from the amoeba and its food to man and man, as the release of energy, the evocation or the calliny forth of new powers one from the other.

This is the stuff of experience. This is the challenge of experience.